In the Light of Agape

In the Light of Agape

Moral Realism and Its Consequences

WILLIAM GREENWAY

CASCADE *Books* • Eugene, Oregon

IN THE LIGHT OF AGAPE
Moral Realism and Its Consequences

Copyright © 2024 William Greenway. All rights reserved. Except for brief quotations in critical publications or reviews, no part of this book may be reproduced in any manner without prior written permission from the publisher. Write: Permissions, Wipf and Stock Publishers, 199 W. 8th Ave., Suite 3, Eugene, OR 97401.

Cascade Books
An Imprint of Wipf and Stock Publishers
199 W. 8th Ave., Suite 3
Eugene, OR 97401

www.wipfandstock.com

PAPERBACK ISBN: 978-1-6667-6924-1
HARDCOVER ISBN: 978-1-6667-6925-8
EBOOK ISBN: 978-1-6667-6926-5

Cataloguing-in-Publication data:

Names: Greenway, William, 1963–, author.

Title: In the light of agape : moral realism and its consequences / William Greenway.

Description: Eugene, OR: Cascade Books, 2024 | Includes bibliographical references and index.

Identifiers: ISBN 978-1-6667-6924-1 (paperback) | ISBN 978-1-6667-6925-8 (hardcover) | ISBN 978-1-6667-6926-5 (ebook)

Subjects: LCSH: Christian ethics. | Agape. | Emmanuel Levinas, 1906–1995.

Classification: BJ1251 .G70 2024 (paperback) | BJ1251 (ebook)

05/09/24

"Animals: Beyond the Enlightenment Eclipse" first published as entry for "Animals." Originally published in *Dictionary of Scripture and Ethics* by Joel Green, ed. Copyright © 2011. Used by permission of Baker Academic, a division of Baker Publishing Group.

New Revised Standard Version Bible, copyright 1989, Division of Christian Education of the National Council of Churches of Christ of the United States of America. Used by permission. All rights reserved.

"The Flower of Faith Blooming in the Light of Agape," artwork and photograph, William Greenway, 2018. Used by permission. All rights reserved.

With fond memories of and loving hope for our greater Rigby
family—the Celebration, DW, Toronto, and Zoom gang!
Scott, Jasmine, and Erika
and
Mark, Alice, and Oscar

Contents

Acknowledgments		ix
Introduction: In the Light of Agape		xiii
Chapter 1	Peter Singer, Emmanuel Levinas, Christian Agape, and the Spiritual Heart of Animal Liberation	1
Chapter 2	Jesus as Moral Philosopher: The Parable of the Good Samaritan	17
Chapter 3	Seized by Love: Teaching, Ministry, and Augustine's "Teacher"	26
Chapter 4	Eternally Incarnate: Advent in Genesis	29
Chapter 5	Before and Above All: Agape	38
Chapter 6	To Love as God Loves: Animals and the *Imago Dei*	41
Chapter 7	Karl Barth, Albert Schweitzer, Emmanuel Levinas, and "Love for All Creatures" as a Quintessential Aspect of Christian Spirituality	46
Chapter 8	Life Sacred: Recovering the Seven Days of Creation Narrative	58
Chapter 9	Tragedy of the Commons: Agape, Creation Care, Polis	74
Chapter 10	Animals: Beyond the Enlightenment Eclipse	82
Chapter 11	*Saying* Grace	88
Chapter 12	Barth and Universal Salvation: A Neo-Calvinist Spiritual Affirmation	102
Chapter 13	From Cagayan de Oro, Mindanao, Philippines: September 23, 1989	125
Chapter 14	Dear Gail, About Stan	136

Chapter 15	Extinction	138
Chapter 16	The Passion of Torah Is the Passion of Jesus Is the Passion of Lent	142
Chapter 17	The Flowering of Faith in the Light of Agape	149
Bibliography		175
Index of Names		181

Acknowledgments

I would like to thank the board of trustees and the faculty, staff, and students at Austin Presbyterian Theological Seminary, who provided support and encouragement over the years as I worked to research and compose these essays. Last year I completed a two-year term as faculty representative to our board of trustees, where I was assigned to the finance committee. I now have newfound appreciation for the donors and administrators who provide and shepherd the resources necessary to ensure, among other things, that faculty have time and resources for research and writing. I am dependent upon and grateful for their gifts and stewardship.

At Cascade Books, I want to thank Matthew Wimer, managing editor, for his coordination of the project, his support, and for his patience. I am also happy once again publicly to offer thanks to Rodney Clapp. Long before we knew each other or I had published any books, Rodney paused in passing and took time to provide a junior scholar with vital publishing advice. In the years since, he has become not only one of my editors but a treasured conversation partner, a friend, and, especially vis-à-vis the threats of neoliberalism, my teacher. Thanks also to Jesselyn Clapp for her careful copyediting, and to the rest of the staff of Cascade for designing and producing a beautiful book.

The essays in this collection complement one another and are organized in accord with a thematic logic, but they need not be read in order. There is considerable repetition of basic themes, but variety in their application vis-à-vis influential figures and topics. Several essays appear in print here for the first time. Others were published in scholarly journals or as chapters in books, and I owe thanks to the anonymous readers and editors whose careful work helped to refine my thinking and writing. All these essays, together with all the other books and articles I have written over the last decade, are attempts to unmask and redress a modern systemic distortion that cuts us off conceptually from moral reality—the force of agape, the force of the divine, the force of God insofar as God *is* love—and to detail clearly the momentous and wondrous consequences of awakening to agape.

"Peter Singer, Emmanuel Levinas, Christian *Agape*, and the Spiritual Heart of Animal Liberation" was published in *Journal of Animal Ethics* (Fall 2015). "Jesus as Moral Philosopher: The Parable of the Good Samaritan," written in honor of my friend, former colleague, and chess nemesis (I did beat him once!), Dr. Ismael Garcia, was published in *Insights* (Fall 2012).

"Seized by Love: Teaching, Ministry, and Augustine's 'Teacher,'" is from Austin Seminary's *Windows* (Winter 2016). "Eternally Incarnate: Advent in Genesis," is from *Journal for Preachers* (Advent 2015). "Before and Above All, *Agape*: On the Essence of Faith" was published on the SARX web site in December 2015.

"To Love as God Loves: Animals and the *Imago Dei*" is the accepted final version—the printers mistakenly published the penultimate version—of an essay published under the title "Animals and the Love of God" in *The Christian Century* (June 21, 2000). "Karl Barth, Albert Schweitzer, Emmanuel Levinas and 'Love for All Creatures' as a Quintessential Aspect of Christian Spirituality" was published in *Issues in Ethics and Animal Rights* (2011). "Life Sacred: Recovering the Seven Days of Creation Narrative" appeared in *God's Earth is Sacred* (2012), and sections of the essay were excerpted and developed far more exhaustively in *For the Love of All Creatures: The Story of Grace in Genesis* (2015).

"Animals: Beyond the Enlightenment Eclipse" appeared as "Animals" in the *Dictionary of Scripture and Ethics* (2011). "Saying Grace" is a revised version of a lecture delivered at the *Oxford Centre for Animal Ethics Summer School* at St. Stephen's House, Oxford University (July 26, 2016). "Karl Barth and Universal Salvation: A Neo-Calvinist Spiritual Affirmation," was delivered at *The Legacy of Karl Barth* conference at Austin Presbyterian Theological Seminary (November 14, 2007).

"From Cagayan de Oro, Mindanao, Philippines," is an unrevised (some phrasing and ideas are obviously dated) letter I sent to sponsoring individuals and churches in 1989 as I was serving for a year as an ecumenical associate with the United Church of Christ in the Philippines. "Dear Gail, About Stan" is the unrevised text of an e-mail I sent to my friend, the late Reverend Gail Snodgrass, upon learning of the untimely death of her husband and my friend and colleague, the Reverend Professor Stan Hall, on February 3, 2008. "Extinction" appeared in the progressive Christian online journal, *Unbound: An Interactive Journal on Christian Social Justice* (April 23, 2020).

ACKNOWLEDGMENTS

"The Passion of Torah Is the Passion of Jesus Is the Passion of Lent" and "The Flowering of Faith in the Light of Agape" are revised versions of sermons I preached at Shelton Chapel, Austin Presbyterian Theological Seminary (March 8, 2022, and April 24, 2018, respectively); both are published as videos on my YouTube channel. All previously published material appears with permission, all rights reserved.

Introduction

In the Light of Agape

THE REALITY OF AGAPE

We see children squealing with delight in new-fallen snow. We see the shocked faces of the survivors of the tsunami, broken bodies strewn about the background. We are not first objective, detached, neutral, and only then deciding what we think. No, insofar as we are not by nature or through repeated hardening of heart psychopathic, whether they are scenes of joy or scenes of horror, we are *instantly*, before decision or even reflection, joyful or horrified. The singular passion by which we are seized in both contexts, the singular passion enflaming our joy or, in other circumstances, our horror, the palpable spiritual force over and against which we must exert ourselves if we decide to harden our hearts and react differently, that spiritual force is agape.

Agape is the wellspring of the good in a moral realist sense. I stress "moral realist" to make clear that "moral" here is not indexed to what is pleasurable, desired, preferred, biologically or socioculturally selected for, expected, reciprocated, legally required, or implicitly or explicitly contracted or agreed upon. "Moral" here is rooted in the real and independent force signified by "agape," a force as real as gravity, though different in kind. Agape is the force over and against which evil is discerned. In complex ways it is also the wellspring of spiritual peace, spiritual community (*koinonia*), joy, and forgiveness—the wellspring of forgiveness not only for others, but also the wellspring of the gift of forgiveness and love for we ourselves.

Initial defense of the reality of agape is best achieved through invocation of scenes that provoke joy or horror, for even people whose philosophies leave no place for realist affirmation of agape are profoundly awakened to it in their daily lives. Seized by agape, they are joyful when they see children squealing with delight in the snow and horrified by the anguished faces of the survivors of the tsunami. Psychopaths, somehow cut off from agape, do exist, but they are no more an argument against the reality of agape than people who are colorblind are an argument against a difference between red and green.

Unfortunately, potent streams of modern rationality have perpetuated spiritually devastating systemic distortions that cut us off conceptually, if not spiritually, from agape. For instance, the epistemological ideal of modern Western rationality has long been to begin our reflections from an objective, disengaged, neutral epistemological stance. This has been an epistemological ideal not only in the sciences, where it is wholly appropriate, but even in ethics, to devastating effect, for this has idealized for modern Western ethical theory the existential stance of the psychopath. The result has been an infamous and enduring "crisis of foundations" in ethics and a "legitimization crisis" in political theory.

Fortunately, as indicated by philosophy's infamous late twentieth-century "turn to religion" and intellectual elites' early twenty-first-century embrace of "mindfulness" and talk of norms in "expansive" or "liberal" naturalism, the moral poverty of modern Western rationality is widely appreciated. But because systemic distortions in predominant forms of modern rationality elide all conceptual space for naming agape, the urgent need to address the moral poverty of modern Western rationality endures.[1]

My efforts to theorize agape are inspired by the work of the Jewish modern Western philosopher, Emmanuel Levinas (1906–1995). A French officer in World War II, Levinas was captured when General Rommel's forces defeated the French Tenth Army on June 18, 1940. He was sent to a Nazi forced labor camp, Stalag IXB, where he was segregated with other

---

1. Today this problem is so evident that representatives of predominant streams of modern rationality are publishing books with titles like *Naturalism and Normativity* and are modulating their metaphysical naturalism into "expansive" or "liberal" naturalisms in an attempt to carve out a place for ethics in their metaphysics. See de Caro and Macarthur, eds., *Naturalism and Normativity*; see also Ellis, *God, Value, and Nature*, and Williams, *Truth and Truthfulness*. Some streams of psychology, which emerged as a discipline discrete from philosophy only in the late nineteenth century, are borderline in this regard, and are struggling to find ways to address existential and spiritual questions; this is visible, for instance, in the likes of Self-Determination Theory, or psychological explorations into "mindfulness," "moral distress," and "moral injury"— though typically practitioners secure modern scientific *bona fides* by declaring they are metaphysical naturalists (see especially Ryan and Deci, *Self-Determination Theory*).

Jews.² While captive, Levinas was overwhelmed by concern for all the pleading, tortured, dying, murdered captives surrounding him in the Nazi camp.³ Levinas speaks of this fundamental moral event in terms of being taken "hostage" or "commanded" or "put in the accusative" by the face of the other. The significance of this event for Levinas's thought is manifest in his only, very brief, autobiographical statement, where he says that his biography is "dominated by the presentiment and the memory of the Nazi horror."⁴ In a small but significant shift, where Levinas speaks of being commanded directly *by the face* of the other, I speak of having been seized *by agape for* every face, including one's own.

Naming agape, we can distinguish two predominant forms of modern rationality wherein agape is conceptually elided and describe a third, awakened rationality, which is distinguished by its naming and theorizing of agape. First, there is *naturalistic rationality*, which takes the bounds of natural explanation and the bounds of reality to be coterminous. Thus, naturalistic rationality affirms natural explanations and celebrates modern science, but it elides all conceptual space for affirmation of free will and of agape. Second, there is *secular rationality*, which affirms natural explanations and celebrates science *and* affirms free will and celebrates authentic self-creation. But secular rationality also elides all conceptual space for affirmation of agape. Third, there is *awakened rationality*, which affirms natural explanation and celebrates modern science *and* affirms free will and celebrates authentic self-creation *and* affirms the reality of agape and celebrates life lived in fidelity to agape.⁵

Agape is among the most significant forces in existence. The causal forces of the sphere of nature—nature and nurture; genes and memes—described by the natural and social sciences, are in many respects more powerful than agape, and they are certainly aesthetically, erotically, and existentially significant insofar as they can be the source of tremendous happiness or pain and even death, but they are morally significant only insofar as they support or violate agape.

---

2. Malka, *Emmanuel Levinas*, 6.

3. After the war Levinas would learn he had lost his entire family, his mother, father, and two brothers (Dvora and Gurvitch, Boris and Aminadav Levinas) to the Nazi horror. His wife and daughter (Raïssa and Simone) were hidden and saved by nuns of the Monastery of Saint Vincent de Paul (see Malka, *Emmanuel Levinas*, 64–81).

4. Levinas, *Difficult Freedom*, 291.

5. Elsewhere I unfold awakened rationality as a post-representational (Rorty), falsifiable scientific theory, Moral Realism Theory, in which the incommensurable families of vocabularies which constitute a Sphere of Nature, a Sphere of Poetic I's, and a Sphere of Agape are all affirmed.

Obviously, agape can be violated. Our world is filled with brutality. But the existence of natural and intentional evil—that is, the reality of nature's ability to be the source of horrendous suffering and the ability of poetic I's willfully to create the same—does not tell against the reality of agape. In fact, contrary to the confused idea that the reality of evil presents a problem for affirmation of agape, the reality of agape is often most powerfully manifest in the face of the most horrific evil. Precisely in our horror the force of agape is all the more evident, screamingly manifest in our protest and tears, for it is by virtue of agape that we see evil as evil. Agape names the force enflaming our passionate response to suffering and injustice.

Agape is often set in straightforward opposition to eros. This is a mistake. Not only is there nothing wrong with eros, but the delights of eros—delicious food, the beauty of a sunset, sex—are all to be celebrated. I can be filled with eros even as I live surrender to agape. Ideally, I have both eros concern for myself and am awakened to agapeic affirmation of myself. Conflict between eros and agape arises only when eros drives me to violation of agape. For instance, "sexual abuse" names instances when eros towards an I violates agape for that I. Romantic relationships, on the other hand, should name instances where *eros* and agape are both in play, in harmony, and reciprocal.

AGAPE AND THE DIVINE

Agape is often rightly named as the essence of divinity: God *is* agape. This can be read without importing any extra meanings into the signifier "God." So, "God *is* agape" is equivalent to "agape *is* God." God may be more than agape. God may be personal, as in monotheistic traditions, or triune, as in Christianity. I do not deny God may be more than agape, but here I consider God or the divine only insofar as agape *is* God/the divine. The essential meaning of this classic confession—God is love—though articulated differently in different faith traditions, lies at the heart of all the world's historic faiths, both monotheistic and monistic. Viscerally, even children know agape. Indeed, in the visceral, a-conceptual sense of myriad mystical traditions, children may be awakened to agape with unparalleled purity.

Insofar as God *is* agape and agape *is* God—again, we are not yet speaking of a personal, let alone a triune God, though such is certainly not foreclosed upon—living out in one's day-to-day life surrender to having been seized by agape describes wholly reasonable faith in God/the divine. "Faith" in this sense is not intellectual assent to propositions but awakening and fidelity to agape. "Faith" in this sense is common to monotheistic and monistic traditions from Judaism, Christianity, Islam, and Wicca, to Hinduism, Buddhism, Taoism, and Secular Humanism.

In terms of conceptual understanding, the complexities we signify with the vocabularies of agape are as difficult to comprehend as the complexities we signify with the vocabularies of physics. "God is agape" and "$e=mc^2$" are both easy to say. But both can also be understood with varying degrees of depth, and the deepest comprehension of each requires intellectual gifts and disciplined study. Comprehension of "God is agape" requires, in addition, emotional balance, deep and open self-understanding, and the wisdom of diverse communities.

Unfortunately, all the world's faith traditions have been afflicted with simplistic understandings leading to superstitions and actions contrary to agape. While the world's great faith and wisdom traditions are rooted in the reality of agape and are full of ethical and spiritual wisdom, in large part they remain in a state of conceptual disarray, riddled with superstition in a fashion that parallels the state of "science" before the scientific revolution, and they provoke, even among intellectuals, irrational affirmation of "leaps of faith."

Let me stress that while predominant streams of modern theology have been plagued by irrationality, considerable insightful and important work has nevertheless been done by theologians across faith traditions. My philosophical brief for agape could supplement that work by helping to set diverse faith traditions on the path of epistemologically and ontologically rigorous disciplines.

While theological reflection is plagued by irrationality, scholars of religion, especially those influenced by modern Western rationality, are overwhelmingly captured by naturalistic and secular rationalities, so vast regions of religious studies are dedicated to study of the history, sociology, or psychology of religion, not to rigorous exploration of the dynamics of agape. In large part, then, elite academic study of faith traditions is systematically cut off from the living heart of every faith. It is important to study the world's faiths within the parameters of the natural and social sciences, but insofar as scholars at modern universities understand the world's faiths only within scientific parameters, they study the world's religions with no theoretical comprehension of the spiritual reality at their heart.

Let me stress that while predominant streams of modern Western rationality are indeed spiritually impoverished by devastating systemic distortions rooted in naturalist and secular rationalities, considerable insightful and important work has nevertheless been done by a multitude of self-proclaimed naturalist and secular theorists who transgress the truncated parameters of their stated theoretical commitments in fidelity to agape. Just as for millennia people with no theoretical idea about gravity nonetheless took account of its reality in their daily lives, so these theorists reject agape in theory even as they know and treasure its reality in their living. Indeed, many self-proclaimed atheists confusedly reject "God" or "faith" on passionately moral grounds, vibrantly awake to agape. Reckoned in accord with faith defined in terms of surrender to having been seized by agape for all faces, including one's own—where God *is* agape/agape *is* God—this means that the community of self-proclaimed atheists includes many people of true faith.

Bad theory does not wholly cut us off from agape. But theory makes a difference. Unable to name and affirm the call of agape, people who are truly faithful and loving but theoretically bound within the parameters of naturalism or secularism—this is the paradigmatic conundrum of *awakened* naturalists and secularists—are hobbled in their efforts to affirm love, to promote flourishing ethical communities, to find personal peace, and to resist global greed, injustice, and oppression.

Finally, let me note that I am not only a philosopher, and not only a philosopher profoundly influenced by the Jewish philosopher Emmanuel Levinas, but also a Christian, a follower of Jesus Christ, who was crucified because of his fidelity to clearly and publicly speaking agape to an oppressive empire. Because of these influences, my reflections upon agape are primarily written in conversation with Christian and Jewish texts and traditions, and often in a Christian vernacular.[6] My philosophical spirituality, however, is not special-pleading, question-begging, or irrational. I remain within the parameters of what is globally and generally considered reasonable and good.[7]

---

6. It would be natural but incorrect to assume I write in conversation with Gene Outka's important 1972 work *Agape: An Ethical Analysis*, and by extension with Anders Nygren's famous 1930s work *Agape and Eros* (Outka is largely responding to the conversation provoked by Nygren). As a diverse collection of essays published in 2016 in honor of Outka illustrates, the anglophone conversation is important and flourishing (Simmons and Sorrells, eds., *Love and Christian Ethics*). However, the essays in *Love and Christian Ethics* manifest the ongoing reign of naturalistic and secular rationality, for even the most insightful essays in the volume are compromised because they remain confined within the conceptual parameters of naturalist or secular rationality, which is to say, in terms of the typology of Moral Realism Theory, that their explanations of agape are confined within the conceptual parameters of the Sphere of Poetic I's or even the Sphere of Nature. For entirely accidental reasons, my immediate philosophical conceptual heritage is not Nygren, Outka, and the anglophone conversation, but Heidegger's *Being and Time*, Richard Rorty's post-representationalism, Augustine's work on time (in conversation with Aristotle and Plotinus), the work of Marcel Mauss, Jacques Derrida, and Jean-Luc Marion on "counterfeit money" and "gift" and, above all, the philosophy of Emmanuel Levinas.

7. I sometimes get vague calls to define more precisely what I mean by "reasonable and good." I could note that I begin, in all my works, from the contention that it is

I read Christian and Jewish Scriptures and theologians precisely as I read Plato, Aristotle, the Bhagavad Gita, Kant, Heidegger, and Levinas. I do not presume any Scriptures are inerrant or infallible. Faith traditions, like all traditions, can carry systemic distortions and perpetuate harmful prejudices. However, insofar as the world's Scriptures are typically texts that originally proved to be spiritually profound and were then edited and re-edited and/or interpreted and reinterpreted over centuries by diverse generations of peoples living through both times of prosperity and times of terror, so that predominant interpretations of each scriptural tradition come to represent the most profound collective life-tested spiritual wisdom of a people, the world's Scriptures and their interpretive traditions deserve respect on a par with the works of acknowledged philosophical or literary giants and their interpretive traditions.

Accordingly, as my closing essays make clear, I eagerly welcome complementary explorations of agape from other faith and wisdom traditions—from Buddhism to Humanism to Wicca. In the light of agape, we should respect, learn from, and love one another as fellow travelers, we should all be thankful that we are among multitudes who are awakened and striving to live out fidelity to agape, and we should be thankful that there are diverse texts and traditions of spiritual genius helping us to understand how to live gloriously and faithfully in its light.

William Greenway
Austin, Texas
March 2023

---

reasonable and good to think torturing infants, or the Holocaust and similar ethical horrors are genuinely evil, not simply happenings that, due to conditioning or choice, I happen not to prefer. But let me suggest a more precise approach: you name a conceptual move or assertion I make that does not qualify as "reasonable and good" and I will defend myself (such concrete criticisms are to date wholly lacking in response to my work).

Chapter 1

Peter Singer, Emmanuel Levinas, Christian Agape, and the Spiritual Heart of Animal Liberation

> Animal liberation will require greater altruism on the part of [humanity] than any other liberation movement.
> —Peter Singer, *Animal Liberation*[1]

Peter Singer is rightly celebrated as the father of the modern Western secular animal rights movement, and also for influential arguments condemning global inequities.[2] In "Famine, affluence and morality," Singer introduced his famous "shallow pond" analogy.[3] Singer imagines he sees a small child drowning in a shallow pond. He can save the child, but that would muddy his expensive shoes. Should he save the child or walk on by? "Save the child," Singer responds emphatically. Likewise, he argues, if the rich do not aid the poor when faced with a similar ratio of benefit to cost, what they are doing is morally equivalent to walking on by. Reasoning similarly in *Animal*

---

1. Singer, *Animal Liberation*, 29.
2. Generally, Andrew Linzey is considered to be the father of the late twentieth-century Christian animal rights movement.
3. Singer, "Famine, affluence and morality."

Liberation, Singer documented horrific treatment, to relatively little gain, of animals in medical and industrial experiments and in factory "farms." A significant swath of the Western public drew an emphatic moral conclusion, and the late twentieth-century animal rights movement was born.

We who are passionate over the well-being of nonhuman animals and global inequities owe Peter Singer our gratitude. I argue from within this horizon of gratitude. I focus upon a twofold lacuna in Singer's thought (and in modern Western ethics generally) of which Singer himself is fully cognizant, namely, his inability objectively to ground his ethical theory (and avoid moral skepticism) and his inability to provide a compelling answer to the question, "why act morally?"

I suggest Jewish philosopher Emmanuel Levinas unfolds an essentially Christian notion of agape that resolves this twofold lacuna by unveiling a reasonable moral ground for ethics that answers the question, "why act morally?" A Levinasian ethic also forecloses upon some of Singer's more notorious conclusions and better articulates and legitimates the ethical contentions and moral dynamics that made "Famine, affluence, and morality" and *Animal Liberation* so influential. Singer himself thinks these important works pivot upon *ad hominem* argument (namely, they work by unveiling inconsistent ethical reasoning).[4] From a Levinasian perspective, Singer's pivotal works are models of sound ethical reasoning morally grounded in agape.

PETER SINGER'S METAETHICAL CONUNDRUM

Let me follow Singer's lead in *Practical Ethics* and begin by roughly specifying what, for Singer, ethics is not. First, ethical norms and moral motivation do not come from religion. In relation to the twofold lacuna, for reasons familiar since Plato, appealing to God in order to ground ethics begs the relevant questions.[5] With regard to the reward/threat of heaven/hell as a source of moral motivation, many people who believe in heaven and hell are immoral, and many people who do not believe are moral. So, appeals to religion neither ground ethics nor provide reliable motivation for being moral.[6]

Second, in the course of human evolution as social mammals we "developed a moral faculty that generates intuitions about right and wrong."[7] Such intuitions, including those related to kinship, reciprocal, and group altruism, were selected in accord with survival potentials, not in accord with

4. Singer, "Reply to Michael Huemer," 390–92.
5. Singer, *Practical Ethics*, 3.
6. Singer, *Practical Ethics*, 3–4.
7. Singer, *Practical Ethics*, 4.

ethical truth, so there is no reason to conclude evolved intuitions track ethical truth.[8] This, says Singer, is why intuitions appropriate to small, primitive human communities, such as "be fruitful and multiply" or "homosexuality is evil" are no longer reliable guides.[9] It is equally confused to equate what is natural with what is good (as becomes clear the moment we fight disease). Ethics, Singer concludes, should not be dictated by nature.

Once we are "free" of God and nature, Singer says, our task is to "work out" which intuitions to affirm.[10] The plot thickens as we try to discern how precisely we are to work this out. Singer insists ethics cannot be relative to society, for if ethics were relative to society then in some societies slavery would be ethical. That, Singer says, is clearly incorrect. Nor can ethics be subjective—a matter of personal taste or individual choice—for that would be more relativistic than sociocultural relativism.[11] At the same time, Singer concedes, two centuries of attempts to deduce substantive ethical norms from reason alone have failed.[12]

If ethics cannot be relative to society, cannot be the product of subjective preference or choice, is not (so far) the product of reason, and does not come from nature or God, how do we "work out" which intuitions to affirm as truly ethical, and why act morally? At this conceptual juncture in *Practical Ethics*, Singer detours. Even though we cannot say how we can establish ethical norms, Singer insists, we can still make demands about reasoning if it is to be ethical reasoning. For instance, appeals to self-interest may be rational, but they are not ethical. At a minimum, Singer contends, in order to be ethical the reasoning must adopt a universal perspective.[13] On this point, Singer says, all the famous names agree: Moses, Jesus, the Greek philosophers, Stoics of the Roman era, and modern Western thinkers as varied as R. M. Hare, Adam Smith, John Rawls, Jean-Paul Sartre, and Jürgen Habermas.[14]

As this disparate list of ethical thinkers illustrates, the formal contention that ethics must involve appeal to the impartial/universal does not entail any particular, substantive ethical theory. Singer recommends preference utilitarianism because, in contrast to theories that invoke "rights," "sanctity

---

8. de Lazari-Radek and Singer, "Objectivity of Ethics and the Unity of Practical Reason," 13–15.
9. Singer, *Practical Ethics*, 4.
10. Singer, *Practical Ethics*, 5.
11. Singer, *Practical Ethics*, 5–8.
12. Singer, *Practical Ethics*, 13.
13. Singer, *Practical Ethics*, 8–11.
14. Singer, *Practical Ethics*, 10–11.

of life," and the like, preference utilitarianism involves minimal metaphysical commitments. You begin with individual self-interest (i.e., preferences/desires), typically called "rational egoism," and you add only impartiality (i.e., consideration for every affected being's preferences/desires), typically called "universal benevolence."[15]

In all of this, Singer is solidly in line with classic utilitarianism, which arose in the nineteenth century in an effort to establish ethics as a science. Utilitarianism seemed especially promising because it anchored good and bad firmly in the natural world: pain is bad and pleasure is good. This helped secure ethics' claim to scientific status, for pain and pleasure are measurable phenomena and, all else equal, animals move to avoid pain and to gain pleasure. Since animals with advanced cognitive capacities sometimes prefer pain to pleasure (e.g., humans), Singer uses the richer vocabulary of preferences.[16] Singer also inherits the well-known problem of the "dualism of practical reason" (the essence of which I am unfolding in terms of the twofold lacuna).

The dualism of practical reason follows directly from utilitarian theory's foundational definition of "good" and "bad" in terms of pain and pleasure, for the pain and pleasure in question is some being's pain and pleasure, and so bad and good, are indexed to that individual being's desires/happiness/preferences. That is, good and bad are anchored in "rational egoism"—each being's passion/desire above all for her or his own well-being/preferences. This foundational good and bad, then, is not an *ethical* good and bad, for the rational egoist's good/pleasure/preferences and bad/pain/the undesired are good or bad in a self-interested sense—they only become ethical in light of commitment to impartiality/universal benevolence. In order to do ethics, utilitarians must add impartiality/universal benevolence to rational egoism. Rational egoism, however, does not in itself generate any reason to adopt an impartial/universal benevolence perspective. To the contrary, rational egoist desires and the ethical demands of an impartial/universal benevolence perspective often conflict. Moreover, it is not *unreasonable* for the rational egoist to prefer not to be ethical.

Hitting these conceptual obstacles in *Practical Ethics*, Singer promises to return to the issue in the final chapter and, pointing out that we can argue rationally among ethical theories without resolving the twofold lacuna/dualism of practical reason, Singer (as already noted) detours, putting preference utilitarianism into conversation with other major ethical theories. Amidst all the rigorous, comparative ethical reasoning in the balance of

---

15. Singer, *Practical Ethics*, 10–14.
16. Singer, *Practical Ethics*, 12–14.

Practical Ethics, it is easy to forget we lack any decisive argument grounding ethics and any answer to the question, "why act morally?" Singer invites readers to judge for themselves which of the ethical theories is superior, but he provides no criteria for readers to use to make their decisions.[17] Throughout the book he appeals to readers' moral intuitions (e.g., vis-à-vis the shallow pond or the evil of slavery).[18] To be sure, all this describes the situation and approach of modern Western ethics generally.[19] Singer should be commended for frankly acknowledging his inability to ground ethics and his inability to answer the question, "why act morally?" (i.e., the twofold lacuna haunting modern Western ethics).[20]

BASIC ASPECTS OF SINGER'S PREFERENCE UTILITARIANISM

Singer does not assign ethical significance to species membership.[21] For Singer, extant capacity for preferences/desires/pleasures anchors ethical consideration. I *do not* injure a cat or a comatose child by refusing to teach them to read, for no extant preference/desire is violated. I *do* injure a seven-year-old girl if I refuse to teach her to read or a cat if I keep him in a cage,

---

17. Singer, *Practical Ethics*, 15.

18. Huemer, "Singer's unstable meta-ethics," 373.

19. Consider Beauchamp and Childress's widely acclaimed and entirely typical *Principles of Biomedical Ethics*. Their "moral foundation" is at root a straight decision to take "the common morality as the universal morality" (2–3). The chapters on theory and method come at *the end* of the book; after all the concrete ethical bioethical reasoning is completed. Mirroring standard practice in modern Western introduction to ethics courses, they review all the major modern Western ethical theories and explain how all have been invalidated because, vis-à-vis diverse ethical situations, they each entail conclusions that are grossly *counterintuitive*. At the same time, Beauchamp and Childress, in accord with mainstream modern Western ethics, officially dismiss appeals to intuition.

20. Or a bit more precisely, all this applies to modern Western ethics insofar as it remains committed to ethical realism. Thomas Hobbes, rejecting ethical realism, explains how we can still go a long way toward legitimating civil society through appeal to *enlightened* selfishness (*Leviathan*). Hobbes, a naturalist, would have thought Sidgwick/Singer's "dualism of practical reason" to be fundamentally confused (Sidgwick, *Methods of Ethics*). To put the point in Hume's terms, insofar as all that "is" is "physical" or "nature" in the modern Western sense, once one establishes that "ought" cannot be derived from "is," one has entirely dissolved the sphere of "ought" in any realist/objective sense. There is no moral realm, no ought, no benevolence (aside from what I, for my own reasons, prefer to extend), no motivation that is rooted in or responsive to objective good. When the is/ought distinction is related to naturalistic ontology in this fashion, it is significant.

21. Singer, *Rethinking Life and Death*, 202–6.

for in both cases extant preferences/desires are violated. If a human child and rabbit are equally susceptible to pain when shampoo runs into their eyes, then to cause equal pain in a child or rabbit is equally wrong. This inclusive understanding is intuitive when looking at pictures of eyelid-less bunnies strapped to the vivisection table, and its public power is visible in the impassioned movement for animal rights inspired by *Animal Liberation*. At the same time, Singer's preference utilitarianism diminishes our overall moral sensitivities and at points leads to conclusions just as horrifying as walking on by the child drowning in the shallow pond.

For instance, for Singer, any animal that imagines a future and prefers to live into that future (e.g., does not prefer euthanasia) has a right to life. Likewise, no animal who experiences pain and prefers to avoid it should be made to suffer. All else equal, no animal with a preference to live into the future should be killed, and no animal who can experience pain should be made to suffer.

Singer understands that often all else is not equal.[22] For instance, if a human must kill a deer in order to survive, then, balancing the full depth and range of preferences and desires of the human in comparison to the deer, a utilitarian calculus (i.e., maximize good), dictates that the human should kill the deer. At the same time, if the human could survive by eating snails and grubs, then the snails and grubs, not the deer, should be killed. With respect to the same hierarchy of value and utilitarian calculus, it would be better yet for the human to eat only scallops and mollusks, which may be unable even to feel pain. Best of all, Singer affirms, there is no ethical problem in eating cabbage, rice, soybeans, and the like, for, with nothing akin to a brain or nervous system, there is no reason to think plants, any more than rocks, experience anything at all.[23] In areas of biological ambiguity, Singer urges us to err on the side of caution (he now avoids eating scallops), but in most cases we can be fairly sure of the pertinent capacities of various beings.

Singer's approach diminishes moral sensitivities in two ways. First, plants and all animals with rudimentary or impaired cognitive capacities wholly or largely vanish from our sphere of moral concern. Second, Singer's theory of ethical argument fosters a methodological disengagement that marginalizes the felt reality of moral passion—this in marked contrast to the intuitive appeals (e.g., the drowning child, the tortured monkeys) that anchor his most influential works. In the case of the human killing the deer for life-sustaining sustenance, Singer would have us perform the utilitarian calculation, realize that killing the deer is the right thing to do, and kill

---

22. Singer, *Rethinking Life and Death*, 202–6.
23. Singer, *Rethinking Life and Death*, 203.

the deer, period. Singer has no place for lament, no naming of the tragic character of existence, no talk of choosing the lesser of two evils, no place for confessing oneself a killer in a fallen world. Singer's ethical calculations are cold-blooded because Singer is faithful to mainstream modern Western philosophy, which idealizes above all the objective conclusions of dispassionate reason.

Cold-blooded becomes chilling when Singer applies his theory to human infants. Since human infants can feel pain and hunger, can desire to move, and so forth, to deny such would be unethical. However, insofar as human infants have no time-consciousness, no sense of themselves as beings with a future, nothing extant is taken from them if no future comes. That is, provided it can be done painlessly, and that the preferences of the parents make it desirable, Singer holds it is ethical to kill human infants.

There is some question as to when time-consciousness develops, so with regard to infanticide Singer recommends a biologically conservative twenty-eight-day limit. Accordingly, if a child is unexpectedly born with Down syndrome (as in Singer's example) or, by the same reasoning, when there is nothing remarkable about the baby, but the parents have recently fallen in love with an expensive, time-consuming hobby or gotten new jobs, and their infant is less than twenty-eight days old, then the parents should have the right to have that infant killed if they so prefer (provided the killing is painless).[24]

Singer defends infanticide with clinical detachment.[25] I find Singer's infanticide scenarios just as horrifying as the idea of walking on by while the child in the shallow pond drowns. It is chilling to imagine a society in which parents' right to kill infants has been institutionalized. Singer suggests we might establish some sort of neo-birthday type celebration to mark the parents' decision to accept—that is, not to kill—their infant.[26] Singer claims cultivation of altruism is essential if we are to create a maximally ethical world, but his ethical theory not only has no conceptual space for altruism as a manifestation of love, it seems unlikely to cultivate altruism.

Let me be quick at this juncture to remember our debt to Singer and the moral passion of "Famine, affluence, and morality" and *Animal Liberation*. Singer's most influential works display and presume the very moral passions that should lead us to evaluate his ethical theory with caution and, at points, to reject it in horror. From my perspective, Singer is at these problematic

---

24. Singer, *Rethinking Life and Death*, 213–18; Singer, *Practical Ethics*, 151–67.
25. Singer, *Rethinking Life and Death*, 213–18; Singer, *Practical Ethics*, 151–67.
26. Singer, *Rethinking Life and Death*, 217.

points a victim of modern Western rationality's unqualified celebration of dispassionate reasoning.

SINGER: "WHY ACT MORALLY?"

In the concluding chapter of *Practical Ethics*, "Why Act Morally?," Singer reconsiders heaven and hell as moral motivators. He rejects the possibility not because of its wholly selfish (i.e., not impartial, not ethical) motivational structure, but because there is insufficient evidence of an afterlife. The selfish (and, by the way, wholly un-Christian) motivational structure would be no problem for Singer. Indeed, he explicitly affirms a rational egoist "ulterior motive" in relation to moral motivation for acting in accord with impartiality/universal benevolence.[27]

Singer's surprising stance is explained when he gives what for decades was his best answer to the question, "why act morally?" His answer: because your greatest and deepest happiness in the long run will be found in leading an ethical life.[28] Singer even musters studies showing ethical people are happier. Singer is aware of the paradoxical nature of appealing to self-interest in order to justify adopting an impartial/universal benevolence perspective. He identifies the "paradox of hedonism"—act so as to secure the happiness of others in order to secure your own happiness—but he cannot resolve it. This is no small problem, for when he resolves the dualism of practical reason by affirming the ulterior motives of the rational egoist for acting ethically, he loses the ability to distinguish between people who act *as if* they are impartial/universally benevolent *in order to be themselves happy* and people who *actually are* universally benevolent for reasons Singer cannot yet imagine (and who are, as an unintended consequence, happier).

Singer is unconvinced by his own responses to the twofold lacuna. Singer concludes a 2005 essay, "Ethics and Intuition," with his most concise statement of the current challenge: "In light of the best scientific understanding of ethics, we face a choice. We can take the view that our moral intuitions and judgments are and always will be emotionally based intuitive responses, and reason can do no more than build the best possible case for a decision already made on non-rational grounds."[29] This option, "leads to ... moral skepticism."[30] On the other hand, "we might attempt the ambitious task of separating those moral judgments that we owe to our evolutionary

---

27. Singer, *Practical Ethics*, 285–86.
28. Singer, *Practical Ethics*, 283–95; Singer, *How Are We to Live?*, vii–x, 235.
29. Singer "Ethics and Intuitions," 351.
30. Singer "Ethics and Intuitions," 305.

and cultural history, from those that have a rational basis." This, Singer contends, is "the only way to avoid moral skepticism."[31]

Recently, Katarzyna de Lazari-Radek and Singer have taken up the "ambitious task" of defending the objectivity of ethics by clarifying its rational basis.[32] In brief, de Lazari-Radek and Singer argue that while evolutionary theory *can* explain kinship, reciprocal, or group altruism (for they are indexed to Darwinian potentials), it cannot explain "pure altruism," namely, "universal altruism of the sort that is required by the axiom of [universal] benevolence."[33] Our "intuitive grasp of the principle of universal benevolence," they argue, is "like our ability to do higher mathematics" or physics and can, likewise, "most plausibly be explained as the outcome of our capacity to reason."[34] Moreover, the "intuition" of the "axiom of universal benevolence" has never been discredited by any philosophy.

Furthermore, de Lazari-Radek and Singer claim, the axiom is consistent with the Jewish, Christian, Confucian, Hindu, and Buddhist traditions.[35] They concede it is not irrational to affirm rational egoism and reject universal benevolence, but insofar as we "form the intuition [i.e., of the axiom of universal benevolence] as a result of a process of careful reflection"—namely, we realize

31. Singer "Ethics and Intuitions," 305.

32. de Lazari-Radek and Singer, "Objectivity of Ethics," and de Lazari-Radek and Singer, *Point of View of the Universe*; the quote is from "Objectivity of Ethics," 9.

33. "Objectivity of Ethics," 19. The text says, "rational benevolence" (which is the phrase de Lazari-Radek and Singer end up using) but it is more consistent at this juncture in my/their argument to say, "*universal* benevolence."

34. "Objectivity of Ethics," 26. The precise ontological status of "objective" ethical facts in Singer remains ambiguous. Singer sometimes says they have the same status as mathematical facts (which is potentially troublesome, since mathematical facts are usually considered to be objective in an analytic sense), but he sometimes says they have the same status as facts in physics (which would indeed give them significant ontological heft, but it is not clear that I bump up against the axiom of rational benevolence in the same way that I bump up against gravity [compare de Lazari-Radek and Singer bottom of 16, "mathematics or physics," and middle of 26, only "mathematics"]). Notably, a Levinasian argument for the "objective" reality of agape will meet de Lazari-Radek and Singer's criteria for "establishing that an intuition has the highest possible degree of reliability" (*Point of View of the Universe*, 195; "Objectivity of Ethics," 26). Significantly, having been taken hostage to passion for others is different from having an intuition. In contrast to Singer, who thinks of intuitions (including the axiom of rational benevolence) as something "we form" (de Lazari and Singer, "Objectivity of Ethics," 25), on a Levinasian account "agape" names a reality by which we are taken hostage (hence its distinct ontological status is different from mathematical axioms and is as basic/discrete—though different in kind—as the realities named by physics, for insofar as we are not psychopathic we are seized by agape differently but every bit as concretely as we are seized by gravity). Note also that a Levinasian agape ethic does not affirm multiple ethical or moral intuitions, but a single, moral reality.

35. de Lazari-Radek and Singer, "Objectivity of Ethics," 19.

it is reasonable to extend our altruism beyond kin, reciprocal, and group parameters—reason takes us beyond evolutionary parameters to affirmation of impartiality/universal benevolence.[36] Pure altruism, then, has a strong claim to objective truth status because (a) its appearance and endurance is not indexed to evolutionary forces, (b) it is widely affirmed, (c) it is nowhere discredited, and (d) it is grounded in reason.[37]

Moreover, de Lazari-Radek and Singer notice that the "egoism" of so-called "rational egoism" *is* directly explicable by evolutionary dynamics, which means the "rational" is unjustified, for egoism's appearance and endurance is not indexed to reason or the good.[38] Egoism is a brute evolutionary product. It is universal benevolence, "pure" altruism that, like the truths of higher mathematics and physics, is the product of reasoning and so is likewise indexed to rationality/truth. This resolves the dualism of practical reason in favor of impartiality/universal benevolence because "rational egoism" is displaced by "brute egoism" and "impartiality/universal benevolence" is replaced by "*rational* impartiality/universal benevolence." As a matter of reason there is no contest between brute egoism and rational benevolence: rational benevolence prevails.

A shadow of the dualism endures insofar as this affirmation of the axiom of universal benevolence's claim to truth status still leaves us with a split between desire/passion/partiality and dispassionate rationality/impartiality. We may not have established a "motivating reason" to act morally, de Lazari-Radek and Singer concede, but we have strongly defended the truth of "normative reason." We have a rational answer to the question, "why act morally?" then, because it is reasonable to affirm the truth of the axiom of rational benevolence and a desire to act rationally can reasonably direct action.[39]

De Lazari-Radek and Singer significantly advance our understanding, but the price of their strict bifurcation between passion/desire and reason amplifies the cold-bloodedness of Singer's ethical theory. "Pure altruism" on their account names our logical recognition of the legitimacy of an axiom's claim to be true. Strictly speaking, on their account when we witness the girl abused, the monkey tortured, or the smoke from the camp ovens, what so disturbs us is violation *of an axiom* that we reasonably affirm to be true. On their account, in all such cases we are disturbed in *precisely* the same way we are disturbed when we witness violation of what

---

36. de Lazari-Radek and Singer, "Objectivity of Ethics," 25; de Lazari-Radek and Singer, *Point of View of the Universe*, 193.
37. de Lazari-Radek and Singer, "Objectivity of Ethics," 25–26.
38. de Lazari-Radek and Singer, *Point of View of the Universe*, 197–99.
39. de Lazari-Radek and Singer, *Point of View of the Universe*, 197–99.

we reasonably affirm to be true in higher mathematics or physics (e.g., when we "witness" mathematical miscalculations). Their account utterly fails to capture the lived passion of our moral horror over the violation of others (e.g., the girl, the monkey, Jewish people).

EMMANUEL LEVINAS AND THE "ETHICS OF ETHICS"

Jewish philosopher Emmanuel Levinas focuses his work upon the twofold lacuna that bedevils Singer and modern Western ethics. Levinas studied with Martin Heidegger in 1926 and 1927. In 1940, Levinas, by then a French officer, was captured by the Nazis and segregated with other Jews at a labor camp, Stalag XIB. When released in 1945, he learned his mother, father, two younger brothers (his entire immediate family), and mother-in-law had been murdered by the Nazis.[40] Heidegger was an ardent Nazi. Levinas's judgment of Heidegger was not ambiguous. Nonetheless, he thought Heidegger's *Being and Time* was critical to legitimating what Levinas called "the ethics of ethics."[41]

In brief, Heidegger answered this question: what could exist other than nature in a naturalistic sense? Heidegger distinguished between the ontic and the ontological. Ontic basically designates nature in the naturalistic sense. Ontic being is the being of chairs, balls, planets, and nature (i.e., "nature" in the naturalistic sense). In this sense, we are ontic beings, our bodies and brains are ontic. However, Heidegger argues, the ontic character of some beings makes them also ontological. *Ontological* names the be-ing of beings that distinguish things as such and that are, moreover, concerned about being and be-ing. Chairs do not distinguish chairs in reality or care at all. So far, the same is apparently true for smartphones, which "see" in a metaphorical sense, but which do not see chairs as chairs or care about the be-ing of being. Chairs have being but no be-ing. Some beings, however, *also* enjoy be-ing, they see the being of chairs as chairs, and they are concerned over their own be-ing. The character and concern of beings with be-ing cannot be adequately described in ontic/physical categories.

Heidegger names beings with be-ing, (i.e., ontological beings) *Dasein*, which, literally translated, means "there-be-ing," and marks the emergence of concerned, ontological be-ing within the midst of raw ontic being. Dasein is what we humans are (Heidegger remains anthropocentric): passionate loci of be-ing within being. We are, moreover, passionate be-ings aware of our own coming deaths. In a word, we are each passionate be-ing-toward-death.

40. Malka, *Emmanuel Levinas*, 6.
41. Heidegger, *Being and Time*.

I may have passion for others, but that is authentically my own concern only if it is my freely self-chosen concern, not a product of the "they" (i.e., of nature and/or nurture).

Levinas uses Heidegger's argument for ontological be-ing to move beyond naturalism.[42] He thinks Heidegger is wrong, however, to think humans are above all else passionate over their own lives and deaths. For insofar as we are truly awakened to the lived, impassioned dimension of be-ing in this vale of tears, we invariably find ourselves taken hostage by the Faces of others (I capitalize "Face" to signal the neologism). You see the child drowning in the shallow pond; the gallows at Auschwitz; the starving baby with Down syndrome; the child burnt, running, and screaming as the napalm fireball lights up the sky behind her; the bull bloody and staggering in the ring; eyelid-less bunnies strapped to the vivisectionist's table; a paralyzed but conscious cockroach dragged into the nest by the wasp, and you are not initially neutral and dispassionate in deciding what to think or what theory to bring into play, you are taken hostage directly by the suffering, pleading, murdered Faces. You may also be taken hostage by Faces amidst happy circumstances. You see the birds singing happily at sunrise, the woman playing in the field with her dog, the children rolling in the grass, and you are happy, smiling, rejoicing, taken hostage by passion for those Faces.

The Face that takes us hostage is not the physical face, the color of the eyes, the nationality, the intelligence, or any other natural or social factor, not even—and here I step beyond Levinas's overt specification, but not beyond his logic—the be-ing's species. The Face is precisely that which is discerned in the event of our having been taken hostage to concern for another.[43]

The reality of the Face can be especially powerful in awful circumstances, where one is taken hostage by the faces of those who are suffering, persecuted, murdered. The hostage language is harsh but true to Levinas's wartime experience, and to the fact that in awful circumstances we do not want to be taken up by such pain, we would love from a selfish perspective to turn away, not to witness the horror, but we realize we are not really free to turn away. As the Nazi *Schutzstaffel* (SS) officers illustrate, we can harden

---

42. See especially: Levinas, *Entre-nous*; Levinas, *Of God Who Comes to Mind*; Levinas, *Otherwise Than Being*.

43. At this conceptual juncture we need to guard against widespread reductionistic readings of Levinas that reduce the otherness of others precisely to sociocultural distinctions such as ethnicity, gender, culture, species. Levinas is aware of otherness in this sociocultural sense, but this is not the otherness with which he is concerned. Levinas is concerned with the transcending *moral otherness* of sociocultural, gendered, and species others, that is, that of others that renders us hostage to passion for them.

our hearts, but we cannot do so freely, for we cannot harden our hearts without doing violence to passion for the other by which we have already been taken hostage.

From this perspective, the modern demand that ethics begin from an objective, dispassionate stance is revealed to be confused. To idealize initial dispassion in the presence of moral horror is not reasonable, it is monstrous. The moral response comes first, before theory. This is why Levinas speaks of ethics as "first philosophy"—this in marked contrast to modern Western epistemological prioritizing of dispassionate, objective reason.[44] I suspect this is the reality de Lazari-Radek and Singer attempt to describe when they speak of "our intuitive grasp of the principle of universal benevolence," but their description is inexact, most especially in its alienation from the lived reality of having been taken hostage by passion for Faces.[45] We do not "intuit" or "form an intuition" of an axiom of benevolence. We after the fact (transcendentally) name the reality of having been taken hostage by passionate concern for Faces.

The passion of being taken hostage by the Faces of others is, for Levinas, the most immediate, plainly undeniable, and significant of realities. It does not originate in nature in the material sense (nor, derivatively, as a meme). It does not come from God in the sense of an oral command or directive written down somewhere that I believe and obey. It is not a product of reason itself, nor a product of my own intentionality or choice. This passion for others is not from me. It has me. What Levinas is describing is what Christians call agape—love for others and passion we surrender to or against which we harden our hearts. There is no neutral, objective, or dispassionate starting point. In concrete circumstances we find ourselves from the first taken hostage by the Faces of particular others. Our free will is not wholly negated, but our option is not, from a dispassionate, impartial perspective to choose (*ex nihilo*) whether or not to be ethical. Our only self-assertive choice is negative, to harden our hearts. Or we surrender and act decisively in response to having been taken hostage by concern for Faces.

Levinas says the reality of having been taken hostage by the Faces of others is how God comes to mind.[46] This is God insofar as God *is* love. I would argue that this understanding is far more faithful to classic Jewish and Christian understanding, and for that matter to Hindu or Buddhist understanding, than is the case with Singer's "Golden Rule" interpretation. For Levinas, the whole point of the Torah is to flesh out the implications

---

44. Levinas, "Ethics as First Philosophy."
45. de Lazari-Radek and Singer, *Point of View of the Universe*, 193.
46. Levinas, *Of God Who Comes to Mind*.

of agape for real life. I would contend Christian theology takes up the same task. Insofar as God *is* love, *is* agape, *is* having been taken hostage by passion for all Faces, the reality of God *is* the reality of agape *is* the reality of the moral. We might call an ethics grounded in agape in this sense an agape ethics.

For agape ethics, "the moral" and "ethics" are different. The "moral" names agape, having been taking hostage by passion for every Face—for every child, every deer, every mollusk, even every cabbage. Taken singly, each Face seizes us absolutely, infinitely, incomparably. Insofar as we are wholly awake, we are taken hostage by a glorious sea of Faces. Insofar as we live in this vale of tears, wholesale awakening is simultaneously joyous and searing—and we are consumed with desire to maximize the joy and minimize the violation of Faces.

The "ethics" in agape ethics names the reasoning and judgment necessary when we need to adjudicate among Faces, when we need to discern as wisely as possible how to and/or what will maximize joy and minimize violation for all Faces. The need for ethics, then, arises when we confront what Levinas calls "the third," which is the third or three thousandth Face that appears in a context when we must adjudicate among Faces. Given my distinction between "the moral" and "ethics," what Levinas calls "the ethics of ethics" I would call "the moral ground of ethics."

Ethics without agape is empty, devoid of passion, but agape without ethics is hapless, devoid of critical discernment. Often, as in the shallow pond scenario, or with regard to slavery or useless and cruel medical experiments, there is no question what love desires for others' Faces. If forced to adjudicate among Faces in irremediable conflict as described in the example of the human needing to choose between starvation and eating a deer, mollusk, or soybean, I would largely affirm Singer's utilitarian ethic, including the delineation of a hierarchy of value indexed to creaturely capacity—though I would give more ethical weight than does Singer to unrealized life potentials (e.g., of a fetus)—but the shift to agape makes a decisive difference.

To illustrate, a trolley is coming down the track. On the track is a two-month-old human baby. I can throw a switch diverting the trolley, so the baby will be saved, but that will kill an earthworm on the other track. There are no other options. Should I throw the switch? Forced to "compare incomparables" (i.e., the Face of the baby and the Face of the worm), I affirm Singer's ethical hierarchy of value and utilitarian calculation and throw the switch, saving the baby and killing the earthworm. However, in contrast to Singer, for whom based upon a utilitarian calculation doing so is right, *period*, in the light of an agape ethic I *mourn the worm* and acknowledge I have been forced in a fallen world to do evil, to become a killer. To proclaim the world fallen in the agapeic sense (which is not a historical sense) is to acknowledge that we find ourselves inextricably caught in situations where we must compare incomparables, where we must choose among bad alternatives, *where to do what is ethically best may simultaneously be to do what is morally evil.*

The shift to agape ethics also makes a decisive difference vis-à-vis infanticide. Insofar as we are taken hostage to passionate concern for every Face, even the Faces of cabbages, it is unimaginable we would kill infants because that is the preference of their parents (this is not to foreclose upon the question of euthanasia for an infant, or anyone else, in untreatable, near-term terminal agony, but infanticide is decisively rejected).

While agape ethics is radically pro-life, however, it is not automatically antiabortion. If we are comparing the autonomy and preferences of a pregnant woman to a zygote, for instance, the differences are much the same as those we faced when comparing the human baby and the earthworm. So, we radically privilege the preferences of the woman. Later in pregnancy, as the differences between fetus and baby become vanishingly small, ethical weighting should shift accordingly (i.e., to an increasing degree over time in pregnancy, we should no more kill a fetus than we should kill a baby). I will not delve further into the fierce debates over abortion, but this illustrates how with regard to ethical quandary cases agape ethics marginalizes extreme positions (e.g., infanticide, absolute valuing of the zygote, wholesale devaluing of the late-stage fetus) even as significant areas of uncertainty remain (e.g., what trumps when there are extenuating circumstances? What about scenarios at twenty-two weeks?).

Agape ethics reframes key ethical issues in critical and intuitively powerful ways, then, but it does not provide magical shortcuts vis-à-vis quandary cases. It may sometimes remain unclear what is the most loving action or how to adjudicate among Faces. While agape ethics does not eliminate all ethical quandary cases—no ethics does that—it has a major virtue beyond its critical reframing of key ethical issues. Namely, it eliminates the twofold lacuna. Agape ethics understands moral motivation to be intrinsic to having been taken hostage by passion for all Faces, so the question, "why act morally?" never arises. Indeed, the very appearance of the question "why act morally?" betrays the privileging of the monstrous, wholly dispassionate, neutral stance. It is no accident that Singer ends up addressing psychopaths in *Practical Ethics*, for the standard modern Western idea that "rational" entails "dispassionate" not only presumes but idealizes the absence of any initial moral inclinations—sheer egoism is thereby baptized as the default, rational, neutral stance.[47] In real life, this would be someone who has either hardened their heart completely or someone who, for physical, psychiatric, or psychological reasons, lacks any moral sensitivity. With regard to grounding ethics from a Levinasian perspective, in the event of having been taken hostage by passion—not an evident product of physical evolution, culture, choice, or reason, nowhere credibly discredited, celebrated by all the world's major religions—the objective reality of agape is manifest.

Moreover, if we understand "altruism" in terms of having been taken hostage by passion for all Faces (i.e., as agape), then we can affirm and enhance Singer's hunch about altruism being essential to movements for the liberation of all Faces to lives of minimal pain and maximal flourishing, for agape ethics allows us more accurately to describe the moral and ethical dynamics that make Singer's shallow pond and *Animal Liberation* arguments so *legitimately* powerful (not merely *ad hominem* attacks). In part, Singer did catch our attention by pointing out inconsistency in our ethical reasoning, but what anchored us morally—so we did not just shrug our shoulders and (gaining consistency) say, "so let the child drown," or "experiment on the bunnies"—was the altruistic/agapeic awakening Singer stimulated by placing the Faces of all those suffering, tortured, murdered creatures right in front of us. Awakened, taken hostage by passion for all those hurting Faces, people responded, global poverty relief efforts gained traction, and an animal liberation movement was born—all in response to agape, all because, on a Levinasian reading, Singer, stepping in where historic Western faiths were falling short, helped bring awakening to agape vis-à-vis all Faces of every kind more fully to human hearts and minds.

---

47. Singer, *Practical Ethics*, 288–91.

Chapter 2

Jesus as Moral Philosopher

The Parable of the Good Samaritan

I am privileged to write this essay in honor of my colleague, friend, chess teacher, and chess nemesis, Ismael Garcia. While this essay draws upon my own areas of expertise in theology and ethics, I consider it to provide an independent line of support for the rich and interdependent notions of *dignidad* and community that Garcia unfolds in *Dignidad: Ethics Through Hispanic Eyes*. Not surprisingly, I discern considerable common ground between the ethical wisdom Garcia discerns among Hispanic peoples and the ethical wisdom of Jesus.

The parable of the good Samaritan, Jesus' globally admired interpretation of "love your neighbor as yourself," is the fount of innumerable thoughtful and inspiring sermons and commentaries. What remains largely underdeveloped, however, is full appreciation for the philosophical genius of Jesus' parable and, as a result, full appreciation for the parable's significance in the face of influential modern Western conceptual trajectories that are threatening for classic moral realism (i.e., the idea that "good" and "evil" are more than products of human history).

Let me explain three especially influential and damaging trajectories: 1) metaphysical naturalism, 2) existential atomism, and 3) the equating of legitimate reasoning with objective reasoning. "Metaphysical naturalism" is the belief that ultimately everything is natural or physical in a modern scientific sense. As one metaphysical naturalist, Wayne Proudfoot, professor of religion (!) at Columbia University, put it:

> The inquiries into language and culture that have occupied the humanities and the social sciences for most of the twentieth century, along with progress in the natural sciences, have led to beliefs that conflict with what [William] James took to be the religious hypothesis. Any moral order, any more that is continuous with the higher parts of the self, any forces that might help to bring our ideals about, can be understood only as the emergent social products of the beliefs, desires, and actions of men and women. At the end of the nineteenth century, a number of thinkers subscribed to a kind of panpsychism, which they took to be compatible with the science of their day. At the end of the twentieth century, that belief is no longer plausible.[1]

Proudfoot goes on to explain that while there "is an unseen moral order," this moral order exclusively "consists of the social and cultural world that is a product of history."[2] All this, Proudfoot explains, is why for the past century, "the humanities and social sciences have been preoccupied with the ways in which language is constitutive of agency, experience, social practices, and everything identified with *Geist* [i.e., "spirit"] in the *Geisteswissenschaften* [i.e., sciences of the spirit, social sciences, humanities]."[3]

In other words, the mainstream modern Western natural and social sciences, and even the humanities, have presumed and in many elite circles now find unquestionable (i.e., treat as dogma) the truth of metaphysical naturalism, an affirmation that entails the denial of moral realism in the classic religious and philosophical senses, for moral "realities" are considered to be wholly a product of human linguistic capacities.

The second influential modern Western conceptual trajectory, existential atomism, is in significant tension with metaphysical naturalism, for the mainstream of philosophers who are metaphysical naturalists find the idea of free will to be unintelligible. They acknowledge that we are self-conscious and thinking beings. Nonetheless, our brains/minds, which are understood to be physical in the modern scientific sense, can in no way transcend the deterministic/random progressions of nature. "Existential atomism" is incompatible with metaphysical naturalism because it maintains that ordinarily we are, within some natural and sociocultural limits, free to decide whether we will do one thing or another in any particular circumstance. That is, it affirms a power that transcends the determined and random, a power that transcends the "physical" or "natural" in the modern sense.

---

1. Proudfoot, "Religious Belief and Naturalism," 85.
2. Proudfoot, "Religious Belief and Naturalism," 85.
3. Proudfoot, "Religious Belief and Naturalism," 85.

For the existential atomist, notably, the only thing that distinguishes me from the deterministic/random machinery of reality is my ability to decide for myself, to create myself, my autonomy. The danger is subservience to external conditioning, the possibility that I will never be anything but a product of sociocultural and genetic conditioning (of memes and genes), that I will never have a real "I" at all. The ideal is authenticity, creating the "I" each of us wants to create, accepting the power of choice that distinguishes us from the brute machinery of existence. As the celebrated American philosopher Richard Rorty summed up this conceptual trajectory, our greatest potential possibility, the sole potential source of our dignity as humans, "is the one Coleridge recommended to the great and original poet: to create the taste by which he will be judged."[4]

Momentously, this conceptual trajectory sets up an either/or between autonomy/authenticity and heteronomy/servitude. So, all ethical imperatives—the God of Judaism, Christianity, and Islam, the reality of any external "ought" that delimits my ability to create the very taste by which I will judge myself—become a threat to the sole possible source of human dignity. Furthermore, in this modern Western conceptual context, what is "natural" and "rational" (e.g., see modern "decision theory") is for me to pursue my own interests and desires. Even if my actions look altruistic, to the degree I am not determined or deluded, to the degree my actions are free and rational, then the real reason I ever engage in any action must be because it fulfills my own desires.

In the wake of metaphysical naturalism and existential atomism, altruistic motivation in the classic sense is rendered unreal and irrational by definition. The question "why be moral?" rises up with unprecedented force and finally, at best, allows for only one answer: "because it is in accord with my own enlightened self-interest." What can be "ethical" in the wake of these two conceptual trajectories, then, bears no relation to moral reality in the classic sense (for there is no such). The ethical at best relates to what *I have rationally agreed to treat* as ethical (if only implicitly, as in social contract theory). Moral realism and ethics as classically understood have been rendered unintelligible.

The third conceptual trajectory, the equating of legitimate reasoning with objective reasoning, is devastating because it demands not only that we distance ourselves from self-interest and subjective preferences when reflecting ethically (a classic ethical recommendation to guard against prejudice), but also that we distance ourselves from any feelings of sympathy, any moral intuition, any sense of call from another. We are to reason dispassionately

---

4. Rorty, *Contingency, Irony, and Solidarity*, 97.

and construct ethical theories using only explanations that are natural and reasonable within modern parameters (i.e., the parameters of metaphysical naturalism and existential atomism). This requirement methodologically shuts us off from moral reality as classically understood.[5]

Numerous theologians and philosophers have recognized and responded to these devastating conceptual trajectories. Indeed, our own reading of Jesus' interpretation of the love command is decisively informed by another Jewish interpreter of Torah, Emmanuel Levinas, whose understanding we consider strikingly similar to Jesus' own. But, again, the philosophical significance of Jesus' parable of the good Samaritan, most especially for modern ethics, has yet to be unfolded.

The parable of the good Samaritan is Jesus' interpretation of "love your neighbor as yourself." Jesus' parable is part of his ministry to a lawyer seeking "eternal life." Jesus first elicits and affirms the standard twofold summary of the Torah: 1) love God with all your heart, soul, strength, and mind, and 2) love your neighbor as yourself. "Do this," Jesus affirms, "and you will live."

There was no debate over this summary of the Law, but there was debate over who counted as "neighbor." So the lawyer asks, "who is my neighbor?" For centuries commentators, noting that in Jesus' day Samaritans were considered to be enemies by Jews, and noting also that the Samaritan proved to be neighbor, have read the parable as a call to radically expand the parameters of "neighbor."[6] Who is neighbor? Answer: everyone, even those who profess other faiths, even enemies. This interpretation is certainly not incorrect. Moreover, Jesus' portrayal of an enemy as the one who fulfilled the Law is significant, especially given the historic and enduring power of "us" versus "them" sectarian impulses, for the parable makes clear that anyone, regardless of national or religious identity, may prove to be neighbor.

But to think that Jesus is straightforwardly extending the category of "neighbor" is to miss the depth of his spiritual genius. Jesus realizes that what is keeping the lawyer from true "living" ("do this and you will live") is his all-consuming self-interest. For the lawyer any "neighbors," whoever

---

5. Not surprisingly, this naturalistic turn gave prominence and plausibility to "ethical" theories indexed to pain and pleasure; unsurprisingly, it was never made clear why I should be concerned with anyone else's pain and pleasure (unless such concern related ultimately to my own pain and pleasure).

6. On Samaritans as enemies and for an excellent brief survey of some problematic and common tendencies in interpreting the parable, see Amy Jill-Levine, "Many Faces of the Good Samaritan—Most Wrong," 20–21. Note that Jill-Levine understands "neighbor" in the ordinary sense, thereby joining a virtually universal consensus that stretches at least back to St. Augustine, who in his interpretation gives the ordinary meaning of "neighbor" and interprets the parable accordingly (*On Christian Doctrine*, I.XXX.31).

they might be, will only be means to realizing his own self-interested desire for eternal life. Jesus realizes that the lawyer, and for that matter everyone who accepts the standard framing of the debate over "who counts as neighbor?" is confused over the meaning of "love." Accordingly, it is the meaning of "love" in the *agape*/altruistic sense that is movingly conveyed by the parable.[7]

Jesus displaces the standard debate by radically changing the meaning of "neighbor." Jesus draws our attention to this profound shift when he asks the lawyer, "who proved neighbor?" For Jesus' question regarding "neighbor" directs our focus away from any other (e.g., the man in the ditch) and toward the one who was seized by compassion for another (e.g., the Samaritan). In short, in Jesus' understanding, the meaning of "neighbor" in "love your neighbor" has nothing to do with the identity of the man in the ditch. In the parable not only is "neighbor" not every other; "neighbor" is not any other.

In contrast to standard definition, in the parable "neighbor" names the spiritual orientation of the Samaritan, the spiritual orientation of the one who was seized by compassion for the man in the ditch. "Neighbor" names a way of be-ing, a spiritual orientation, a way of living in this world. "Neighbor" names the spiritual orientation of the prodigal's father, who was also (same Greek word) seized by compassion. "Neighbor" names the spiritual orientation of those who feed the hungry, welcome the stranger, clothe the naked, care for the sick, visit the imprisoned. "Neighbor" names the spiritual orientation of sheep (Matthew 25).

Note the passive character of this love in and by which we find ourselves seized. This love comes from without and cannot be heard (no "ears to hear") if one insists that authentic life depends upon the atomistic (intentional) self and its power of choice being absolutely primary. The Samaritan is not obeying any command in the sense of *choosing* to be obedient to any concept, principle, divinity or any other inert external authority. The Samaritan is directly seized in and by love for the wounded man. "Love of neighbor" commands with utter immediacy and orients our desire, which becomes essentially a desire *from* love and *for* another.

All this reveals the brilliance and necessity of Jesus' use of narrative, which compels passionate engagement, to unfold the meaning of the love command. In order to discern existential/moral/spiritual truths one must open oneself up subjectively, for existential/moral/spiritual truths cannot be discerned dispassionately. Indeed, an objective, dispassionate stance

---

7. Though I cannot unfold the point here, note that affirmation of *agape* constrains but does not entail rejection or condemnation of *eros* (i.e., aesthetic, including erotic, desires).

shuts one off from existential/moral/spiritual truth. The "command" of the twofold call to love, indeed, the command of Torah, cannot be objectively and dispassionately discerned. Spiritual talk of "command," then, should be understood in terms of call, in terms of having been seized, in the case of the twofold love commands, in terms of having been seized in and by love.

While agape commands us with absolute intimacy and directness, then, it is not a coercive, power-based command to obey an objective external imperative, let alone an inducement to act in selfish response to potential reward or punishment. Moreover, as the two who passed by illustrate, the command of love is not irresistible. It does not negate our autonomy. Indeed, ominously, those who over time have hardened their hearts may barely feel it. In any case, there is an asymmetry with regard to having been seized in and by love for others. Our autonomy is neither primary nor negated: we cannot choose to love, but we can choose to harden our hearts. Our autonomy is affirmed, then, even as the reality of the love of having been seized is made primary.

For those with "ears to hear" the command is received in a radically passive, subjective dynamic. Love in the agape/altruistic sense is never something we initiate, cause, create, choose, or give. The love we give and share is always a love in and by which we first find ourselves seized.[8] One finds oneself having been seized in and by love for those who are needy and wounded (in which case one finds oneself immediately/intimately troubled and moved to help), and also by those who are happy and rejoicing (in which case one finds oneself immediately/intimately joyful and smiling). Of course, we also find ourselves seized in and by love not only for other people, but also for cats, dogs, horses, seals, rats, and (hopefully) all manner of other animals, even, in our most spiritually sensitive moments, by plants.

Most famously, loving God with all our heart, soul, mind, and strength is not something we initiate, but begins in response to having been seized in and by love ("This is love, not that we first loved God, but that God first loved us"). Indeed, loving God with all our heart, soul, mind, and strength names the radical passivity of allowing oneself to be seized fully in and by love for all others and acting accordingly ("insofar as you have done it for the least of these, you have done it for me"). Just so, the second great command is "like unto" the first.

Insofar as one has been awakened to having been seized in and by this love the question "why be moral?" has been rendered utterly superfluous, for the motivation is intrinsic to the dynamic of having been seized in and

---

8. My understanding of the dynamics of love in this regard was profoundly shaped by an essay by Jean-Luc Marion, "Phenomenological Sketch of the Concept of Gift."

by love. Moreover, one has *de facto* and without any reason for real doubt rejected both metaphysical naturalism and existential atomism. This makes clear the full significance of global admiration for this parable, for it amounts to a massive, overwhelmingly positive, millennia-old, cross-cultural, and multi-faith affirmation of its truth. And given the power and profundity of this affirmation, which presupposes the legitimacy of engaged, passionate reasoning, we quite reasonably reject the equating of legitimate reasoning with objective reasoning.

Certainly, in our world, where so many legitimate needs conflict, and where it is not always clear what action is most loving, we will always be faced with ethical quandaries. There is no reason to expect that theoretical closure will ever be within our grasp. But there is no basis for any real doubt over this moral reality, over the reality of the command of having been seized in and by love for others, over the call to *be* neighbor, and no question of what those who are neighbor are called to do when there is no conflict of legitimate needs and it is clear what action is most loving (this means that while we will ever face ethical quandaries, it is unreasonable to affirm ethical relativism).

Granted, it is logically possible that this "love" is wholly a product of sociocultural and physical forces (of genes and memes). But there is no reason to worry over this logical possibility. For as Proudfoot's very precise précis unwittingly reveals, there has been no argument establishing the truth of metaphysical naturalism. Instead, as Proudfoot acknowledges, for nearly a century metaphysical naturalism has been both the working presupposition and the preoccupation of mainstream modern thought. This nearly century-old preoccupation has been buoyed by the success of the natural sciences, and this has created a massive bias in favor of metaphysical naturalism.

But since any actual argument for metaphysical naturalism is still lacking, and since only methodological naturalism, not metaphysical naturalism, is required to practice modern science (as a multitude of first-rate, morally realistic and even theistic scientists illustrate), and since the vocabularies/rationalities of metaphysical naturalism, while clearly accurate and wonderfully productive within certain boundaries, are so woefully inadequate to the spiritual/moral/existential dimensions of human experience (lament on this score is a standard trope in the literature even among metaphysical naturalists), a heavy burden of proof lies decidedly with metaphysical naturalism.

Since there is no good reason to conclude that agape must come from either one's own or others' intentionality, or from "nature" in the modern sense, there is no good reason to doubt that this love is as real as the sound you hear when a tree falls in the woods. That is, while this love is not "physical" in the modern sense, it is "natural" and most reasonably received as a part of "reality" (typically the part designated as "divine") in the classic sense.[9] If "faith" names living in the light of having been seized in and by love, and if "God" is understood strictly in the sense of "God is love," then to understand oneself to be living by faith which is the gift of God, while certainly not the product of human reasoning or argument, is entirely reasonable.

My reading of Jesus' interpretation of "love your neighbor as yourself" is confirmed by two striking aspects of Jesus' exchange with the lawyer. First, in the New Testament, "eternal life" typically signifies an immediately effective and ongoing state of affairs. That is, while in the New Testament "eternal life" does refer to life after death, life after death is not the defining characteristic of "eternal life." "Eternal life" names a way of living here and now. But Jesus tells the lawyer that if he keeps these commands, he "will" (future tense) receive eternal life. If "eternal life" for Jesus does not typically specify life after death, why does Jesus use the future tense in "do this and you will live"?

An answer becomes apparent in light of the second striking aspect of Jesus' interchange with the lawyer. Note that though the parable defines "love your neighbor" in terms of a spiritual orientation, a way of *being*, Jesus does not say, "go and *be* likewise," but "go and *do* likewise." On my reading, this is because Jesus brilliantly relates intentional action and agape, which is neither self-interested nor directly intended. In brief, one cannot decide to love people experiencing homelessness, but one can decide to work in a soup kitchen. And as one gets to know them personally in the context of

---

9. Like the sound of the tree falling, if there is no hearing being in range of hearing it, then there is no sound. But the reality (i.e., the sound waves) that the sound manifests to hearing beings when they are in range of hearing is really there, whether there is a hearing being in range or not. Likewise, if there is, for instance, no being capable of having been seized in by and by love in the presence of some unconscious and wounded creature, then there is no having been seized in and by love for that creature. But the reality of the love that is realized when someone is present and seized in and by love for that creature is as real as the sound waves, though, unlike the sound waves, it is not a part of "physical" reality in the modern sense. That is, not only is there no argument for metaphysical naturalism, but one of the most powerful and treasured of human experiences (though not "experience" in the modern sense), an experience for which there is widespread and revered testimony throughout history and across cultures, an experience whose power and exquisite character commonly calls forth talk of the divine, this widely shared experience quite reasonably leads to the classic and near-global conclusion that the parameters of the "physical" in the modern sense are not coterminous with the parameters of reality.

acting in loving ways toward them, one will begin to find oneself having been seized in and by love for them.

Furthermore, and this is a cliché in ministry, mission, and social services circles, one finds oneself, even in devastating circumstances, full of a sense of meaningfulness and certain of purpose, and insofar as good results, one finds oneself overcome with the fullness of joy. That is, insofar as one begins in this sense to live "love your neighbor," one finds *oneself* having been seized in and by love, one finds that one has oneself received the gift of being loved, one receives and lives the gift of the "as thyself." This too is a cliché in mission and service circles. Folks come back from mission trips inspired, excited, loving, loved, gifted, full of a sense of purpose and meaningfulness, they can hardly wait to do it again, and they say things like, "I went there to give to them, I thought they were the needy ones, but it turns out that I was more needy than I ever imagined, and I received not only far more than I gave, but far more than I realized was even possible."[10]

Acting as neighbors, doing likewise, they taste what it is to be neighbor, what it is in this world right now to be living eternally, and they are filled with joy, happiness, and love (they receive the "as thyself"). All of this names lives lived in the light of having been seized by agape. All of this describes, here and now, eternal living. All of this depicts Jesus' understanding of "love your neighbor as yourself" and reveals the spiritual genius of his counsel to the lawyer: go and do likewise.

---

10. Many have thought that "love your neighbor as yourself" must be interpreted in accord with the logic of selfish self-love. In short, "just as much as you love yourself, you must love your neighbor." But if one abides by the Torah sequence and grasps Jesus' holistic interpretation of "love your neighbor as yourself," one realizes that the love that is the concern and compassion of the having been seized in and by love for others is precisely and simultaneously the love in and by which one finds oneself seized for oneself (a reality for self which is made most obvious vis-à-vis others). This love of self is not selfish because it does not originate in oneself at all, let alone in self-love in the selfish sense. Significantly, this is a real love and valuing of self and so decisively rejects any denigration or neglect of self. To be clear, this means that to *be* neighbor is not to allow oneself to be abused, suckered, taken advantage of, cheated, or discriminated against. One loves enemies of the good, but insofar as they remain enemies of the good, one works and in extreme circumstances fights for what is good.

Chapter 3

Seized by Love

Teaching, Ministry, and Augustine's "Teacher"

". . . it is not I who teach him. He is taught not by my words but by the things themselves which inwardly God [the Teacher] has made manifest to him."

—St. Augustine, *The Teacher*[1]

In Romans Paul says, with regard to those who "by their wickedness suppress the truth," that, "what can be known about God is plain . . . since the creation of the world [God's] eternal power and divine nature, invisible though they are, have been understood and seen through the things [God] has made."[2] If this is true of the wicked, "what can be known about God" must be even clearer to the faithful. Today God's power and nature is indeed plain to a multitude of *hearts*, but modern rationality has clouded the *minds* of even many faithful.

Does Paul help clear away the haze? Paul says all commandments are "summed up in this word, 'Love your neighbor as yourself.'"[3] Recently a host of celebrated philosophers have read in Paul's summary a decisive

---

1. *Augustine: Earlier Writings*, 96–97.
2. Romans 1:18–20 (NRSV).
3. Romans 13:9 (NRSV).

break with Jesus, for Paul drops "love your God with all your heart, soul, strength and mind." Seizing upon this, they champion Paul for fellow atheists because he keeps love of neighbor but drops God. But without God they read, "love your neighbor as yourself" backwards and upside down. Since the only love they know is *eros*—desire, perhaps desire for others to flourish, but still *one's own desire to desire* others' flourishing—all "love" must be at root "love of self." But for Paul—this is why they champion Paul—you must decide to universalize this love, you must decide to love everyone just as you love yourself, and this decision to universalize love is faith.[4]

These philosophers have good hearts (they are sincerely committed to universal neighbor-love), but their minds are clouded. Their reading is backwards because it starts with love of self. It is upside down because faith is now rooted in us, in our conviction/decision, not in God. It is insufficient, for they have no explanation as to why I would/should decide to love everyone as much as I love myself. Finally, their reading is utterly contrary to common experience of agape.

Jesus unfolds "love your neighbor as yourself" with the parable of the good Samaritan. The parable depends upon hearers discerning the plain truth of who proves neighbor. What inspires us has nothing to do with self-interest. The essential dynamic is unfolded precisely by celebrated philosopher and Talmudic scholar Emmanuel Levinas (not an atheist) in terms of our being taken hostage to care for others. What we recognize as "neighbor" is the Samaritan's having been seized by love for the wounded man.

Insofar as we do not harden our hearts, this is the love by which we are seized in horrific and also wondrous circumstances. We see the survivors of the shooting, the tsunami, or the earthquake, we see fearful, silenced immigrants laboring at dangerous jobs, we see desperate families crowding boats to cross the Mediterranean, and we are seized by concern for those others, our love immediately made manifest in our grief and protest. Or we see the little girl laughing happily at her birthday party, or the smiling newlyweds descending the church steps, and we are seized by love for those others, now manifest in our joy. These responses are not a product of our own initiative, reasoning, or decision. We are directly seized by love for others. Let me be very clear, we are not seized directly by others, we are seized directly *by love for* others, we are seized by love, seized by agape, which is to say, since God is love, we are seized by God for others.

---

4. See especially, among many others, Giorgio Agamben, *Time That Remains: A Commentary on the Letter to the Romans*; Alain Badiou, *Saint Paul: The Foundation of Universalism*; Jacob Taubes, *Political Theology of Paul*; and Slavoj Žižek, *Puppet and the Dwarf: The Perverse Core of Christianity*.

Thereby, says Jesus, when you surrender to having been seized by others and comfort, clothe, visit, or feed them, you comfort, clothe, visit, and feed God, for you are directly surrendering to agape (to God) for others. Insofar as you do not harden your heart but surrender you *are* neighbor, faithful. Paul cites only "love your neighbor as yourself" because, in full accord with Jesus, he recognizes the spiritual unity of the two commands. You love God with all your heart, soul, strength, and mind precisely by surrendering to agape for every other with all your heart, soul, strength, and mind. In surrender to God, you become neighbor, for you are surrendering to/receiving love for all—love for all others, and for yourself ("as yourself").

Insofar as people since the creation of the world have been seized by concern for all others—this reality is as real as horror over the suffering wrought by tsunami or exploitation, as real as joy for the laughing little girl—a dimension of God's eternal power and divine nature, invisible though they are, has been understood and seen through all God has made. All this remains within bounds of what is generally considered reasonable and good. More about God's nature is equally plain—remember, the Teacher's teaching famously seizes Saul the oppressor, therefore, "while we were yet sinners..." and all which that entails. None of this general revelation, however, is a matter of natural theology (inferring God from nature or reason). For it is not a matter of argument, conclusion, decision, or assertion, but rather of openness and surrender to the Word behind the words, awakening to the Teacher who truly teaches when teaching is ministry.

Chapter 4

Eternally Incarnate

Advent in Genesis

I kept on braking, stopped, pushed on the flashers, and got out of my car. There were no obvious injuries. No blood. But the possum lay motionless, her young eyes bright, her tongue draped out the side of her mouth. As I drew close, she screamed softly and turned her eyes toward me. I knelt beside her, speaking gently, apologizing. A moment later she exhaled audibly and went utterly still. I could have done no more when she darted in front of me, but I felt to the core my existing as part and parcel of a reality suffused with pain, suffering, and injustice. In this case I was only complicit, not culpable, but for those few moments nothing was more real, moving, or significant to me than the suffering and death of that young possum.

Ever since the Council of Nicea in 325, the mainstream Christian tradition has rejected the idea that God changed on a particular day in first-century Israel (roughly, the Council of Nicea rejected Arianism). The Word was in the beginning. God is eternally triune, eternally incarnate. This is familiar Christian teaching. At the same time, however, we who are Christian also confess that the eternal reality of God incarnate was specially realized and fully revealed—and, we always add quickly, most perfectly hidden—in a particular person, Jesus of Nazareth. Nonetheless, "the Word became flesh" does not name a change in God.

Despite classic insistence upon the eternal character of incarnation, because of the historical character and significance of the Christ event, it has been easy to neglect incarnation as an eternal reality, a reality spiritually present to all peoples at all times. In a word, it has been easy to neglect incarnation as an omnipresent spiritual reality manifesting the eternal character of God.

A question immediately arises: *how* can we confess both that the Word became flesh at a particular point in history *and* that there was no change in God? I do not address this question. My concern here is with the eternal aspect of incarnation, that is, with incarnation as an omnipresent spiritual reality, and in particular with proclamation to the spiritual reality of God as eternally incarnate in the primeval history of Genesis.

Insofar as we think about incarnation exclusively in terms of an empirical, temporal-historical event, we will understand "Advent" exclusively in terms of a period of time in the first century. With regard to the reality of the eternally triune, eternally incarnate God, however, Advent should also be understood in terms of the eternal, spiritual arrival/descent/approach/kenosis of God, an Advent equally present spiritually (insofar as hearts are not hardened) to the Jews wandering in the wilderness, to the disciples of Jesus, and to you and me this very day. In popular terms, this reality is confessed when Christians sing with thanks, "And He walks with me, and He talks with me"—which should be understood as a literal confession about a spiritual reality (not about an empirical reality).[1] On the other hand, Jesus Christ as an empirical reality walked beside all sorts of people who never discerned the spiritual reality.

Insofar as the incarnation is an eternal reality, then even if, as we Christians confess, it is specially realized in Jesus Christ, it has always and everywhere been spiritually present, has always and everywhere been the saving, spiritual arrival of God to those who have not hardened their hearts. In this sense, I will argue, testimony to the eternal, spiritual reality of incarnation lies at the heart of the flood/rainbow covenant and the seven days of creation narratives in the primeval history of Genesis. In relation to the eternal aspect of incarnation, that is, in relation to God as eternally incarnate, these are narratives of the birth of the God of grace, they proclaim the eternal, spiritual reality of Advent.

A final qualification about this reflection: I will remain within the parameters of a philosophical spirituality, that is, I will remain wholly within the parameters of what is generally considered to be reasonable and good. Obviously, a philosophical spirituality cannot presume the truth of

---

1. Miles, "In the Garden."

Scripture. With regard to spiritual concerns, however, it is wholly reasonable for a philosophical spirituality to seek guidance from the classic texts of the world's great wisdom traditions, for instance, to seek guidance from the flood/rainbow covenant and seven days of creation narratives. Obviously, the claims I can make about incarnation within the parameters of philosophical spirituality will be delimited. Some may think these parameters unduly constrictive but consider that I will be arguing that *all who are reasonable and good should affirm the essence of the proclamation of the flood/rainbow covenant and seven days of creation narratives about the spiritual reality and character of the eternally incarnate God.*

A familiar way to define justice, mercy, and grace in relation to complicity or culpability (i.e., in relation to some wrong) is to say that *justice* is getting what you deserve, *mercy* is not getting what you deserve, and *grace* is getting what you do not deserve.

The impulse to *justice*, including a sense that a wrong committed demands a proportionate penalty, a reality discerned not only vis-à-vis others (i.e., they must pay) but vis-à-vis we ourselves (the voice of conscience, consuming guilt), is potent and evidently global (considering everything from interaction among monkeys to the world's religious and legal systems). The incredibly complex relation among justice, mercy, and grace becomes apparent when one comes to mercy. Why mercy? Not only is there no widespread impulse to mercy, that is, no widespread impulse not to redress wrongs committed, but the potent and global impulse to justice stimulates an accusing question: "How is mercy just? Indeed, is not mercy unjust?"

From the perspective of justice, mercy (not getting a deserved penalty) is at best a failure of justice, nowise justified. By definition, no *justification* of mercy is possible (likewise for grace if grace is thought of in terms of "getting what is not deserved"—we will have to think "grace" differently). Nor can mercy justify or account for itself, for there is no widespread impulse simply to ignore wrongdoing. To the contrary, the impulse to justice is incredibly potent. At the same time, mercy is a reality, and is even celebrated as good. So, justice and mercy taken alone are conceptually unstable, for impulses toward and affirmations of mercy imply something beyond either justice or mercy. "Grace" appears as a necessary third. But what help is grace? Can grace account for mercy and be itself adequately accounted for? The saving answer, I will argue, is *yes*.

Remember the story of the possum or bring to mind similar experiences involving all sorts of creatures, beloved household animals, or perhaps other people, mothers, fathers, and children you see on *Huffington Post* or CNN, strangers to you, emerging from the horror of the earthquake or tsunami. The philosopher, Talmudic scholar, and Holocaust survivor Emmanuel Levinas unfolds the dynamic of such encounters with revealing precision. In such contexts, all who do not harden their hearts find themselves seized to the core by concern for suffering faces. You do not decide to be seized. You do not respond to some religious or ethical system that tells you to be concerned (to the contrary, religious, and ethical systems themselves flow from people having been seized by concern). Just as I did not decide to be concerned for that possum but found myself having been seized by passionate concern for her—and did not harden my heart—in all such moments we find ourselves seized by passionate concern.

Notably, because we can choose to harden our hearts, our autonomy is not violated when we are seized by concern, and in that sense the concern to which we surrender is authentically our concern even though it is not something we initiate or create.

The reality of having been seized by concern often emerges with unparalleled force in contexts of pain, suffering, and injustice. But we are also seized by concern in wonderful circumstances, where we take joy in the flourishing or happiness of the friend who got the job, or the smiling newlyweds or parents. Levinas claims those who are awakened are even seized by concern when passing strangers in the street. Even there, he says, those awakened hear a call to acknowledge concern and smile "hello."

At precisely such moments, says Levinas, whether the context is joyful or horrifying, whether the occasion is momentous or passing, God comes to human hearts and minds. That is, God is manifest in the concern which seizes us, and to which we do not harden our hearts. Indeed, to describe having been seized by passionate concern for others (a having been seized which is not a product of personal decision or self-interest) is to give a precise description of love as agape, what Christians mean when they say, "God is love." The passion to which we surrender is God immediately and intimately present to us, is the manifestation of the spiritual, omnipresent, eternally incarnate God. In this sense, to say, "having been seized by passionate concern for the flourishing and well-being of all" is to say, "having been seized by agape" or "having been seized by God."

Focusing upon the eternal aspect of incarnation as an omnipresent, spiritual reality, then, we discern profound continuity between Levinas's Jewish spirituality and classic Christian proclamation. Moreover, to return to the main thread of our discussion, we have now identified a reality that is incredibly powerful and everywhere celebrated, that is, a reality that is at least as potent and global as the impulse to justice, the reality of agape, the reality of our having been seized by passionate love for all. This includes, let me be sure to specify and stress, love for ourselves. Notably, this love for ourselves is not from us, but is rooted in God's love for us, rooted in agape, so it is not a selfish love for self, for it flows from surrender to agape, which in this way is surrender to ourselves-as-eternally-beloved.

We can plunge deeper. What is the character of the "impulse to justice" (an impulse most potent in the face of injustice)? What spurs our protest when we see an injustice? What is at the heart of our impassioned "that is wrong!"? What makes something wrong? Ultimately, insofar as "justice" is understood ethically, that is, in relation to what is good or wrong, the answer is that we are moved to protest and name something wrong when we see violation of the passionate concern for all faces by which we have been seized and to which we have surrendered. In short, we passionately protest whenever there is violation of agape (with regard to any others or, let me say explicitly one more time, with regard to ourselves).

Justice and agape, then, are not equally primordial. Agape is primordial. Agape does not need justice. Justice as an ethical concern only exists because there is agape, for injustice is only discerned as an ethical concern because it violates agape. Grace should not be understood in terms of justice; justice should be understood in terms of grace. So, it is not merely the case that agape is just as potent and global as justice. Justice is a potent and global ethical reality only because agape is a potent and global reality. If there were no injustice, if we lived in a world where agape was always and for every creature perfectly realized, we would never even think of "injustice" nor have cause to develop the category of "justice."

Agape, then, provokes passion for justice even as it is autonomous from and transcends justice. This is dry but momentous, for it means agape is primordially and ultimately *gracious love*. It says God provokes passion for justice even as God is autonomous from and transcends justice. It says that while God remains passionate about injustice God is ultimately and primordially a God of grace. So, it says that insofar as we surrender to God, we surrender to a reality that awakens us to passion for justice even as it awakens us to the even more primordial and ultimate reality of grace (thus the priority of *iustus* in Luther's *simul iustus et peccator*). Awakening and surrender to agape in this world of pain, suffering, and injustice, then, is immediately awakening to judgment upon this world and upon ourselves, but simultaneously it is awakening to primordial and ultimate gracious love for all creatures, including ourselves.

Awakening to agape, then, is saving awakening to the gracious love of God, is awakening to God come to us in a most immediate, intimate, profound, and powerful fashion, is awakening to the eternal aspect of Advent, to God eternally incarnate (again, as Christians say, it is saving awakening to Jesus, who walks with me and talks with me). We are saved from all complicity and culpability, saved to loving embraces for all, including ourselves. This love is appropriately called a gift because, insofar as we do not harden our hearts, we are always already seized by it and, insofar as it is the source of our love for others, the love we give (or, perhaps better, the love we share and share in together) is love we first receive. Obviously, this means regularly celebrating the incarnation by giving gifts (e.g., Christmas) is a great idea.

For whatever reasons, we are often seized most powerfully by violations of agape. As a result, we tend to speak first and with the greatest conviction about injustice, and the category of justice appears to be predominant and autonomous. These reflections support, to the contrary, the Christian proclamation that grace is primordial and ultimate, an omnipresent spiritual reality transcending and standing at the root of justice as an ethical concern.

Let me add one more observation before hastening on to the question of Advent in Genesis. This understanding of the relationship between grace and justice helps us to understand and to see our way past the inability of justice to restore fellowship and to bring healing and peace, for these are all fruits of love. This is not to reject legal penalties. This does not mean we forget or fail to address injustice, but it does explain why attempts to find restoration and healing through justice are bound to fail. This explains, for instance, the sad futility of vengeance—and the powerful spiritual gift bestowed upon all of us by those who forgive (without excusing) people who have wronged them or their loved ones.

The primeval history famously begins with an impossible vision that represents the realization that agape, gracious love, stands alone as the primordial and ultimate reality. The seven days of creation narrative does not tell but shows us this in its vision of a perfectly perfect world in which there is no pain, suffering, or injustice (and so no category of justice), where agape for all is perfectly realized.

In real life, however, the ancient Israelites always lived in our world, a world of pain, suffering, and injustice. Every bit as much as us, they understood how reaction to injustice and an impulse to justice could cut us off from grace. This, I will argue, is the point of the flood/rainbow covenant narrative, which is in its own way a narrative of Advent, a narrative of the birth of the God of grace. To be clear, in order to communicate important truths Genesis portrays a momentous change in God and the Gospel of John talks about the Word becoming flesh. In neither case, however, need we conclude God changes, nor should we criticize such texts for taking ordinary literary license.

The flood narrative sets us up to think wholly in terms of justice. Wickedness covers the face of the earth. Only one appears righteous: Noah. We are tempted to view God's killing of every creature of the land and air except those on the ark as not only justified, but as a path back to the perfectly peaceful world of the seven days of creation: global wrong undone by global penalty; restoration within the parameters of justice. We are tempted straightforwardly to see the flood as just and good. We are tempted to forget the multitudes of crying, dying, drowning faces, of all families, of all kinds. This means, to be clear, that we are tempted to harden our hearts to having been seized by gracious love for all creatures. We are tempted to understand God to be first and last a God of justice—indeed, this is precisely the God we are presented throughout the bulk of the flood narrative.

The narrative, however, ends up decisively attacking all such understanding. Evidently, God was immediately present to and did not ignore or forget all those crying, dying, drowning faces. Evidently, God was profoundly moved. Evidently, God's sensitivities were amplified to the nth degree, so that the pivotal, seemingly insignificant event that finally unleashes the floodgates of grace, transforming God utterly, giving birth to the God of grace, comes when Noah, remaining wholesale within the sphere of justice, not yet discerning the futility of attempting to restore peace through violence, not recognizing that he is amplifying the horror, kills several beloved creatures.

In the very next verse, the divine transformation is apparent. The narrative to this point tempts us to expect God to react with pleasure to Noah's sacrificial offering, tempts us to expect God to speak with hope of a new future, where Noah and his descendants would initiate an age of righteousness on earth, where peaceful fellowship among people and with God will cover the earth. But God says no such thing. God smells the sweet odor of the burning flesh and God says in his heart, "I will never again curse the ground because of humankind, *for the inclination of the human heart is evil from youth*" (Gen 8:21, NRSV, emphasis mine).

The following verses describe the way the world will be. This is a world we know all too well, a world where animals dread humans, a world of carnivores, a world full of murder and capital punishment. This is not the ideal world a God of love would have, but the world as we have it. Nonetheless, after abandoning any hope of dealing with perfect people ("evil from youth") and recognizing that the world to come would be full of the same wickedness that provoked the flood, God reiterates the "never again" in the rainbow covenant that is then made with Noah and "every living creature of all flesh."

In other words, without forgetting *justice*, and without failing to be offended at injustice, God nevertheless will show *mercy*: "never again." At the most obvious level, the rainbow covenant, which explicitly says only "never again," manifests mercy, not yet grace. But for millennia readers have discerned not only mercy in the rainbow covenant but also grace. They have discerned in this passage a proclamation that God is indeed a God of justice, but that primordially and ultimately, transcending the realm of justice, that God is a God of grace. In light of our philosophical reflection, we can explain why readers have been right to discern a proclamation of the God of grace in this passage, for we now understand that mercy already indicates awakening to the fact that grace stands behind and transcends justice, and so we realize that the grace of God is implicit in the "never again" of the rainbow covenant.

At this point the meaningfulness of the seven days of creation narrative that the redactors placed at the very opening of the primeval history becomes even more apparent. For the picture of God in that passage, namely, the picture of God creating places for all creatures, blessing all creatures, delighting in all creatures, wanting all creatures to flourish in a perfectly peaceable realm of delight and love, in short, this depiction of actions that portray and so proclaim that God is seized by passionate concern for every creature: this is joyful proclamation that God is before and above all a God of grace.

When I preach on the seven days of creation I always step out from behind the pulpit and say, "If a single image could capture the Seven Days of Creation narrative's testimony about God it would be this," and then I open my arms wide as I bend low, embracing all that is beneath me and bringing it up in a loving embrace. This is a picture of divine grace. We see here again the profound continuity between Jewish and Christian spirituality, for the Christian doctrine of incarnation in Jesus Christ takes this same notion of God's radical, gracious, kenotic concern, this passionate, gracious love for everything beneath God, this idea of grace that lies at the very heart of the Jewish Scriptures, to a radically amplified, empirical extreme.

We can also note that if this gracious, loving, kenotic bow is the very image of God in the seven days of creation narrative, then, if we are faithfully to live out our creation in the image of God, we should live loving embrace of every creature before us—every person, every possum—we should love as God loves. This is another way of describing awakening and surrender to having been seized by love for every creature of every kind on the face of the earth (i.e., surrender to having been seized by agape, by God, *for* every creature, including we ourselves).

Although it has more potential than I have had space to unfold here, a philosophical spirituality probably cannot reach all aspects of classic Christian testimony about the incarnation. Perhaps I have said enough, however, to begin to establish that insofar as we are concerned with the spiritual reality of God as eternally incarnate, a philosophical spirituality does allow us wholly reasonably, based only upon what is generally considered to be reasonable and good—for instance, upon our having been seized by possums and all other sorts of hurting, dying faces—a philosophical spirituality does allow us to proclaim that primordial and ultimate reality, divine reality, the reality of God, is manifest in agape, the gracious love by which, if only we do not harden our hearts, we always everywhere already find ourselves seized.

The doctrinal reach of philosophical spirituality may be limited, but it does allow us with full assurance to proclaim the primordial and ultimate reality of grace. Not only is this claim utterly reasonable and good, but it is also critical in an age in urgent need of awakening to the blessings and joy of surrender to divine grace. In a day when even pastors reportedly worry over the reasonableness of faith, I hope this meditation helps to instill confidence and reinforce conviction over the truth of God's primordial and ultimate benevolence toward us. We live in a trying, challenging age. On some days it feels as if wickedness is smothering the face of the earth. We cannot make everything better, but annual, liturgical celebration of Advent and Christmas, an annual tradition of gift giving, and proclamation that grace is primordial and ultimate, that God is above all a God of grace: all strive after awakening to a wondrous, desperately needed gift. Since it is wholly reasonable and loving, we should proclaim the saving truth of the eternal arrival of divine grace passionately, lovingly, confidently, and with glad hearts, for we bring good tidings of great joy.[2]

---

2. I develop and expand upon these arguments in *For the Love of All Creatures* and *Reasonable Belief*.

Chapter 5

Before and Above All

Agape

By the time I published my first "animal rights" essay, "Animals and the Love of God," in *The Christian Century* in June of 2000, the animal rights movement birthed by Peter Singer's *Animal Liberation* (1975) and Andrew Linzey's *Animal Rights: A Christian Assessment* (1976) was already a quarter-century old and encompassed diverse ethical perspectives from many disciplines (for a great representative sampling, see Waldau and Patton's anthology, *A Communion of Subjects* [2006]). What is distinctive about my contribution to this rich and ever-growing discourse is my attempt to adopt the thought of preeminent Jewish philosopher Emmanuel Levinas in order to articulate a wholly reasonable, essentially (but not exclusively) Christian spirituality that is awakened from the start to infinite love for all creatures. My work does not focus upon nonhuman others *per se*. In conversation primarily with Christian testimony and the philosophy of Levinas, I have struggled to discern some essential contours of a wholly reasonable, loving, difference-making faith—and I contend awakening to love for *all* creatures is an essential part of such faith.

When the animal rights organization *Sarx* asked me to reflect briefly upon the distinctive characteristics of my work, they stressed their appreciation for my emphasis upon grace and the displacement of guilt. This is right and significant, so I will briefly sketch how in a neo-Levinasian spirituality guilt is wholly displaced by the dynamics of faith; how all moral/spiritual resolve and action, including even confession of sin and acknowledgment that we emerge from the start as a part of a fallen (pain and strife-ridden) world, is rooted in awakening to agape; how, while keeping us alive to real-world realities and responsibilities, agape displaces both guilt (a hostility toward self) and blame (a hostility toward others).

Levinas holds that true philosophy begins, before any intending, resolving, or deciding on our part, in awakening (and not hardening our hearts) to having been seized by infinite concern for the flourishing of every other. This precisely describes agape. Following Levinas and Christian Scripture and tradition, I identify this from-without, infinite concern for all others by which we find ourselves seized, with God ("God *is* love"—hardly a claim exclusive to Christianity). To be seized by concern for others is to be seized by agape/God for others. Living surrender to having been seized by infinite concern for every other *is* living surrender to God *is* faith (not to be confused with beliefs, ideas concerning faith).

Faith, then, is the gift of agape, the gift of God. This faith in/from God is as reasonable, sure, and powerful as our joy over the flourishing of others, and as reasonable, sure, and powerful as our horror over the violation of others. Moreover, insofar as we live surrender to having been seized by agape for all creatures, we live *ourselves having been seized* by agape. That is, we live surrender to a love for ourselves. This is not self-love in the modern, I-centric, selfish sense, but a love from without, a love received for ourselves.

Notably, evil is often seen as an obstacle to faith. Levinas helps us realize, to the contrary, that conviction over the reality of agape arises powerfully in the face of violation of others (that is, in the face of evil). Levinas unfolds this dynamic not in terms of a violation of justice (it is not a sense for a system of justice which is offended), but in terms of a violation of agape (I am moved directly by the violation of the one for whom I have been seized by infinite concern).

Paradoxically, then, the reality of agape is powerfully manifest in the most horrific circumstances. In such circumstances, all hope for justice is overwhelmed and lost. In such circumstances, we are offended by the very idea anything could compensate/make things right. More generally, the painful and overwhelmingly obvious conclusion that our world is fallen, on the whole unjust, a vale of tears, defeats any reasonable affirmation that existence is just. This sober conclusion does not, however, defeat agape. For, to the contrary, this morally sensitive conclusion *depends upon* awakening to agape. And while agape keeps us wholly alive to our own harmful actions and the awful realities suffusing this vale of tears, agape primordially and ultimately delivers neither blame nor guilt, for agape is, before and above all, our having been seized by love for every creature, including ourselves.

These spiritual dynamics are incredibly complex. Here I only note that because agape lives *beyond* the tit-for-tat economies of justice, then, insofar as we live surrender to having been seized by agape for all creatures, including ourselves (insofar as we live by faith), we live spiritually beyond guilt and blame. Because agape is primordial and ultimate, confession of moral wrong that—after all, appears as wrong *only in the light of awakening to agape* (which transcends the tit-for-tat, guilt and blame economies of justice)—confession of moral wrong, surrender and confession bring only release, deliver forgiveness of self and forgiveness of others.

Because agape simultaneously unveils evil and transcends it, thereby bringing release from guilt and blame precisely as we frankly confess evil, people of faith emphasize that agape names *gracious* love, and they give thanks for and live in the light of the transcending, gracious love of God.

Release nowise entails quiescence. To the contrary, insofar as we surrender to agape, we immediately act in the world. Seized by infinite concern for each and every creature—every human, cat, cockroach, daisy—we immediately act to resist every violation and we immediately act to enhance the flourishing of every creature (including ourselves). Living surrender to having been seized by love for all creatures, infinitely alive to every violation but living beyond guilt and blame, wholly moved by agape, we ever strive toward an impossible dream—a dream the ancient Hebrews knowingly cast as eschatological—we ever strive toward a world where the "wolf will lie with the lamb," where "the lion will eat straw," where no one anywhere will "hurt or destroy . . . for the earth will be full of the knowledge of the Lord as the waters cover the sea" (Isaiah 11:1–11).

Chapter 6

To Love as God Loves

Animals and the Imago Dei

Many of us feel a little silly if we react strongly to the death of a pet or the plight of an animal. "Well, it was just a cat," we say, embarrassed over our grief. Where does this attitude come from? It's certainly not biblical. Our modern view of animals can be traced primarily to such Enlightenment philosophers as René Descartes, who argued that animals are biological machines unable to feel pain or experience emotion and unimportant except as they affect the lives of human beings. In the Bible, by contrast, value and redemption extend not only to humans but to all animals.

In Genesis 1:1–2:4, God first creates the heavens and the earth, then the plants, fishes, birds, and all the other animals. And God repeatedly declares that this creation is good. Finally, God creates male and female human beings in God's image and gives them dominion over the earth. They are to fill and subdue it.

We are all familiar with these parts of the creation story, but we often overlook what God then says to the man and woman: "See I have given you every plant yielding seed that is upon the face of all the earth, and every tree with seed in its fruit; you shall have them for food. And to every beast of the earth, and to every bird of the air, and to everything that creeps on the earth, everything that has the breath of life, I have given every green plant for food." The passage concludes, "and indeed, it was very good."

The message is startlingly clear: we were given plants and fruits for food, and so were all the other animals who have "the breath of life" in them.

Not only are all the creatures of the earth proclaimed to be pleasing to God, but neither animals nor we are given other animals to eat. The beginning of Genesis depicts a harmonious creation where none kill to live.

This first creation account, known as the Priestly, or "P," account, was written during the Babylonian captivity. As the people of Israel worried that the Babylonian gods might be superior to their God, this narrative boldly asserts that despite all appearances the God of Israel is lord of all. Amazing though that declaration is, even more amazing is the people's assertion not only that their present suffering is not what God intends, but that suffering is not God's intention for any of the rest of creation, human or animal.

The writers of these words were not romantic idealists unfamiliar with nature's harsh realities. They were people who struggled to survive in what we would consider a desolate wilderness. They fought lion and viper. They knew that suffering suffuses nature, just as they knew the harsh realities of defeat and captivity. Yet they were convinced that none of this was God's intention. With the audacity of faith, they declared the present order to be fallen, and articulated a vision of a diverse and harmonious creation.

This vision is the context in which we should read the P strand of the flood account, in which God tells Noah that people now have God's permission to eat other animals: "Every moving thing that lives shall be food for you; and just as I gave you the green plants, I give you everything" (Genesis 9:3). This accommodation within a fallen order does not negate the previous vision. The next verse explicitly instructs people not to eat the animal's life, that is, its blood. And God's covenant with Noah is also and explicitly with "every living creature that is with you, the birds, the domestic animals, and every animal of the earth" (Genesis 8: 9–10).

Not only did the Israelites claim that the world we know is not the world that God intended, but they also expressed their hope in a messianic age when God's intention would be realized. They proclaimed an eschatological vision of a creation that has realized perfect harmony. Isaiah 11:1–12, the classic text, begins by describing an end to the political injustices afflicting the Israelites, but extends the vision beyond human concerns:

> The wolf shall live with the lamb, the leopard shall lie down with the kid, the calf and the lion and the fatling together, and a little child shall lead them. The cow and the bear shall graze, their young lie down together; and the lion shall eat straw like the ox. The nursing child shall play over the hole of the asp, and the weaned child shall put its hand in the adder's den. They will not hurt or destroy on all my holy mountain; for the earth will be full of the knowledge of the Lord as the waters cover the sea.

The commentaries on these texts almost exclusively emphasize how glorious it is to be human. They stress the hierarchy within creation. Repeatedly they remind humans that only we are created in God's image, that only we have been given dominion and told to subdue the earth, that only we are directly addressed by God, and that only we have speech and the right to name all other creatures. But amidst all the exegetical energy bent on glorifying humanity, a pivotal theological teaching is neglected: that all life is sacred, that we are to love all creatures.

The hierarchy on which the exegetes focus is indeed present in these texts. Humans are elevated over the rest of creation by being formed in the image of God. But the primary hierarchical division in Genesis is not between us and the rest of creation; it is between God and creation. True dominion lies not in us, but in God. So, if we are rightly to understand how to exercise our dominion, we must strive to understand and imitate God's dominion.

This realization returns us to a classical theological confession: that first and foremost, God's creative act testifies to the love of God, to the willingness of God to make and bless that which is other than God. Indeed, God so loves all that God has made, that God acts in love for us and all the world through Jesus Christ.

If God exercises God's dominion over creation through love, how can we reflect the image of God in our own dominion? If God graciously loves us, even in our humble and fallen state, how should we regard animals?

The conclusion is clear, but we are tempted to turn the unmerited gift of our creation in the image of God into a claim of greatness, into a reason not to love those who are not our equals. We often resemble the man in the parable of the unmerciful servant, who owed a king a great debt, was forgiven it, and then did not extend the same grace to those "beneath" him.

We pervert the image of God in ourselves when we do not love all which is "beneath" us. That is the critical spiritual insight of St. Francis of Assisi and of Albert Schweitzer. Schweitzer argues that one is holy only if one

> assists all life as one is able, and if one refrains from afflicting injury upon anything that lives. One does not ask in what way this or that form of life merits or does not merit sympathy as something valuable ... Life as such is holy ... When working by candlelight on a summer night, one would rather keep the windows closed and breathe stuffy air than see insect after insect fall on the table with wings that are singed. If one walks along the street after rain and notices an earthworm which has lost its way ... one carries it from the death-dealing stones to the grass.

> If one comes upon an insect that has fallen into a puddle, one takes time to extend a leaf or a reed to save it. One is not afraid of being smiled at as a sentimentalist.[1]

Karl Barth, citing these words, observed that "those who can only smile at this point are themselves subjects for tears." Barth goes on to argue that if we are to obey God, the killing of animals is only possible as a deeply reverential act of repentance; and that it is permissible "as we glance backward to creation and forward to the consummation as the boundaries of the sphere in which alone there can be any question of its necessity."[2]

Like Barth, Schweitzer was a realist. He regularly killed insects, viruses, and other animals in order to protect patients at his hospital in Africa. In a fallen world, one does take other animals' lives when protecting human life demands it. But Schweitzer undertook such actions with a heavy heart, as a lamentable necessity in a fallen world. He never considered it his uncontested right as a superior creature.

Most people deny the sacredness of animal life not out of pride but because it is too painful to acknowledge. There is simply too much animal suffering, and we too often find it necessary to hurt animals. It is far easier simply to turn away from the problem. Consequently, we seldom talk about or even allow ourselves to be conscious of our conflicted feelings. We live with animals, name, feed, and play with them and value their companionship. We wonder at their beauty and grieve when they die. And we also eat, wear, and experiment on them.

I became a vegetarian several years ago.[3] But as I write this, I'm wearing a belt and shoes made of cowhide. When I walk to my office I see the gleaming smokestacks atop the University of Texas animal research facility, and I depend on drugs developed through excruciating animal testing. There's no way out. And it's hard enough to cope with human suffering without worrying about the suffering of other animals. When we see the

---

1. Albert Schweitzer, *Kultur und Ethik*, 331–32, as quoted in Karl Barth, *Church Dogmatics III/4*, 349.

2. Barth, *Church Dogmatics III/4*, 349.

3. I was a strict vegetarian for thirteen years, and I still see veganism (not just vegetarianism) as an ideal. For a variety of reasons related to limits in adjudicating among conflicting goods, I am no longer vegetarian, though I strive to live as close to the ideal as possible (this is just one of many ways my life in this world is compromised—for the same sort of reasons I see pacifism as ideal, but I am not a pacifist). Nonetheless, with regard to the ideal of veganism and all the other ways we wish and strive to live perfectly within this fallen world, the compromises that reality forces upon us should not lessen conviction regarding the ideals we violate—we live by grace (see chapter 11, "*Saying* Grace"). Notably, this is to reject a commonplace of modern Western ethics, namely, that "ought implies can" (i.e., this is typically read as disqualifying any "ought" that we cannot fulfill).

consumptive, destructive ways of nature and realize our own inevitable participation in the carnage, it's easiest to say, "They're just animals," or "That's just the way it is."

But the Bible asks us to have the courage displayed by the people of Israel, the courage of people who know full well what it means to be carnivores and yet who dream of a day when lions eat hay. Repressing our sympathy for animals can lead to an all the more destructive disrespect for them and for all of creation.

Schweitzer knew that allowing ourselves to love all creatures would not suddenly deliver us into an easy and carefree life. He wrote that for the person who loves and shows concern for all creatures, life will "become harder . . . in every respect than it would be if [one] lived for [oneself], but at the same time it will be richer, more beautiful and happier. It will become, instead of mere living, a real experience of life."[4]

---

4. Schweitzer, *Out of My Life and Thought*, 268.

Chapter 7

Karl Barth, Albert Schweitzer, Emmanuel Levinas, and "Love for All Creatures" as a Quintessential Aspect of Christian Spirituality

LOVE FOR ALL CREATURES

In 1967 Lynn White Jr. published a famous essay in the prestigious journal *Science* in which he argued that Christianity bore a "huge burden of guilt" for the global ecological crisis.[1] When I, a Christian, relate White's accusation to Christian audiences, I stress that the first thing Christians should do is *confess*, for there is no doubt that White's accusation is wholly justified.

For the past few centuries, predominant Western Christian interpretation, both scholarly and popular, elevated humans above all else. Everything else was relegated to the status of "natural resources." In particular, the Genesis creation narrative in which humans are given dominion over all creation was taken to mean that humans should appropriate for themselves the earth and everything on it (Genesis 1:26–28).

Of course, people have not exploited the earth so recklessly over the past few centuries because of Christian teachings. A far larger role has been played by raw desire for power, pleasure, and profit. But not only did mainstream Christianity fail to speak against exploitation and urge us toward reverence for, or at least stewardship of, all creation, but the predominant

---

1. White Jr., "Historical Roots of Our Ecological Crisis," 1206.

Christian interpretation positively sanctioned the activities of those whose aim was exploitation.

Much has changed in the four decades since White issued his indictment. As Christians have awakened to the myriad ecological crises pervading most every landscape on earth, sensitivity to the biblical and traditional call to be good stewards of creation has risen among Christian conservatives and progressives alike. Indeed, it may not be too much to claim that the sense that humans are called by God to be good stewards of creation may finally be emerging as the predominant Christian understanding at both scholarly and popular levels.

But the same cannot yet be said with regard to "animals." Already in 1976, only a year after the publication of Peter Singer's influential *Animal Liberation*, Christian theologian Andrew Linzey dedicated an entire book, *Animal Rights: A Christian Assessment*, to advancing a Christian argument for animal rights.[2] Ever since then a small but significant and steadily growing number of Christians at both the scholarly and popular levels have been working to include nonhuman creatures as subjects of ethical and spiritual concern. At present, however, the contention that "love for all creatures" names a quintessential aspect of Christian spirituality would strike most Western Christians (and likely the majority of Christians across the globe, not to mention those who observe Christianity from the perspective of other faiths) as absurd.

Though in this brief essay I cannot establish that "love for all creatures" names a quintessential aspect of Christian spirituality, I can establish ample warrant for Christians and those of other faiths to consider with utmost seriousness the possible truth of this claim about Christian spirituality. Such will be the prime goal of this essay, and I will attempt to do this by making clear that this claim about Christian spirituality is affirmed by one of the most prominent Christian theologians of the twentieth century, Karl Barth.

I appeal to Barth not because I am a Barthian, and certainly not because Barth is famed for his sensitivity to ecological or animal concerns. Indeed, Barth is regularly and with considerable justification accused of thinking only in terms of God and humanity. For instance, in *The Travail of Nature*, an influential study of theology and ecology, Paul Santmire accuses Barth of "theanthropocentrism," that is, of constructing a theology that forgets the world and thinks only in terms of God and humans.[3] But precisely that is why I appeal to Barth. For if even Karl Barth, when confronted with the question of animals, clearly supports the contention that "love for

---

2. Singer, *Animal Liberation*; Linzey, *Animal Rights*.
3. Santmire, *Travail of Nature*, 147–55.

all creatures" names a quintessential aspect of Christian spirituality, then there is ample warrant for taking this spiritual contention seriously, and the widespread and easy confidence that currently enables the marginalizing of those Christians who argue for "animal rights" or "love for all creatures" should be seriously shaken.

As we will see, Barth's work and perspective on animals was inspired by the life of Albert Schweitzer. In significant ways, I will suggest, Barth and Schweitzer supplement one another. Moreover, I will suggest that ambiguities in their thought quite naturally bring the work of Emmanuel Levinas into constructive play, and that it is helpful to read Barth, Schweitzer, and Levinas together. Unfortunately, in the space allotted I can only sketch the essentials of this claim, and there is no space to explain or defend my interpretation of Levinas's esoteric vocabulary.

BARTH, SCHWEITZER, LEVINAS

It was the work of Albert Schweitzer, and in particular his doctrine of "reverence for life," that confronted Barth with the question of animals. In an uncharacteristic gesture, Barth is so moved by the spirit of Schweitzer's work that he adopts "reverence for life" as the title of a long section of his *Church Dogmatics* (a fact somewhat obscured in the English translation, which translates *Ehrfurcht*, the word used by both Schweitzer and Barth, as "respect" instead of "reverence").[4]

As we will see, Barth rejects Schweitzer's methodology, but this rejection only makes Barth's powerful affirmation of Schweitzer's spirituality all the more stunning. Moreover, as we will see, Schweitzer would have been more consistent with the essence of his own spirituality if he had abandoned his paradigmatically modern methodological quest.

Barth's profoundly sympathetic encounter with Schweitzer also created profound and unprecedented openings at junctures where Barth's own methodology is open to significant critique. For instance, Barth is often critiqued for being a revelatory positivist (e.g., for making dogmatic appeals to Christian doctrines or Scripture), and for being religiously exclusive. Barth certainly provides ample warrant for these critiques. With regard to reverence for life, for instance, Barth claims first that, "Life does not itself create this respect. The command of God creates respect for it."[5] And he contends, second, that, "We may confidently say that the birth of Jesus Christ as such

---

4. Compare, Karl Barth, *Church Dogmatics*, *III/4* and Karl Barth, *Kirchliche Dogmatik*, *III/4*.

5. Barth, *Church Dogmatics III/4*, 339.

is the revelation of the command as that of respect for life. This reveals the eternal election and love of God."⁶ Barth even goes on to claim, third, that with respect to reverence for life, "the Christian Church and Christian theology have an incomparable weight to throw into the scales. They and they alone know exactly why and in what sense respect for life is demanded from us."⁷

While the first claim is primarily misleading, the second is sheer, nonsensical assertion, and the third is arrogant and offensive. Unfortunately, at this juncture in Barth's theological journey all three of these claims are typical. Fortunately, in later works Barth will significantly qualify the second and third claims. In any case, given these problematic claims, it is especially notable how, in the face of Schweitzer's testimony to reverence for life, Barth is also moved to make other claims that sound very different.

For instance, Barth says, "Respect is man's astonishment, humility and awe at a fact in which he meets something superior—majesty, dignity, holiness, a mystery which compels him to withdraw and keep his distance, to handle it modestly, circumspectly and carefully."⁸ Note that there is no question in this quote of reverence for life being mediated through knowledge of Jesus Christ or of any specifically Christian understanding. To the contrary, the astonishment, humility, and awe describe response to an immediate encounter.

Significantly, it is in this immediate context that Barth asserts, "life itself does not create this respect," for it is the "command of God."⁹ That is, the "command of God" names the experience of being irresistibly grasped by reverence for life. "God" names the surpassing, sacred, awe-inspiring character of the reverence. And the "command" is not external, is not found in a book or in some orthodox teaching, but names the irresistible, nonintentional character of the call of the lived encounter. This is classic Barth, for Barth stresses throughout his corpus that the command of God is always encountered as a living and present event, it is encounter with the living Word of God *in* the world, *in* history.

The "life" Barth is rejecting as the source of reverence, then, is "life" as it is known in the world, life as it is known biologically or theorized philosophically. With "command of God" Barth means to be gesturing to a source beyond history, beyond philosophy and science, beyond any understanding, reasoning, or willing. Indeed, Barth stresses that the command

---

6. Barth, *Church Dogmatics III/4*, 339.
7. Barth, *Church Dogmatics III/4*, 340.
8. Barth, *Church Dogmatics III/4*, 339.
9. Barth, *Church Dogmatics III/4*, 339.

of God is, "an incomprehensible and in relation to ourselves intangible fact . . . Those who do not know *respicere* in face of it, those who are not startled and do not feel insignificant and incompetent in its presence, those who think they can understand and master and control it, do not know what obedience is."[10]

Once we have encountered the command of God that seizes us in the form of reverence for life, Barth says, we must not, "at any price . . . relinquish or even to lose sight of this perception. We must be awake . . . and always be wakeful . . ."[11] Moreover, Barth argues, if one is truly awakened to reverence for life, truly seized by the "command of God," then action necessarily follows, for "real respect for life" is "more than passive speculation."[12]

I think it is no accident that Barth stumbles here into using classic Levinasian categories and terms (e.g., "awake"). On this philosophical frontier Barth lacks the rigor of Levinas, who speaks of the awakening brought about by the in-breaking of the Other within the sphere of the Same as a non-intentional consciousness finds itself taken hostage by the Face of some other. But while Barth's attack upon metaphysics is less rigorous than that of Levinas, his concern is quintessentially Levinasian, and thus I would suggest that we rightly read Barth in a Levinasian light.

Let me also note, finally, how explicitly Barth, when inspired by Schweitzer's testimony to reverence for life, and so writing in the grip of a quasi-Levinasian focus upon the "command of God," makes statements that push back against his more arrogant, offensive, and exclusivist claims. For instance, later in this section Barth reflects upon the spirituality of a "good horseman," namely, one who "is so completely one with his horse that he always knows exactly to take out of it no more and no less than what it can not only give but is willing and glad to do so."[13] Somewhat stunningly, Barth without any mention of Christianity asserts that a person who enjoys such a relationship with an animal, "cannot possibly be an ungodly person."[14]

Barth's Levinasian instincts are also on display when he expresses a concern that Schweitzer betrays his own reverence for life when he attempts to set it up as the "fundamental principle of ethics."[15] Schweitzer himself has a vague awareness of this problem. It may seem, he acknowledges, that "Reverence for Life" sounds "too general and too lifeless to provide the

---

10. Barth, *Church Dogmatics III/4*, 340.
11. Barth, *Church Dogmatics III/4*, 341.
12. Barth, *Church Dogmatics III/4*, 341.
13. Barth, *Church Dogmatics III/4*, 352.
14. Barth, *Church Dogmatics III/4*, 352.
15. Barth, *Church Dogmatics III/4*, 324.

content of a living ethic," but, he continues, anyone who "comes under the influence of the ethic of Reverence for Life will very soon detect... what fire glows in the lifeless expression."[16]

While Schweitzer continually specifies that real "thought" refers not to any thinking, but to the ethical awareness named by reverence for life, he continues to name reverence for life as a "logical consequence" of thought. For instance, Schweitzer contends that his doctrine of "Reverence for Life" is "the ethic of Jesus, now recognized as a logical consequence of thought."[17] Moreover, Schweitzer never gives up on what turns into a decades-long and ultimately unsuccessful quest to ground "reverence for life" and all ethics in a first principle. From a Levinasian perspective, Schweitzer's failure on this score is saving, for he has confusedly taken up the misbegotten and paradigmatically modern epistemological quest to reduce and negate the in-breaking of the Face of the Other by grasping it within reason and drowning it within the Same.

Schweitzer's confusion on this score is overt. For instance, he specifies that he wants to make an "assertion" the prime and continual object of our consciousness. Schweitzer explicitly presents this assertion, which he now puts forward as "the most immediate and given fact of [one's] own consciousness," as his own substitute for Descartes's *cogito ergo sum*.[18] Rejecting the *cogito*, Schweitzer maintains that, "the most immediate fact of [a human's] consciousness is the assertion: 'I am life which wills to live, in the midst of life which wills to live.'"[19]

The first and really significant problem here, one obvious from a Levinasian perspective, is that Schweitzer elides the Faces of others from view when he urges us to focus primarily and continually not upon other creatures but upon an assertion. On this score, Barth's Levinasian instinct to keep us focused upon the "command of God," the living encounter which irresistibly awakens astonishment, humility, reverence and awe, is far more consistent with the spirit of Schweitzer's reverence for life than is Schweitzer's own attempt to make an assertion the most immediate focus of our consciousness.

Second, Schweitzer's epistemological project fails on its own terms because his fundamental assertion ("I am life which wills to live, in the midst of life which wills to live") is wholly compatible with a wholly individualistic, hyper-competitive and amoral vision of the world as "red in tooth in

---

16. Schweitzer, *Out of My Life and Thought*, 180.
17. Schweitzer, *Out of My Life and Thought*, 180.
18. Schweitzer, *Out of My Life and Thought*, 125.
19. Schweitzer, *Out of My Life and Thought*, 125.

claw." Schweitzer quickly goes on to assert that "the man who has become a thinking being feels a compulsion to give to every will-to-live the same reverence for life that he gives to his own," and he asserts that such a person "accepts as being good: to preserve life, to promote life, to raise to its highest value life which is capable of development; and as being evil: to destroy life, to injure life, to repress life which is capable of development," and that this "is the absolute, fundamental principle of the moral, and it is a necessity of thought."[20] But Schweitzer never articulates any logic that would move one from his prime assertion (i.e., "I am life which wills to live amidst . . .") to a compulsion to revere the lives of all creatures equally, and there is no reason to think any such logic exists.

Again, Schweitzer's theoretical ambition urges us to replace the Face of the other with an idea and so shuts us off from awakening to the Faces of others and to the realm of the Other. Neither of the two problems noted above can arise if one simply dismisses the misbegotten epistemological quest to derive all ethics from a principle. But Schweitzer never stopped affirming epistemology as first philosophy. Fortunately, Schweitzer's theoretical frustration never lessened the passion with which he acted upon and testified to a compulsion to reverence for life.

To be clear, I am criticizing Schweitzer's philosophy, not his spirituality. The phrase "reverence for life," and the naming of the "compulsion" to do good that it irresistibly inspires, wonderfully captures Schweitzer's love for all creatures. But "reverence for life" never gained traction as a philosophical principle, as the lynchpin of an entire ethic, not even, despite decades of efforts, for Schweitzer himself. Sadly, Schweitzer never realized the secret wisdom in his failure. That is, he never realized, as is now clear, that the epistemological quest for a first principle was itself wholly inconsistent with the essential spiritual character of reverence for life.

As the following quote illustrates, at his best, Schweitzer sounds something like Levinas, though his need to think in terms of a basic principle continually short-circuits his ability simply to name and own the having been grasped by the Faces of others that brings forth a compulsion to protect, aid, and comfort all creatures. "Reverence for life," says Schweitzer, "means to be in the grasp of the infinite, inexplicable, forward-urging Will in which all Being is grounded. It raises us above all knowledge of things and lets us become like a tree which is safe against drought, because it is planted among running streams. All living piety flows from reverence for life and the compulsion towards ideals which are given in it."[21]

---

20. Schweitzer, *Out of My Life and Thought*, 126.
21. Schweitzer, *Philosophy of Civilization II*, 214.

Precisely because Barth thought the immediate, living encounter with the "command of God" transcended all human categories, he was protected from Schweitzer's quintessentially modern quest to delineate a foundational principle. And in summing up the essence of Schweitzer's spiritual stance Barth wisely cites not Schweitzer the would-be foundational epistemologist, but the Schweitzer whose life and testimony helped awaken multitudes, including Barth, to the Faces of all creatures.

Barth cites the following long quote in its entirety, for he considers it to manifest the essence of Schweitzer's spirituality:

> A man is truly ethical only when he obeys the compulsion to help all life which he is able to assist, and shrinks from injuring anything that lives. He does not ask how far this or that life deserves one's sympathy as being valuable, nor, beyond that, whether and to what degree it is capable of feeling. Life as such is sacred to him. He tears no leaf from a tree, plucks no flower, and takes care to crush no insect. If in summer he is working by lamplight, he prefers to keep the window shut and breathe a stuffy atmosphere rather than see one insect after another fall with singed wings upon his table. If he walks on the road after a shower and sees an earthworm which has strayed on to it, he bethinks himself that it must get dried up in the sun, if it does not return soon enough to ground into which it can burrow, so he lifts it from the deadly stone surface, and puts it on the grass. If he comes across an insect which has fallen into a puddle, he stops a moment in order to hold out a leaf or a stalk on which it can save itself. He is not afraid of being laughed at as sentimental.[22]

This sort of testimony awakens people to the Faces of other creatures. And for his part Barth, whose work is justifiably criticized for being theanthropocentric, quickly and decidedly insists that his readers take Schweitzer's testimony here with utter seriousness by contending that those "who can only smile at this point are themselves subjects for tears."[23]

All of this brings us to our primary objective, which is to make it even more clear that Barth would affirm that "love for all creatures" is a quintessential aspect of Christian spirituality. Before proceeding, however, let me pause to suggest some preliminary conclusions we might draw from this brief sketch of the ways in which Barth, Schweitzer, and Levinas constructively correct and supplement one another.

22. Schweitzer, *Philosophy of Civilization II*, 243, quoted by Barth, *Church Dogmatics III/4*, 349.

23. Barth, *Church Dogmatics III/4*, 349.

First, I am suggesting that what Schweitzer called the "compulsion" to reverence for all life, and what Barth called an encounter with "the command of God," and what Levinas describes as being taken hostage by the Faces of others, are all attempts to gesture toward the same ethical having been seized. Of the three, it is Schweitzer whose spiritual sensitivities were profound and subtle enough to extend to every creature, and who bequeathed to us a phrase, "reverence for life," that beautifully testifies to that all-inclusive spirituality. Schweitzer, however, was hampered by a belief that he had to *theorize* "reverence for life," even though there are clear indications in his work that at some level he knew he was dealing with a form of "thought" and a "compulsion" that came to him apart from the "logical consequences" of any theory.

Levinas most rigorously describes the encounter with the Faces of others, and offers an anti-foundational, anti-theoretical, and wholly reasonable argument for ethics as first philosophy. As noted, Levinas's displacement of epistemology and delineation of ethics as first philosophy offers a critical correction for Schweitzer and adds rigor to instincts extant but unevenly developed in Barth. At the same time, Levinas's rigor necessitates the creation of an esoteric vocabulary that is inaccessible to general audiences. More significant, Levinas notoriously remains even more anthropocentric than Barth. Quite inconsistently, given that the Face, according to Levinas, is not supposed to be about things like eyes and noses or, *mutatis mutandis*, fur and tails, Levinas only ever sees Faces in encounters with other humans. In this regard the all-inclusiveness of Schweitzer's ethical sensibilities offers an important correction to Levinas.

Barth is nicely supplemented by Levinas' philosophical rigor, and he evidently owes Schweitzer thanks for awakening him to a sense of reverence for the life of every creature—an awakening that apparently leads him to make claims that resist some of the more problematic aspects of his theology. While Barth's appeal to "the command of God" is indeed susceptible to dogmatic (in the negative sense) appropriation, it is now clear that Barth's understanding of the command is neither dogmatic nor positivistic. Moreover, while Schweitzer's life provides the most dramatic living witness of the three, he is marginal to major world wisdom traditions. Levinas's technical vocabulary, meanwhile, is generally inaccessible. Barth, however, speaks from and to one of the most influential wisdom traditions in the world, and while one must guard against the very real danger that his work will be appropriated towards dogmatic, positivistic, and exclusive ends, it also has tremendous potential for exerting substantial influence among the adherents of a major world religion. This last observation partly explains and returns us to the prime objective of this essay, which is to establish that Barth would full-heartedly affirm that "love for all creatures" is a quintessential aspect of Christian spirituality.

BARTH'S AFFIRMATION OF REVERENCE FOR LIFE

Barth is clearly moved and convinced by Schweitzer's conviction that we should reverence all life as sacred. He goes far beyond explicitly adopting Schweitzer's signature line, "reverence for life," as the title of a major section of his *Church Dogmatics*. For Barth believes that if "we are really listening in relation to the human life of ourselves and others, we cannot feign deafness with regard to animal and vegetative life outside the human sphere" and so we must give significant and passionate attention to the question of animals.[24]

For fear that it could lead to a belittling of the responsibility people will assume with regard to people, Barth will not equate the responsibility we owe other humans with the responsibility we owe to "animal and vegetable life." Nonetheless, he insists that with the vegetative and animal we face a "serious secondary responsibility."[25]

Taking on the predominant and oppressive modern Western understanding of the character of human dominion on earth, Barth agrees that humans are indeed set up as "lords" on the earth, but he takes care to stress that animals and plants belong not to humans but to God. Thus, Barth argues, lordship conveys upon humans not license but serious responsibility.[26] Of course, animal and vegetative life are humans' "means of life," and responsibility to humans is primary, so there are times when the appropriation of plants and animals for human ends may be necessary.

Even with regard to plants, however, Barth contends that we face serious ethical questions. There is no problem, he maintains, when the question has to do with the superfluidity of vegetable life, that is, with a harvest of seeds and fruits, since in such instances there is no destruction of a plant's life.[27] But where the destruction of plant life is in question, Barth stresses that we face a serious ethical issue. In the first place, there must be no needless or cavalier destruction of plants: "No one should behave in wood or field 'like the boy who beheads the thistle.'"[28] On the other hand, Barth does allow that vegetation may be destroyed if it is necessary for essential human

---

24. Barth, *Church Dogmatics* III/4, 349.
25. Barth, *Church Dogmatics* III/4, 350.
26. Barth, *Church Dogmatics* III/4, 351.
27. Barth, *Church Dogmatics* III/4, 351.
28. Barth, *Church Dogmatics* III/4, 351.

purposes (e.g., the cutting down of trees in order to provide warmth or shelter).

With regard to animal life the ethical issues become even more serious. Barth stresses that humans and animals are profoundly close as fellow creatures. He finds the biological and behavioral similarities, especially with regard to some mammals, to be undeniable and striking.[29] Indeed, Barth contends that we "may well have to reckon on an animal soul, at any rate in the biblical sense of a principle of life."[30] Barth notes that the proximity of humans and animals is affirmed in the Genesis creation narrative, which thereby signals that reverence is due "for the fellow-creature of man, created with him on the sixth day and so closely related to him."[31] Given all this, we might conclude, it is no surprise that in their encounters with animals, those who are spiritually awake encounter the command of God, which calls them to be "careful, considerate, friendly, and above all understanding."[32]

Indeed, it is worth noting once again that Barth considers the spiritual significance of a person's reverence for other animals to be so indicative of a person's spirituality generally that he contends that "a really good horseman," that is, one who "is completely at one with his horse," "cannot possibly be an ungodly person."[33] In the same spirit, Barth insists that animals that are caged or tamed "merely to provide a spectacle or pleasure will always have a doubtful element, and the revolt of a sea-lion, for example, against what is demanded from it will evoke spontaneously the sympathy of all right-thinking spectators."[34]

When it comes to the question of killing animals, Barth does not hesitate to assert that to kill an animal is "at least very similar to homicide."[35] Barth notes the chronically overlooked fructarian ideal (i.e., one only eats fruits and seeds) explicitly articulated in Genesis 1:28—"Behold, I have given you every herb bearing seed, which is upon the face of the earth, and every tree, in which is the fruit of a tree yielding seeds; to you it shall be as meat"—and stresses that this expresses "the true and original creative will of God."[36]

---

29. Barth, *Church Dogmatics III/4*, 348.
30. Barth, *Church Dogmatics III/4*, 348.
31. Barth, *Church Dogmatics III/4*, 352.
32. Barth, *Church Dogmatics III/4*, 352.
33. Barth, *Church Dogmatics III/4*, 352.
34. Barth, *Church Dogmatics III/4*, 352.
35. Barth, *Church Dogmatics III/4*, 352.
36. Barth, *Church Dogmatics III/4*, 351–53.

Barth thinks that in our world the killing of animals is sometimes necessary for the sake of protection, food, shelter, or the like. But given the original creative will of God—which, I would want to specify, we know directly through our encounter with the command of God when we are taken hostage by the Face of a creature—given the original creative will of God, even a degree of necessity that justifies a killing does not make it good. A person, "must always shrink from" the possibility of killing an animal, even at the moment when necessity and the balance of goods at stake demands it.

"Across every hunting lodge, abattoir and vivisection chamber," says Barth, "there should be written in letters of fire" the words of St. Paul concerning the liberation of humans, along with all creatures and all creation, from a world in which it is necessary to kill animals.[37] Indeed, Barth contends, unless a person has killed an animal in whole dependence upon the grace of God, and abandoning any and all assertion of an ethically pure right to kill, then that person "sins in the killing of animals . . . murders an animal."[38] Thus, what distinguishes the "good hunter, honourable butcher and conscientious vivisectionist" from the bad, Barth says, is the fact that even as they kill animals those who are good hear the "groaning and travailing of the creature," and thus "are summoned to an intensified, sharpened and deepened diffidence, reserve and carefulness."[39]

By this point it is clear that Barth would agree that "to love all creatures" is a quintessential aspect of Christian spirituality. I have left out some of Barth's more dubious formulations, and even some of the points I have lifted up would be criticized by theologians today (including myself) who advocate for reverence for all life. On the other hand, we should bear in mind that when Barth wrote this essay in 1951, talking seriously about animal souls, reverence towards vegetation, and the murder of animals was truly radical. That Barth could so seriously and sincerely respond to the fullness and inclusivity of Schweitzer's testimony to reverence for life, all life, even as he vehemently disagreed with Schweitzer's methodology, gives us ample reason to believe that were he alive today, Barth himself would be the first to critique and revise aspects of positions he staked out sixty years ago. In any case, again, by this point it is abundantly clear that Karl Barth, by consensus one of the most distinguished theologians of the twentieth century, and one not at all known for ecological, let alone animal concerns, nonetheless would passionately agree that love for all creatures is a quintessential aspect of Christian spirituality.

---

37. Barth, *Church Dogmatics III/4*, 355.
38. Barth, *Church Dogmatics III/4*, 355.
39. Barth, *Church Dogmatics III/4*, 355.

Chapter 8

Life Sacred

Recovering the Seven Days of Creation Narrative

THE POLITICALLY EFFECTIVE AND THE SPIRITUAL

The ecological crisis we face should awaken us to a spiritual crisis that precedes and enables it. Ultimately, we must resolve the spiritual crisis if we are to resolve the ecological one. And given the severity of our ecological predicament, we must stimulate immediate action. But the motivational dynamics implicit in environmental appeals that are most likely to stimulate immediate action are spiritually suspect.

For instance, authoritarian appeals (e.g., do this because the Bible says so), appeals to fear (e.g., do this or you and yours will be overrun by floods, disease, toxins, or refugees), or appeals to missed opportunity (e.g., do this or lost rain forest may mean lost cures to cancer) may be most effective in the short term. But their motivational dynamics are spiritually questionable and, most likely, ecologically devastating in the long term. This is so because the very motivational dynamics that render such self-interested appeals effective are spiritually equivalent to the dynamics empowering self-interested, abusive relations to creation.

A truly spiritual concern over the rain forest would spring not from concern over lost benefits for us humans, but from concern for each among the multitude of plants and animals killed when rain forest is destroyed. Right concern aimed at preventing others from suffering manifests classic, prophetic spirituality—that is, a biblical spirituality, not servile obedience to perceived biblical imperatives.

By far, of course, most who utilize spiritually questionable environmental rhetoric are acting not out of self-interest, but in line with a political calculus that sees appeal to self-interest as highly effective in stimulating political action. Nevertheless, the energy firing truly moral understanding flows from spiritual conviction. This decisively distinguishes truly spiritual or moral understanding from "enlightened self-interest," "social contract" theories, or varieties of "memetic" rationales (where "memes" are the socio-cultural equivalent of "genes"), any of which may identify an "ethic" of "dos and don'ts," but none of which is truly moral or spiritual (for there is nothing "spiritual" about acting out of self-interest, "enlightened" or otherwise).

Moral action flows from love for the other, is motivated by concern for others. One sees, one loves, one acts: this more describes a single spiritual event than a reflective or logical progression. Ethical principles and systems—second order reflections abstracted from a multitude of such primordial spiritual events—flow from and articulate for particular contexts the extant contour of the realized concretization of such spiritual events.

On the one hand, then, the political calculus which emphasizes the effectiveness of appeals to self-interest and dismisses truly moral appeals as ineffective cannot be dismissed—for appeals to immediate self-interest are indeed potent. On the other hand, such appeals perpetuate precisely the anti-spiritual, self-interested motivational dynamics that stimulate abuse of creation. Since our long-term hope and aim must be for a human society that lives in sustainable harmony with the rest of creation—else we will be caught in an ongoing series of rear-guard actions that will only forestall ecological devastation—it is significant that self-interested appeals empower a spirituality opposite to the one which is, ultimately, essential.

It would be incredible to expect to effect the necessary spiritual transformation on a global or even national scale in time to save numerous endangered species and eco-systems. Thus, we are in a both/and situation: the urgency and dire nature of the crisis requires us to utilize politically effective, if spiritually suspect, self-interested appeals in the short term even as we work toward spiritual transformation in the long term. By this point, then, a pivotal question of balance emerges. When does one utilize self-interested motivational dynamics to effectively address urgent challenges? And when does one focus upon spiritual formation, which is admittedly less effective in the short term but our only hope in the long term?

My goal is not to resolve this tension, but simply to name and frame it. In particular—and this will be the focus of the balance of the essay—I intend to make clear the profound significance of long-term moral/spiritual formation.

Emphasizing the long-term issue of spiritual formation is anthropologically and politically optimistic. It is to consider that we as individuals and societies may act out of love, not only out of self-interest, and it is to hope, however cautiously, that we may act out of moral motivation and might mature into a society living in sustainable harmony with the rest of creation. What is at stake in balancing appeal to self-interested motivational structures with long-term spiritual formation is not only the vouchsafing of a biological future, but the vouchsafing of a spiritual future. Morality itself, spirituality itself, love itself are at stake. The spiritual question to which the ecological crisis should awaken us is not marginal, but concerns precisely the flourishing or depletion of morality, spirituality, and love.

DECISIVE EXPLANATION

Why protect creation? Why consider the earth sacred? Why love all creatures? Even many Jewish and Christian environmentalists—folk who genuinely and profoundly love other creatures and peoples and whose environmentalism is clearly an expression of a deep spirituality—are unable to articulate how their convictions square with, let alone express in its very essence, their faith. "We must protect the earth because creation is sacred," they may say. Or, "we are called to be good stewards of the earth." But they are often at a loss if asked simply, "why think creation is sacred?" or, "why should we consider ourselves called to be stewards of the earth?" If the issue of long-term spiritual formation is to be addressed so that humans might one day live in harmony with creation, then we must be able decisively to answer (or more precisely, *to displace*) such questions.

It is important to displace such ethical "why" questions because a paradigmatically modern cast of mind would see these as preliminary questions which must be answered if we are to justify the National Council of Churches (NCC) statement philosophically or theologically.[1] The NCC statement makes no attempt to answer these questions, and rightly so, for they are morally confused questions. Any attempt to *answer* them would already betray the profound creation spirituality at the heart of Judaism and Christianity. They must not be answered. They must be displaced, such that

---

1. This essay was initially commissioned for a book of essays—Phillips and Carmichael, *God's Earth is Sacred*—written in support of the NCC's 2010 "Theological Statement on the Environment."

our love for all creatures and all creation may be recognized and articulated and so flourish.

That such paradigmatically modern questions seem obvious, necessary, and innocent demonstrates the depth of the spiritual dimension of the ecological crisis. It is as if one were to come upon a little child alone and black and blue from a beating, sobbing bodily in pain and grief and loneliness and abandonment . . . and in that moment of encounter to think it obvious, necessary, and innocent to demand answer to a preliminary question, "Why should I be concerned for and care for this child?"

This demand for theory, which is standard in modern Western ethics, is not rational, it is morally confused. One should make no attempt to *answer* such a question, for any such attempt would only feed the moral confusion of modern rationality afflicting the asker. One should attempt to displace the question in hopes of healing the moral confusion. And one should engage in spiritual formation in an attempt to awaken true moral discernment, to awaken love of God and neighbor (including all creatures).

Insofar as "decisive explanation" with regard to the character of Christian creation spirituality is concerned, the seven days of creation narrative should be the *locus classicus*. But amazingly, this text above all others has been abusively misread as condoning self-interested human domination of creation. My first task is to disarm this misreading via a philosophical exegesis of this stunningly subtle and inspired narrative of God's grace in creating.[2] I will not be saying, "Do this because the Bible says so." I am saying, "Search your hearts and minds. Does not this ancient Scripture awaken you to divine wisdom? Do you not now find yourself loving and filled with desire to care for all creatures and all creation?"

THE IMPOSSIBLY PEACEABLE KINGDOM

There are two distinct creation narratives at the beginning of Genesis. They are popularly known as the "seven days of creation" and the "Adam and Eve" narratives. When it comes to valuing nature, the two narratives have typically been pitted against one another. In recent decades, the Adam and Eve narrative (Genesis 2:4b ff.), has been used when theologians wish to affirm the value of nature and to stress that humans should be good stewards of the earth.[3]

---

2 Of course, this was originally and still is a classic Jewish text. I suspect my argument is equally appropriate for both Jews and Christians, but I will limit my discussion to the bounds of my expertise in Christianity.

3. Adam and Eve are portrayed as caretakers of God's garden, and the link between

Far more influentially, however, the seven days of creation narrative (Genesis 1:1–2:4a) has long been interpreted quite to the contrary: our distinction from and superiority to the rest of creation has been emphasized. The seven days narrative contains some of the best known of all biblical passages. From its majestic opening, "In the beginning God created the heavens and the earth," to the famous passage that portrays our creation in the image of God, one easily reads in the first creation narrative a wondrous celebration and glorification of humanity: humans are created in the image of God, blessed, told to be fruitful and multiply, to subdue the earth and to have dominion over all creatures. In this spirit, a commentary included within the New Oxford Revised Standard Version of the Bible introduced the first creation narrative with this comment: "Out of original chaos God created an orderly world, assigning a preeminent place to human beings."[4]

In recent decades the call to stewardship of the earth in the Adam and Eve narrative has found renewed voice across the theological spectrum. But there remains considerable unease and tension over the implications of the *"imago dei"* (i.e., creation "in the image of God"), the "subdue" and the "have dominion" of the seven days of creation narrative. The seven days narrative has almost universally been considered problematic for environmentalists. But we will explain how the seven days narrative testifies to a profoundly gracious spiritually vis-à-vis *all* creatures and all creation, a testimony which is even more poignant, powerful, demanding, and spiritually invigorating than the Adam and Eve narrative's call to stewardship.

The seven days of creation narrative seemingly depicts a clear hierarchy within creation, with humans at the top. In accord with this picture, many Christians have argued that we alone within creation are significant, that "natural resources" and "animals" were created as gifts for our use and pleasure, and that stewardship is a reference only to our responsibility to preserve resources for our grandchildren and great-grandchildren.

With our focus upon human beings, we tend to rush mentally through the passage until we get to the famous verses about our creation in the image of God. But this does violence to the majestic prose with which this text luxuriates in every day of creating. On the first five days of creating, God

---

humans and the earth is emphasized. Adam, for instance, is created "from dust." In Hebrew, it is "Adam from Adamah." "Adamah" means "earth," so "Adam from Adamah" might best be translated "human from humus." The teaching of the Adam and Eve narrative, then, is clear: humans are intimately related to the earth and are called to be good stewards of it, caretakers of God's garden.

4. *New Oxford Annotated Bible*, edited by Metzger and Murphy (1994), 2. A slightly different version of this sentence was in the 1977 edition of this Bible. A whole new set of notes was introduced in the 2001 edition, and this line no longer appears.

creates the night and the day, oceans and dry land, plants and birds and fish. God is pictured rejoicing in creation. Again and again we hear, "it was good," "it was good." In Hebrew, the "it was good" signals not dispassionate evaluation but pleasure and joy (as when one is swept up in a beautiful sunset or delights in the laughter of a child).

God not only delights in but also blesses creation. In the ancient Hebrew context, blessings are highly significant. Quite rightly, then, tremendous emphasis has been placed upon God's famous blessing of humans. Yet there is another blessing in this narrative that even many scholarly commentaries overlook:

> And God saw that it was good. God blessed them, saying, "Be fruitful and multiply and fill the waters in the seas, and let birds multiply on the earth." (Genesis 1:22)

This blessing of the fish and birds on the fifth day is later extended to all animals on earth (Genesis 8:17).

At the beginning of day six God speaks, and the earth brings forth creatures of every kind; cattle and creeping things and wild animals. Here again, God delights: "God saw that it was good." Then comes the famous passage:

> Then God said, "Let us make humankind in our image, according to our likeness; and let them have dominion over the fish of the sea, and over the birds of the air, and over the cattle, and over all the wild animals of the earth, and over every creeping thing that creeps upon the earth." So God created humankind in his image, in the image of God he created them; male and female he created them. God blessed them, and God said to them, "Be fruitful and multiply, and fill the earth and subdue it; and have dominion over the fish of the sea and over the birds of the air and over every living thing that moves upon the earth" (Genesis 1:26–28).

These are some of the best-known verses in all of the Scriptures. But until recently, very few people noticed the very next verses:

> God said, "See, I have given you every plant yielding seed that is upon the face of all the earth, and every tree with seed in its fruit; you shall have them for food. And to every beast of the earth, and to every bird of the air, and to everything that creeps on the earth, everything that has the breath of life, I have given every green plant for food." And it was so. God saw everything that he had made, and indeed, it was very good. (Genesis 1:29–31)

There is no ambiguity here. The passage is not only explicitly vegetarian, it gestures beyond the vegetarian, suggesting that you need not even kill the plants to live, for you eat their fruit and seed.

It is important to remember that the Israelites lived in wilderness in conditions in which most modern Westerners would struggle simply to survive. They knew how nature worked. The ancient Israelites are obviously not trying to write science here. No one has ever done science quite this badly (i.e., looked around and concluded the world is vegetarian). Moreover, this passage reaches its written form while the Israelites are in captivity in Babylon. As a people attacked, defeated, and forcibly marched from their homeland and into captivity, these Israelites are brutally aware of how the political world works. This is the context within which the ancient Israelites proclaim this incredible, utterly unrealistic, wondrous vision of God's peaceable kingdom.

The first creation narrative, then, is not a stunningly bad stab at doing science, but a stunningly optimistic proclamation concerning God's ideals and love for creation. This creation narrative proclaims a religious and moral ideal, affirming the gracious character of God and naming what is good, and by contrast, what is evil. Thus, this narrative suggests a moral orientation within the world, directing our sympathies, ideals, and actions. The peaceable kingdom pictured in the Genesis creation narrative proclaims an ideal, and as such it might be seen as a blueprint, a guide to righteousness, a basis for a Christian ethic regarding our care of creation.

Of course, achieving the ideal of the peaceable kingdom is literally impossible. It is not possible for us to live, even to breathe, without killing. This world where none hurt or destroy cannot be humanly realized. It is an impossible dream.[5]

The impossibility of achieving the peaceable kingdom, however, is no more an excuse to abuse creation than the impossibility of being sinless or eliminating all suffering, poverty, war, and sickness is an excuse for accepting those realities. Christians are called to struggle and sacrifice in the present, to live as righteously as possible, to realize God's intentions as fully as possible, whether perfection is achievable or not. Christians are called to live toward the impossible dream of the peaceable kingdom. Christianity is realistic about real-world moral possibilities, but it refuses to allow practical realism to compromise its moral ideals. At the same time, it saves us from

---

5. That is why the Christian notion of the fall, which is typically associated with the Adam and Eve narrative (i.e., where Adam and Eve are sent out of the garden) is actually much clearer in relation to this first narrative, where it stands out as a contrast effect. We come to awareness already and inextricably complicit. We are fallen.

the crushing existential implications of fully owning impossible moral ideals by also proclaiming God's grace.

This seven days of creation narrative, then, pictures God delighting in a wondrous peaceable kingdom where all creatures live blessed lives in perfect harmony. Far from being an invitation to wrest the rest of creation to our own purposes, the seven days narrative powerfully affirms the value of all creation and all creatures.

But what about the *imago dei*, the "subdue" and the "have dominion"? Have I not simply dodged aspects of the narrative least friendly to my ecological and animal-loving interests? And have I not so far done exactly what I said I would avoid? That is, have I not simply derived principles from the narrative and said, however indirectly, "do this because the Bible says so"? Yes, certainly so. We remain on dangerous spiritual ground and must hasten on.[6]

A CLASSICALLY CHRISTIAN CREATION SPIRITUALITY

The seven days of creation narrative portrays God delighting in a wondrous peaceable kingdom where all creatures live blessedly in perfect harmony. This is a powerful affirmation of the value of all creation and of God's intention that all creation and all creatures might have joy and flourish. But what of the hierarchy, what of the *imago dei*, what of the command to subdue and to have dominion? Do these not affirm beyond any question humanity's absolute right to dominance within creation? That certainly reflects today's principal reading of Genesis 1. But three questions refute that reading decisively.

First, who in this text has absolute dominion? The answer: God. Second, what is the character of God's rule, of God's dominion? As we have seen: blessing, affirmation, joy, love, and concern for the good of all others, for all who are beneath God. When I preach on this passage I always step out from behind the pulpit and say, "If a single image could convey the picture of God in Genesis 1 it would be this," and then I bow deeply and open and

---

6. That is, though some may already have felt a spiritual resonance, I have not yet offered the promised spiritual argument. Nonetheless, since the misappropriation of this text is so influential and widespread, it was important to clarify its basic ethical parameters. Ironically, and contrary to common presumption, we will discover that it is precisely when one reflects upon the *imago dei*, "subdue," and "have dominion" that the spiritual dimensions of the text emerge most clearly. What becomes manifest is not merely something external—some blueprint, ethic, or set of rules which must be obeyed—but testimony reflecting a loving and life-affirming way of being in the world, a call to a spiritual turning, to love, to dominion (not domination).

extend my arms downward and outward in a gesture of giving and caring. And then I sweep my arms up and together in a gesture of loving embrace.

And then I ask the third question, "If this is the biblical image of God's dominion over us, how would we reflect our creation in the image of God when exercising our dominion over other creatures and over the rest of creation?"

To comprehend the spirituality of this text, to gain insight into the character of God's relation to us, we can begin by bringing to mind the love and joy we have taken in other people, other creatures, or even landscapes. At this point in sermons, I try to stir these memories by sharing stories of loving relationships between people and animals, or even between people and a field, stream, or tree. Many people resonate deeply with these stories. "Now," I then say, "imagine such love perfect and all-encompassing and fully realized." That is the spirit and dream of the impossibly peaceable kingdom. Such is the clear character of God's dominion in Genesis 1. Such is the gracious love for all creatures and all creation that defines the character of human dominion when it accurately reflects the dominion of God.[7]

The standard modern interpretation equates dominion with domination. It replaces love *for* all creatures with love of the use and appropriation of other creatures. It replaces delight in other creatures' delights with delight in their use and appropriation. The standard modern interpretation, long common in conservative and liberal churches alike, is an abusive misreading of the seven days of creation narrative's clear spiritual teaching.

Contrary to the common reading, we should read the call to subdue the earth within the context of God's grace. In the seven days narrative God brings forth the peaceable kingdom from original chaos. That is, God realizes loving dominion by subduing the chaos *for the good of all creatures*. Likewise, we are called in imitation of God not to subdue the earth to our own purposes and desires but to subdue the chaos that continually afflicts the earth toward a more perfect realization of godly dominion and a more complete realization of God's peaceable kingdom.

People sometimes expect that because of the powerful vegetarian ideal I meet with resistance from farmers and ranchers on all this. I've found the opposite to be the norm. I heard a Midwestern pig farmer interviewed about factory farms on NPR one day.[8] George Burge was eighty-four and long since retired, but he was animated about his old pigs and he hated

---

7. An expanded version of my analysis of the meaning of dominion in the seven days of creation narrative and its theological implications appears in my essay, "To Love as God Loves."

8. All citations come from transcript of McChesney, "Changing Face of America" (2000).

factory farms. The interviewer, John McChesney, noted that Mr. Burge's eyes misted as he recounted the story of one old mother pig, Pug. Mr. Burge had built a nest inside a shed so Pug could give birth to her litter. When he went out one night he discovered that she had instead built her own grass nest outside the shed.

This is Mr. Burge:

> She come up there to me, went to loving on me, just a-grunting. I says, "Pug, damn it, you're supposed to go in the shed." And she'd look at me and rub on me. And I fooled around with her and scratched her tits a little bit and scratched her behind the ears. And finally I got her tail and I slapped her butt and I says, "Get your ass in that shed." And, my gosh, she just walked on into bed. I shut the door, and the next morning went down there and she had ten, eleven pigs laying there.

At this point, McChesney breaks away, noting pointedly that those piglets were being raised for the slaughterhouse. So where, he wondered, is the complaint about factory farms? McChesney allows a country lawyer, George Huff, to respond: between birth and death there's life, Huff says, and it makes a difference how you treat animals when they're alive.

This anecdote resonates with my own country upbringing. I didn't grow up on a farm, but I grew up in a rural town of 1,500 in dairy country. We were all aware of how people treated their animals and their land—and we judged them accordingly. Even in cities and suburbs, who admires neighbors who mistreat their pets? Far from being marginal—and despite our corporate and self-interested willingness to avoid thinking about the treatment of animals in, for instance, factory farms or nonessential private research (e.g., cosmetics)—Mr. Burge and Mr. Huff's moral instincts reflect overwhelmingly common sentiments regarding mistreatment of animals, as well as the moral intuitions of the ancient Israelites.

DOMINION AND DOMINATION: LIVING LIFE AND LIVING DEATH

Consider the paradoxical dynamics of friendship. Friendship is characterized by being for the other, love for the other. Paradoxically, *one receives the good of friendship only to the degree one does not pursue the friendship for oneself, but for the other.* This is why, for instance, if one discovers someone is acting as one's friend solely for the sake of making a connection or securing a promotion, one immediately concludes that they are not truly a friend.

At the other extreme, there are those who have given their lives for their friends. Most friendships fall somewhere between these two extremes. But the truth of the paradoxical dynamic applies across the spectrum.

There is nothing wrong with being friendly as you cultivate contacts and build networks. Over time, some contacts may even develop into serious friends. But, again, they become friends only to the degree that a real concern for the other has superseded the cultivation of the relationship for personal gain. In other words, a friendship is true to the degree that it is *not* characterized by the logic of domination, that is, to the degree one is not being a friend out of self-interest.

In certain contexts, the logic of domination is appropriate, for instance, in relation to one's employer or employees (though even in those instances there is ample space for dominion). But the logic of domination should never be one's ultimate end. To the degree that the logic of domination dictates one's relations, one is cut off from true friendship, love, and community. Its endpoint is existentially devastating: utter isolation. For absolute success in using all relationships for one's own interest leaves one with no true love, no genuine friends, no authentic relationships. To the degree one lives the logic of domination, that is, to the degree one is living the reduction of every other to thing-to-be-appropriated-and-used, one is living death.

But what, specifically, is "dominion"? "Dominion" describes love for the other in the context of a hierarchy of power. Think not of peers who are friends, but of the relationship between parents and their children. The logic of domination is evident in parents who are living out their own dreams through the lives of their children. But one sees dominion where, despite the legitimate hierarchy of power and exercise of control, parents live lovingly for their children.

Over the decades, of course, the children may become peers and friends, and late in the parents' lives the relationship of power may even reverse. The critical question may even become, will the child exercise dominion or domination toward an infirm parent? Throughout the passage of successive stages, however, the critical question concerns not who has power over whom, but what is the character of the exercise of that power. Which prevails? The logic of domination or the way of dominion?[9]

---

9. I am gesturing very roughly here to distinctions similar to those drawn with great clarity by Martin Buber in *I and Thou*. My distinction between the logic of domination and the way of dominion echoes Buber's distinction between "I–it" and "I–thou" relationships. Significantly, Buber too explicitly included all life, that is, all animals and plants, within the domain where "I–thou" relations are ideal.

PERIL AND AFFIRMATION

Note now the existential peril into which we throw God in the seven days narrative if God's relationship to creation is construed in accord with the dynamics of the logic of domination. If God exercises domination over creation, that is, if God creates out of self-interest *in order* to have relationships or *for the sake of* God's delight, then, because of the paradoxical dynamic of friendship, even God would suffer devastating existential isolation: no true love, no true friends, no true communion.

The fateful question, then, is what will be the character of God's exercise of power? The seven days narrative is unequivocal and brilliant. God never thinks in terms of the logic of domination. God delights in all creation and blesses all creatures. God thereby creates and increases value, and opens up possibilities for loving relationship. Were God to "lord it over" creation, relate in accord with the logic of domination, then God would belittle and impoverish God Godself. Value is created and sustained in accord with the character of one's relations and exercise of power. The sheer having of power, even absolute power, is not only not enough, it represents the tragic epitome of a living death.[10]

The key insight comes from the paradox of friendship: to gain the value of friendship one must *not* engage in friendship *in order* to gain its value. God exercises dominion, not domination, and thereby creates value for God and creation. Dominion—living out love for the other—creates value, yielding life. Domination—using the other for oneself—negates value, yielding a living death. In short, love delivers life. In this sense, vis-à-vis other creatures and vis-à-vis God, value is created and sustained by love. In this dynamic, rather than living over and against everything else—seeing salvation and security in the ability to dominate, living in a fundamentally conflicted relationship to all others, futilely attempting to value oneself in utter isolation—one finds value delivered on the far side of love for all things. Now one is affirmed and filled with joy and delight because one does not live over

10. A classic theological affirmation, made in the context of belief in a personal God, holds that God plus the world is not more than God without the world. I am affirming the motivation behind this formulation (i.e., to stress that God does not create out of self-interest), but I am suggesting that it is nonetheless imprecise. The point of the formulation is to emphasize that God does not create out of self-interest but out of love, and thus—for the reasons delineated here—that the Creator is capable of entering into authentic loving relationship with creatures. But it is incorrect to render this point in terms of contending that God without the world is no less than God with the world. As the seven days narrative affirms quite explicitly that God's existence with the world is richer, more delightful, more fulfilling. The character of God's existence with the world is superior to God's existence without the world. God is enriched and value is increased through creating, but only because God does not create in order to increase value or to be enriched.

and against all those who are other, but precisely through love for them. All the value available is delivered *through* our love for other people and animals and plants and all the rest of creation.

In raising pigs for slaughter, Mr. Burge did exercise domination. We do not live in paradise. At points we have to dominate. But Mr. Burge apparently also strove to maximize dominion in his love and care for his animals, and he thereby enriched the value of his life—again, only to the degree that he did not love his animals in order to enrich the value of his life. No doubt his love of his pigs also increased his pain at their slaughter.

Albert Schweitzer, whose ideal of "reverence for life" reflects this spirituality, speaks of the consequences of truly loving all of life. Existence, Schweitzer says, "will thereby become harder . . . in every respect than it would be if one lived for oneself," but, he urges, "at the same time it will be richer, more beautiful, and happier. It will become, instead of mere living, a real experience of life."[11] In the terms of this essay: instead of living death, one will live life.

In that NPR story about pigs and factory farms, McChesney also spoke to the manager of a factory farm. The man was not a monster. But he was a manager of a factory concerned with production units and maximizing production. He did not have any interest in naming the nearly twenty-five thousand pigs he processed a year, let alone in loving them. Given the suffering he was responsible for inflicting, this no doubt protected him from significant pain.

But this man was also a victim. His life as a factory farm manager was not nearly as rich, beautiful, happy, or tragic as Mr. Burge's life as a pig farmer. To the degree the factory farmer mechanized the animals and the farm he mechanized himself. To the degree that he needed to see all animals, let alone all plants, as machines, he alienated himself from all creatures and all creation: he drained his world of value. He was more efficient and effectively shielded himself from exposure to significant pain, but also, and to precisely the same degree, he was less alive, the inhabitant of a sorely diminished world.

Given our tendency to relate to the rest of creation in terms of domination, the threat to all of us is that we will increasingly see and treat the whole world, even other animals, as machine, that we will increasingly render the whole world into a factory farm and unwittingly dehumanize, diminish, and devalue all of life, and that we will unintentionally but effectively find ourselves living death instead of living life.

---

11. Schweitzer, *Out of My Life and Thought*, 268.

Even scientists who reject belief in God and see the first creation narrative as backward replicate the dynamics I am critiquing here when they struggle to establish human dignity and worth by isolating some trait that clearly sets humans apart from other creatures. Clearly, humans are at the top of a hierarchy of creatures in terms of intelligence, language, and culture. But one does not establish value by affirming these distinctions from the rest of creation and then in their light devaluing all which is, in terms of this hierarchy, beneath one.

We are a part of the hierarchy along with everything else. We are humans from humus. Moreover, in accord with this reading of Genesis, even God, by virtue of creating, becomes inextricably connected to this hierarchy. Our value is not intrinsic; it is relative to the rest of the hierarchy (a critique of the standard understanding of "intrinsic value" is implicit here). All the hierarchy rises and falls together. To affirm one's worth by stressing one's superiority to that which one devalues is, Looney Tunes style, to saw off the limb upon which one is standing.

As we have seen, the first creation narrative avoids these perils by affirming the value-creating dynamics of friendship and love. It does this by proclaiming God's dominion over creation and calling us to like dominion. Again, at the heart of this way of affirming and sustaining value lies the naming and affirming of loving relationships. For instance, many have known the comfort of a tree, felt its fortitude, its life. More mysteriously, trees participate in an elemental way of being that we too enjoy, and that communion with trees can help us more fully to realize and inhabit. That is, there is a communion and peace one feels when one takes time to be in the middle of a forest, when one learns from a tree, a communion which is not available when, for instance, sitting in the middle of even a very quiet parking lot surrounded by cars, or when sitting in the middle of a forest and obliterating it with the mental filter "board-feet." It is sometimes necessary and appropriate to see board-feet—though even then, just as with the slaughter of Pug, there should always be a sense of painful compromise—but the person who only sees board-feet is lost horribly.

I am suggesting that we pay attention to our primordial experiences of communion and love and sorrow—experiences we have not only in relation to other people, but in relation to animals and trees and landscapes (the wider the reality of these primordial experiences the richer). I am suggesting that we embrace these experiences of good, beauty, and evil as our most primordial revelations of value. Here I have returned to my appeal to the infinite significance of our reaction when we encounter that poor, bodily sobbing child. And while I would not exactly equate the value of that child with the value of Pug, here I have returned to the infinite significance of

Mr. Burge's reaction to Pug.[12] It is not, in the first instance, a matter of Pug having some intrinsic property, some right, which should not be violated. As Mr. Burge illustrates, it is a question of regarding the life of Pug, of loving Pug, and out of that love understanding how ideally one would relate to Pug.[13] Such loving reaction to others is the sole origin of all spiritual valuing. That is the primordial spiritual truth which Genesis 1 strives to awaken in our souls.

Mr. Burge, of course, sent Pug to slaughter. I suspect he would name that as necessary, even as painful, but never as good. Some would argue that it was not necessary to slaughter Pug. Wrestling with such difficult questions over where to draw the lines between tragically necessary domination and dominion will always be a challenge, and it is in this context that the struggle to delineate more specific ethics becomes critical, not now as foundations, but as careful attempts to unfold wisely the implications of our primordial spiritual intuitions within the conflicted and imperfect confines of practical life in a fallen world. The task I have pursued here has been the more basic one of sketching the logic, contour, and significance of a Christian perception of the primordial love that breathes valuing fire into all such ethical equations.

IN SUM

Increasingly, in ways the writers of that first Genesis narrative could never have imagined, we have gained godlike power on earth. The long-prevailing tendency to relate to creation and other creatures in terms of domination is in our day being combined with unprecedented human power. As a result, we now pose an unprecedented threat to the well-being of all life on earth. Thus, the need for both short-term political advocacy (which typically includes self-interested appeals) in order to avert ecological harm and long-term efforts at spiritual formation is profound.

In light of all of these reflections, I would suggest that we resist cynical moral nihilism, which ridicules appeal to spiritual ideals and mocks any expectation that people will transcend their self-interest and act out of a greater love. We should remember the ideal of dominion, and affirm our

---

12. I cannot here pursue the subtle and enormously significant subject of properly understanding the relationship between valuing that child and valuing Pug.

13. This distinguishes my position from anthropocentric environmentalisms (e.g., we should save the rainforests because they may contain a cure for human cancer) and from animal rights positions that ground themselves in some ethical theory (e.g., Peter Singer's utilitarian approach)—though I have considerable sympathy for the spirit suffusing the work of both anthropocentric environmentalists and Singer.

love and the exercise of power in love. This will increase our pain over the tragic dimensions of our decisions, it will make existentially real and painful the inescapable fallenness of our daily living, but it will simultaneously preserve us to a real living of life.

On the other hand, in this imperfect world we will face barriers that may require us to compromise, perhaps radically, upon our ideals. We should resist a stubborn idealism, which is unable to acknowledge the pervasive influence of selfishness or unable to tolerate the necessity of compromise and the profound ambiguities involved in real-world power dynamics and the negotiation of intractable conflicts of interest. This means acknowledging the short-term necessity of politically effective appeals to the logic of domination.

Even as we are realistic, however, we should strive to maximize the realm of dominion, and wherever domination is necessary, we should strive to put it ultimately in the service of dominion. We are dealing here with the concrete future of value itself, of morality itself, of love itself. The stakes are terrific, the danger immense. If we allow immediate barriers and personal interest to distract us from our ideals, from dominion, from the affirmation and maximizing of value, then even if we do survive biologically, we will soon find ourselves hopelessly lost: increasingly potent gods busy dominating a diminishing world for which we have only growing contempt.

Not only biologically but spiritually we are racing down a road to hell, well paved. But as a Midwestern pig farmer and Genesis 1 remind us, a primordial love for others yet burns in our souls. If those embers can be flamed, then perhaps the awesome if fragile power of love might unleash the reign of Godly dominion and return joy and delight to all creation.

Chapter 9

Tragedy of the Commons

Agape, Creation Care, Polis

Waters of baptism," "living water," "water of life": "water" is a powerful symbol in Christianity. But when it comes to water as an environmental, public policy issue, should communities of faith be involved? Do communities of faith have anything distinctive to contribute? I argue the answer to these questions is a resounding *"Yes."* The participation of communities of faith in public policy discussion is vital if we are to realize a vibrant and just ecological future.

In 1967, in a famous essay in the prestigious journal, *Science*, Lynn White Jr. concluded that "Christianity bears a huge burden of guilt" for our ecological crisis.[1] Christianity bears this burden because it long interpreted Genesis to say that "no item in the physical creation had any purpose save to serve man's purposes," and modern Western science and society were formed with this human-centered understanding.[2] It is not science and technology but Christianity that bears responsibility for the ecological crisis, for while science and technology made humans capable of creating the ecological crisis, science and technology are neutral tools. *How* humans use science and technology makes all the difference, and how we use science and technology is "deeply conditioned by beliefs about our nature and destiny—that is, by religion."[3]

---

1. White Jr., "Historical Roots of Our Ecologic Crisis," 1206.
2. White Jr., "Historical Roots of Our Ecologic Crisis," 1205.
3. White Jr., "Historical Roots of Our Ecologic Crisis," 1205.

Because of the profound influence of human-centered Christian understanding, we—including "those who fondly regard themselves as post-Christian"—"are *not*, in our hearts, part of the natural process."[4] Despite Darwin, we remain "superior to nature, contemptuous of it, willing to use it for our slightest whim."[5] "Since the roots of our trouble are so largely religious," White continues, "the remedy must also be essentially religious."[6] The ecological crisis will not be solved by "more science and more technology," we must "find a new religion, or rethink our old one."[7]

White, realizing no one remains free of some overarching understanding of human nature and destiny (i.e., no one remains free from some basic religious vision), and too realistic to consider inventing a new religion, recommends we rethink Christianity and reawaken the spirit of St. Francis of Assisi in his imitation of "the ultimate gesture of cosmic humility," wherein the transcendent "assumed flesh, lay helpless in a manger, and hung dying on a scaffold." Christians should assume a similar humility, love all "beneath" them, and act out of love for all creatures and all creation.[8]

Happily, White was not alone in his ecological concerns and spiritual instincts. Widespread awakening to the ecological crisis in the 1970s spurred interreligious spiritual reawakening to all creation. By the beginning of the twenty-first century, conservative and progressive Christians alike were talking about greening churches, stewardship of creation, and love for all creatures. Scholars, with a newfound respect for indigenous understandings of humans as a part of creation, developed new courses in green theology, eco-hermeneutics, eco-spirituality and, in the vein of new religions, Deep Ecology and Gaia theory. At the grassroots level, people and communities of faith formed a multitude of creation care and local environmental advocacy groups. Across religious traditions, among conservatives and progressives alike, the self-emptying spirit of St. Francis was rekindled and burst forth.[9]

---

4. White Jr., "Historical Roots of Our Ecologic Crisis," 1206.
5. White Jr., "Historical Roots of Our Ecologic Crisis," 1206.
6. White Jr., "Historical Roots of Our Ecologic Crisis," 1207.
7. White Jr., "Historical Roots of Our Ecologic Crisis," 1206.
8. White Jr., "Historical Roots of Our Ecologic Crisis," 1207.
9. The connection between religion and environmentalism has become so tight that in 2003 Dustin Penn, a biologist hostile to any understanding that "opposes scientific materialism and reductionism," consequently rejects a "large segment of the environmental movement," including "ecofeminists," "ecotheologists" and nature writers like Wendell Berry—though he grants that "moralizing" does appear to influence behavior (Penn, "Evolutionary Roots of Our Environmental Problems," 277).

In 1968, *Science* published another famous essay, Garrett Hardin's "The Tragedy of the Commons."[10] A "commons" is an open, shared resource, such as the atmosphere, a watershed, lake, ocean, or fishery, or, in Hardin's example, a pasture open to all. For centuries, Hardin explains, herders may happily share a commons. When the population of cattle and herders reaches the carrying capacity of the commons, however, the "inherent logic of the commons remorselessly generates tragedy," for, "[a]s a rational being, each herdsman seeks to maximize his gain."[11] When a herdsman adds to his flock, the benefits are wholly his while the detriments of overgrazing are shared. From the point of view of each herder, then, the rational course is to add cattle. This is "the conclusion reached by each and every rational herdsman sharing a commons."[12] "Therein is the tragedy," for in an unregulated commons in which everyone pursues his or her own best interests while populations increase, "ruin is the destination" of all.[13]

Hardin's essay affirmed a predominant social scientific understanding of human nature. Humans are conditioned by the genetic and social dynamics of kinship and reciprocal altruism, but insofar as humans transcend biological and social conditioning and make rational decisions, they will seek to maximize individual security and gain. This idea, Hardin argues, is consistent with modern science's revelation that in "real life" the ultimate good is survival.[14] Thanks to "free market" economic theory inspired by Adam Smith, which holds that individuals intending only personal gain are "led by an invisible hand to promote . . . the public interest," people have had a tendency "to assume that decisions reached individually will, in fact, be the best decisions for an entire society."[15] This affirmation of the pursuit of self-interest, Hardin notes, aligns with a policy of laissez-faire with regard to commons, such as atmosphere, water, and fisheries.[16]

Hardin's essay created an immediate sensation because he explained, contrary to confidence in the "invisible hand," why rational action (i.e., pursuit of self-interest) in our finite world will inevitably lead to destruction of commons and ruin for all. Science and technology can only delay ruin as populations increase on local and global commons.[17] Like White, then,

10. Hardin, "Tragedy of the Commons," 1243–48.
11. Hardin, "Tragedy of the Commons," 1244.
12. Hardin, "Tragedy of the Commons," 1244.
13. Hardin, "Tragedy of the Commons," 1244.
14. Hardin, "Tragedy of the Commons," 1244.
15. Hardin, "Tragedy of the Commons," 1244, citing Smith, *Wealth of Nations*, 423.
16. Hardin, "Tragedy of the Commons," 1244.
17. Hardin, "Tragedy of the Commons," 1244.

Hardin agrees there is no scientific or technological solution to ecological commons challenges. A change in morals and regulation of commons—"mutual coercion, mutually agreed upon"—is required.[18] Given the inherent selfishness of human nature, however, how can we expect humans to escape the logic of the commons at collective, political, "mutual coercion" levels? Who will watch the watchers?[19]

Lynn White offered a classic answer to this question. Religions—rich with condemnation of enduring human tendencies to avarice, selfishness, and exploitation—are no strangers to Hardin's understanding of human nature. Like White, Christianity (like most religions) also affirms a countervailing force: human awakening to transcending agape, to desire for good for all creatures. As illustrated by Jesus' fidelity to love even to the cross, the good of survival can be trumped by the good of love and justice for all. This transcending affirmation, so beautifully visible in the life of St. Francis, is revealed when our hearts ache over the suffering of others, and in our pangs of conscience when we recognize ourselves as causes of suffering. When we gather to agree upon "mutual coercion, mutually agreed upon," White suggests, we can in that collective setting awaken ourselves to agape, appeal to our higher nature, to conscience, and agree to public policy that is realistic about human selfishness and also committed to realizing as just and good a future for all creatures as is humanly possible.

But Hardin will have none of it. He judges appeals to love and conscience "pathogenic."[20]

18. Hardin, "Tragedy of the Commons," 1247.

19. Hardin, "Tragedy of the Commons," 1245. Here Hardin cites Plato's famous line. See especially with regard to the "who will watch the watchers" problem, Krier, "The Tragedy of the Commons, Part Two."

20. Hardin, "Tragedy of the Commons," 1246. In 1968 Hardin, along with mainstream evolutionary theory, considered conscience/altruism to be self-eliminating in the long term. By the early 1980s, Hardin, again along mainstream evolutionary theory, had realized his error concerning the purportedly self-eliminating character of conscience/altruism (see his 1982 essay, "Discriminating Altruisms"). With regard to evolved "altruisms," see Sober and Wilson, *Unto Others*. Insofar as he insists upon remaining within Darwinian parameters, which requires selection (i.e., among multiple players), Hardin quite rightly refuses to affirm altruisms beyond a group level (e.g., family, tribal, ethnic, national). By definition (again, because it requires selection), evolutionary theory cannot encompass/explain agape/universal altruism, which Hardin consequently refers to as "promiscuous altruism." By contrast, appeals to universal agape/altruism are common in religions such as Christianity. An appeal to universal altruism is also characteristic of atheistic ethicists such as Peter Singer—whom Hardin names explicitly as an opponent in "Discriminating Altruisms" (172). Singer considers appeal to universal benevolence to be a *sine qua non* for ethics (Singer, *Practical Ethics*, 10). Singer's affirmation of universal benevolence led him to draw conclusions very different from Hardin's concerning the obligation of rich people and rich nations

> If we ask a man who is exploiting a commons to desist "in the name of conscience," what are we saying to him? What does he hear?—not only at the moment but also in the wee small hours of the night when, half asleep, he remembers not merely the words we used but also the nonverbal cues we gave him unawares? Sooner or later, consciously or subconsciously, he senses that he has received two communications, and that they are contradictory: (i) (intended communication) "If you don't do as we ask, we will openly condemn you for not acting like a responsible citizen"; (ii) (the unintended communication) "If you do behave as we ask, we will secretly condemn you for a simpleton who can be shamed into standing aside while the rest of us exploit the commons."[21]

Hardin recommends hard-nosed realism in accord with the scientific revelation that the ultimate good is survival (of the fittest). The most advanced nations enjoy standards of living unimaginable even to emperors of old. Earth cannot support even the current human population at such standards. What posterity demands, Hardin concludes, is "lifeboat ethics." The most advanced nations should close their borders (for the lifeboat is full) and stop sending resources abroad. He literally invites people of conscience to jump overboard.[22]

For religious professionals like myself, who are surrounded by people giving stunning quantities of time, talent, and money in response to their love for all creation and all creatures, the idea that insofar as humans are rational they are irremediably selfish is obviously false. The world's classic faith traditions are well aware of humans' selfish and exploitative tendencies, and they clearly distinguish between the good of sacrificing out of love and the evil of allowing oneself to be taken as a chump. People of faith can accordingly agree to the need for "mutual coercion, mutually agreed upon."

---

towards poor people and poor nations in his well-known essay, "Famine, affluence and morality."

21. Hardin, "Tragedy of the Commons," 1246. Hardin provides no empirical evidence for this conclusion. To be fair, Hardin is reflecting a consensus view among social scientists in the late twentieth century (e.g., consider the so-called "complete theory of rationality" that informed twentieth-century game theory). Note that from Hardin's perspective the divide is not, as it is classically, between people of conscience and people who are wholly selfish (most of us fall somewhere along the middle of this continuum between saints and scoundrels). According to Hardin, the divide is between people who are wholly selfish and clueless chumps (i.e., he provides a neat apologetic for wholesale selfishness—from the perspective argued here, by contrast, wholly selfish people are to varying degrees evil, are likely to cause others concrete harm insofar as they gain power and political influence, and should be, proportionately, subjects of moral disdain).

22. Hardin, "Lifeboat Ethics."

The distinction will be that people of faith will insist that central/overlapping norms (moral ideals) should shape the contours of mutual coercion (public policy).[23]

Hardin's "lifeboat ethics" gained few overt followers, but his view of humans as wholly selfish agents, and his criticism of Smith's "invisible hand," endured in late twentieth-century social and political science. The question, "who guards the guardians" remained open, and religious ethical ideals and communities remained marginal in academic social scientific and political discussions. Most troubling, in many discussions *economic efficiency* came to play the role of "highest good." The problem is that appeals to efficiency alone marginalize creation and all creatures, including concern for the good of humans. If efficiency alone is our measure, then we will not care or even notice if there are severe ecological impacts and radical economic inequities, as long as more wealth on the whole is generated.

For example, Paul Debaere and company, writing in *Water Policy*, note that in Australia's Murray-Darling Basin, water's economic productivity is sixty-seven times more efficient in manufacturing—and ninety-nine times more efficient in mining—than in agriculture.[24] On what grounds, Debaere asks, "should a dynamic market economy shelter agriculture [or, by the same reasoning, endangered species or ecosystems] from structural changes"?[25] Debaere can evidently imagine no such grounds. But if economic efficiency is the sole measure, then there are no grounds whatsoever for sheltering agriculture, endangered species, and ecosystems from devastating ecological change. Thus Peter Hill, writing in *The Independent Review*, can argue that the decimation of bison in North America—from thirty million in 1800, to ten million in 1860, to under one thousand in 1886—was not an ecological tragedy but an unqualified good, for bison were replaced with cattle, which are more efficient in the conversion of grass into dollars.[26] With regard to contemporary global food production, two alarmed scholars, Rebecca Clausen and Stefano Longo, explain how efficiencies of scale are resulting in the "pauperization" of millions of relatively inefficient family farmers and fishers. If economic efficiency is the ultimate criterion, they object, the pauperization of millions, human and

---

23. I refer here to the "overlapping" of John Rawls' "overlapping consensus" (Rawls, *Political Liberalism*).

24. Debaere et al., "Water Markets as a Response to Scarcity," 639.

25. Debaere et al., "Water Markets as a Response to Scarcity," 641.

26. Hill, "Are All Commons Tragedies?," 490.

nonhuman alike, appears as part of an unqualified "good"—a "good" unrelated to justice and creaturely well-being.[27]

Fortunately, by the beginning of the twenty-first century, social scientists began to realize the standard, twentieth-century picture of humans as normless, selfish agents was false. Elinor Ostrom won the 2009 Nobel Memorial Prize in Economic Sciences for helping to establish that humans 1) do act selflessly in accord with norms, 2) change behavior in response to verbal chastisement for violation of community values (even when offenders remain anonymous and personal profit is sacrificed), 3) preserve commons better when policy is a shared creation, and 4) self-regulate and govern commons most effectively when there is significant face-to-face communication and compliance is understood primarily in normative (not legal/financial penalty) terms.[28]

A prejudice against agape and religion endures, however, for Ostrom continues to interpret altruism within self-interested parameters, though she refers grudgingly to the utility of "religious mystification."[29] And, when Ostrom and her colleagues note that their findings affirm the vital role of institutions that cultivate and carry moral norms, the institutions they list are "corporations, charitable organizations, neighborhood groups, organized religions, and public and private schools."[30] The disconnect from reality is stark if one takes a moment to reflect (historically, globally, and with regard to religious and secular states alike) upon the relative moral carrying capacity and influence of "neighborhood groups," "charitable organizations," "corporations"(!), and "private schools"—in comparison to the moral-carrying capacity and influence of religions.[31]

Faith communities and their moral ideals must be vital players in the formation of environmental policies if we are to realize a most loving and just ecological future. White was right to think the ecological crisis can largely be laid at the feet of Christianity. He was also right to think that Christianity's potential for reawakening humanity to love for creation and

---

27. Clausen and Longo, "Tragedy of the Commodity and the Farce of AquaAdvantage Salmonâ."

28. Ostrom, "Coping with Tragedies of the Commons," and Kraak, "Exploring the 'Public Goods Game' Model."

29. Ostrom, "Coping with Tragedies of the Commons," 525.

30. Kinzig et al., "Social Norms and Global Environmental Challenges," 165. See also Van Vugt, "Averting the Tragedy of the Commons."

31. Consider, for instance, that, despite Goodstein's "steep decline" rhetoric, 80 percent of Americans claim a religious affiliation, and of the 20 percent who *do not* claim religious affiliation, 66 percent believe in God, and 20 percent pray daily (Goodstein, "Percentage of Protestant Americans Is in Steep Decline").

all creatures can play a vital role in providing the means through which the crisis can be addressed. White would be thankful that—while the Christian community has a long way to go, and while persons who pursue wholly selfish ends remain distressingly powerful[32]—Christians across the world are increasingly embracing the spirit of St. Francis of Assisi.

---

32. In this context the serious problem with the *Citizens United* decision, insofar as it creates superpowerful, sometimes transnational "persons" whose ultimate and/or sole goal is the maximizing of "their" own profit and power, and who are profoundly influential in the formation of public policy (through the co-option of the energies of real people), begins to become visible. For the reasons Hardin cynically rehearses vis-à-vis people, when it comes to such inanimate persons, who are literally incapable of having a conscience, appeals to "self-regulation" and "voluntary compliance" are a fool's game. What is needed is "mutual coercion, mutually agreed upon" (i.e., public policy), but it is critical that those reaching the mutual agreement are imperfect but partly good, well-informed, living people. Ideally, people who have been selected to play leadership roles in policymaking would be selected in part because they have demonstrated good moral resolve and judgment, and the political system would be structured so as to ensure that it would be difficult for moral concerns to be subverted by those pursuing wholly selfish ends. Otherwise, in a world with an expanding population, Hardin's tragedy dynamics take unmitigated hold with regard to local and global commons, and ruin does become a possible destination for all (even those with lifeboat fantasies). Fortunately, again, across the globe, and (in analogous ways) across religious traditions, the spirit of St. Francis is largely in ascendance.

Chapter 10

Animals

Beyond the Enlightenment Eclipse

Seventeenth and eighteenth-century Western European Enlightenment rationality made a fundamental distinction between the mental and the physical. This distinction categorically distinguished human beings, the only physical beings with mind/spirit, from animals and the rest of brute nature. Notably, this distinction was also used to deny full personhood to women and to some peoples who purportedly lacked full possession of the reasoning capacities that signaled possession of mind. In terms of ethical consideration, then, mainstream Enlightenment rationality was decidedly androcentric, Eurocentric, and anthropocentric.

Over the course of the nineteenth and twentieth centuries, Western rationality's racism and sexism was largely recognized, and ongoing critique initiated. But predominant Western rationality into the twenty-first century remains unwittingly anthropocentric. Consider, for instance, the category "animals." While in biology class humans are commonly categorized as animals, in common ethical, religious, and popular discourse, "animals" is not understood to include humans. In accord with this predominant expectation, for instance, one would not expect to encounter theological anthropology under an entry for "animals." Indeed, in popular speech "animal" remains a term of derision when applied to a person. Or consider how ordinarily talk about animal experimentation would not be expected to include discussion of experimentation upon humans.

Significantly, anthropocentrism even permeates modern Western environmentalism. The environment in question is typically the *human* environment. Animals are part of the environment, and are sometimes even grouped with minerals, soil, and crops as "resources" to be "preserved," "managed" and sustainably "harvested." Humans are not part of the environment. In accord with modern anthropocentric rationality, humans alone are thought to be above brute nature.

In place of the classic scriptural nexus "Creator/creatures/creation," then—and remembering that biblically all creatures have "the breath of life"—modern Western Christians think in terms of the categorically different nexus of "God/humans/animals/nature." This fundamental shift in understanding decisively determines the very vocabularies and concepts *out of which* modern Westerners think. As a result, for instance, in the Adam and Eve creation narrative translators naturally translate a Hebrew word (*nefesh*) as "living being" when they apply it to humans and translate the same Hebrew word as "living creature" when they apply it to the birds and beasts (Genesis 2:7, 19).

Within the parameters of this predominant modern Western conceptual framework, *things* such as animals disappear as subjects of direct divine and moral concern. Humans, as categorically unique kinds of being, are understood to be the sole proper subjects of direct divine and moral concern. "Nature," a category that includes everything that is not human, has only indirect or instrumental value. That is, natural objects, including animals, are considered valuable only insofar as they are valuable for humans.

In this fashion anthropocentrism, not as a considered conclusion but as an unquestioned presumption, pervades mainstream modern rationality. To be sure, the way anthropocentrism plays to human pride and self-interest means that it has always influenced human reflection. In the wake of Enlightenment rationality, however, anthropocentrism gained unprecedented philosophical justification and began to exert unprecedented influence. Animals were simply rendered invisible as subjects of direct divine and moral concern as anthropocentrism was inscribed into modern Western rationality at a primordial level.

Not surprisingly, modern ethical and biblical reflection—and this obtains across the theological spectrum—has been decisively shaped by modernity's anthropocentrism. Consider, for instance, the account of Noah and the flood. In a recent work focused upon biblical creation theology, one distinguished author, explaining the thematic significance of the actual shape of Hebrew narratives, points out that the central verses in Hebrew narratives are also often the thematic "key to the story," thus the "story of

Noah turns around Genesis 8:1: 'God remembered Noah.'"[1] In accord with modern thought, this author simply does not notice that Genesis 8:1 says, "God remembered Noah and all the wild animals and all the domestic animals."

In the same way, it has long been standard to refer to "God's covenant with Noah," or the "Noahic covenant." Until recently, it was not thought significant or even noticed that the text repeatedly (six times in nine verses) specifies that God's covenant is not only with Noah but "with every creature that is with you, the birds, the domestic animals, and every animal of the earth with you, as many as came out of the ark."

Similarly, even as twentieth-century students of the Hebrew Scriptures were taught to attend to the significance of blessings, the blessing of the fishes and the birds in Genesis 1:22 and the call for land creatures to be fruitful and multiply in Genesis 8:17 were typically not really noticed. In the same vein, while the creation of humans in the image of God and the blessing of humans and the call for them to have dominion over the earth in Genesis 1:28 is surely one of the most famous passages of Scripture, the explicitly vegan giving of seeds and fruits exclusively for food to every creature with the "breath of life" in the very next verses (29–30) receives scant notice.

As Western Christians have begun to become conscious of modernity's anthropocentrism, however, they have begun to notice God's delight in and blessing of nonhuman creatures in the seven days of creation narrative. They have begun to notice that the creation God declares "very good" is expressly vegan. They have begun to notice that God covenants with all creatures and even the earth in what many now call the "rainbow" or "earth" covenant. Christians are attending anew to passages such as Psalm 148, where all creatures, from sun to birds to young men, are called upon to praise God. They are noticing the wholly peaceable character of famous eschatological passages such as the so-called "lion and lamb" passage of Isaiah 11, where "lions eat straw" and no creature anywhere, whether human, domestic, or wild, "hurt or destroy" on all God's holy mountain.

Conscious of modernity's anthropocentrism, Christians are noticing Jesus' background assertion that God attends to the death of each sparrow. And they are noticing that Jesus rightly presumes that not even his theological opponents will dare to deny that it is good to break the Sabbath in order to rescue a sheep from a pit (Matthew 12:10, Luke 14:5). They are noticing that the "fire" of 2 Peter 3:11–13 does not destroy the physical universe, freeing souls to be with God in some unearthly reality, but that it burns away

---

1. Barker, *Creation*, 25.

all unrighteousness as it refines a "new heavens (i.e., a new sky) and a new earth in which righteousness dwells."

Examples revealing anthropocentric distortion of Scripture could easily be multiplied. But the clear effect of anthropocentrism vis-à-vis all these familiar texts is sufficient to make the problem evident. For as is now clear, modern Western philosophical, scientific, theological, ethical, and biblical understanding has been pervaded by an anthropocentrism that is alien to the Christian Scriptures. We must reevaluate not merely Scripture and ethics, but theology, history, and worship in light of our newfound awareness that nonhuman creatures together with us human creatures constitute a community of subjects of direct divine and moral concern.

Insofar as all the theological disciplines have developed decisively in the modern West, rigorous reorientation in the wake of our recent and ongoing awakening to anthropocentrism is vital. The issues raised are diverse and complex. Clearly, the Christian Scriptures differentiate between humans and other creatures. But what exactly are the differences? And what are their ethical implications? How do our major translations and mainstream interpretations of Scripture need to change in order to correct for modern anthropocentrism? And what are the theological and ethical consequences of making such a correction? What in the writings of the patristics and the Reformers have we failed to notice or misinterpreted because we have been looking unawares through anthropocentric spectacles? How are we to consider the place and capacities of nonhuman creatures in relation to worship, salvation, or heaven? When, if ever, is it permissible to kill, eat, wear or experiment upon nonhuman creatures? Are there ethically significant distinctions to be drawn among nonhuman creatures? If so, what are the criteria? What are Christians to think ethically and spiritually about pets, zoos, wilderness areas, pesticides, transgenic organisms, the "creation" and patenting of life, extermination of invasive species, human-caused extinction events, and varieties of hunting?

Anthropocentrism still reigns in early twenty-first century scriptural interpretation, theology, and ethics. Non-anthropocentric focus upon nonhuman creatures remains the purview of a small if fast-growing collection of scholars and advocates on the margins of mainstream theological discussion. But with ever-widening consciousness of the distorting influence of modern anthropocentrism, one can anticipate that the next few decades will see the emergence of significant areas of interpretive and ethical consensus about non-human creatures, as well as identification of edges of debate requiring ongoing research.

While non-anthropocentric interpretation of Scripture and ethics remains in its infancy, one can identify three broad currents of non-anthropocentic thought: 1) the "land ethic" or "deep ecology," 2) "animal rights," and 3) "animal theology." The "land ethic" (*circa* 1948, Aldo Leopold) and "deep ecology" (*circa* 1972, Arne Naess) are biocentric and holistic. For Leopold, "a thing is right when it tends to preserve the integrity, stability, and beauty of the biotic community. It is wrong when it tends otherwise."[2] This move beyond anthropocentrism, which becomes self-conscious in deep ecology, deemphasizes individual animals, human or no, and focuses instead upon the health of bio-systems.

Notably, this perspective may be reflected in Psalm 104. Nonetheless, it stands in tension with the vast majority of Scripture, which is overwhelmingly concerned with individual creatures. Christians will reject the position of a small minority of deep ecologists who refuse to distinguish ethically between amoebae and humans. Also, the land ethic and deep ecology should be distinguished from a metaphysical Darwinism (in contrast to a scientific Darwinism) that rejects moral ideals not consistent with biological realities, and that tends to invoke biological distinctions (e.g., capacity to reason, capacity for language) in the course of retaining modernity's categorical anthropocentrism.

Highly marginal nineteenth- and twentieth-century movements on behalf of animals rose to mainstream notice when Peter Singer's *Animal Liberation* (1975) captured the public imagination and stimulated the late twentieth-century "animal rights" movement.[3] Singer's utilitarian argument turned upon the moral significance of animals' capacity to suffer. His frank description of the suffering of animals at human hands stirred widespread indignation and spurred overt resistance to anthropocentric disregard for the well-being of nonhuman animals. Appropriating the most powerful moral and international legal vocabulary available, the movement established itself around an appeal to animal "rights."

A Christian version of animal rights quickly materialized with Andrew Linzey's *Animal Rights: A Christian Assessment* (1976).[4] The modern legal concept of "rights" is alien to Scripture, but globally it is a central ethical and legal category. Just as many Christians adopted the "rights" category on behalf of Christian ideals vis-à-vis humans, Linzey adopted the "rights" category vis-à-vis animals. By the 1990s, Linzey and other Christians had developed arguments using specifically scriptural and theological concepts, and as a result a variety of ethical positions predicated upon "reverence for

---

2. Leopold, *Sand County Almanac*, 224–25.
3. Singer, *Animal Liberation*.
4. Linzey, *Animal Rights*.

life," "creature care," and "love for all creatures" began to undergird Christian advocacy for "animal theology."

In contrast to biocentric perspectives, animal theology remains focused upon individuals. In contrast to animal rights, animal theology is predicated upon a non-anthropomorphic reading of Scripture and the Christian tradition. As illustrated above, the focus upon individual creatures and the inclusion of all creatures among a community of subjects who are all loved by and worship God, and thus who are all subjects of direct divine and moral concern, is consistent with the mainstream of Scripture. However, scriptural, theological, and ethical debates over the precise contours of right regard for nonhuman creatures remain in their infancy. There is general agreement that anthropocentrism has distorted biblical interpretation, theology, and ethics, and that blatant mistreatment of nonhuman creatures is beyond the pale. But a mature, non-anthropocentric reading of Scripture and consensus over right Christian response to a host of theological and ethical questions regarding nonhuman creatures are as yet the vital and still-to-be-realized product of this emerging sphere of scriptural, theological, and ethical reflection.

Chapter 11

Saying Grace

It has been traditional for Christians to say grace before meals. Indeed, most of the world's faith traditions pause for some form of prayer or meditation before eating. In a time of plenty it can be easy to eat without a second thought. But go without food for only a few days and you will feel the primordial need begin to build. Even amidst plenty, it is easy to imagine panic at the threat of starvation, easy to imagine the driving force of the *"I need to eat!"* Eating signifies triumph, if transitory, over mortal danger. It is satisfying, comforting, strengthening, empowering. It marks the moment when the mortal vulnerability, the ever-returning, entirely natural neediness of our flesh is for some short while effectively met.

It is profound spiritual wisdom, then, that insists—at precisely that point between primordial physical need and its fulfillment—upon a full and considered pause. For spirituality has a pace and power that flows against haste, against selfish desire, against what is, physically, natural neediness, against survival as the ultimate value. So, profound spiritual wisdom insists upon a pause, a pause to say grace before we eat.

AGAPE, TO *SAY*, TO *SAID*

But precisely what might it mean to say grace? Emmanuel Levinas draws a powerful distinction between what it is to *said* and what is it to *say*. He develops this distinction in order to name a dimension of reality largely elided by modern Western secular philosophy. The *said* relates to an idea or fact that I communicate. Roughly, success with the *said* comes when an idea I have is communicated with relative completeness, when I have stimulated a thought in your head roughly equivalent to the thought I have in my head.

The *says*, by contrast, while it is mediated through the *said*—that is, through physical signs (we are not telepathic), not only through words but also through clothing and gestures—the *says*, while it is mediated through the *said*, is not an idea I have and seek to communicate to some other. The *says*, Levinas contends, names a quite different relation to others, the *says* designates how I am taken "hostage" by the other or, in my modification of Levinas's formulation, *how I am seized by love and concern for another (and, simultaneously, insofar as I am seized by love, the says designates how I am seized by love and concern for myself)*. When the *saying* referred to by the word *says* is shared, it does not mean that we are connected because we share meanings, ideas, or commitments—it means we are united because we have each surrendered to having been seized by love for one another.

The said is significant with regard to the *says*. Unless the circumstances are extraordinary, one cannot use a harsh *said*—for instance, the *said*, "you are a coward and a fool"—in order to communicate the *saying* of the love by which you have been seized for someone. The said, "I love you," or perhaps one's tears or an embrace, is the sort of *said* needed to express the *saying* of how you are seized by love. The *said* is important for the *saying* because it gives necessary aid in communicating the *says* and directs our attention in the world to the specific Faces the *saying* pertains to.

Frequently and quite properly the *said* is all that matters. For instance, if you're explaining how to change a tire or how to do differential equations, then *said* is quite rightly everything.[1] But people who *only* think or theorize in terms of the *said*, who think that ultimately language and truth is all about correspondence between signs on the one hand and material or socially sustained realities on the other, are in their theory—not necessarily in their actual living—such people are in their theory alienated from the transcending love of the *says*.

There is nothing inherently wrong with the *said*. The *said* is only problematic, a tragic obstruction, when the point should be to *say*. For instance, one can *said* grace before meals—not *say* grace but *said* grace. That is, one can speak a prayer that is all about communicating ideas with others or with God, a prayer that originates in one's own intention, or that simply fulfills a sense of liturgical duty or orthodox correctness. Such "prayers," wholly

---

1. One might think helpfully, if roughly, of the distinction Martin Buber draws between I-It and I-Thou relationships.

said, have no opening to the having been seized, no opening to agape, to the divine. By contrast, to *say* a prayer, truly to pray not only with our words but in the orientation of our very being, to pray in spirit, is to open ourselves wholly to the *saying* of gracious love and to use *said* to express and direct our attention to the concrete subjects that *saying* concerns.

SEIZED BY ALL FACES

Levinas's distinction between the *said* and the *says* can also be roughly clarified in relation to a parallel distinction between "faces" (with a small "f") and "Faces" (with a capital "F"). The (small "f") face names the physical and sociocultural face that we see, the color of the skin, eyes, and hair, the gender, age, nationality, professional identity and, by the same reasoning—here, with significant implications, I push a Levinasian logic beyond Levinas—the species. The (capital "F") Face names what is only manifest in our having been seized by love for a Face.

Think very concretely here of times when you have been wholly seized by love for another, whether the circumstances were joyful or horrific. This love is not a function of our own decision or desire. Though we can harden our hearts to it, we do not initiate it. Moreover, resisting the having been seized takes effort. Very significantly, the reality of the Face is manifest continually among people, and as even a cursory survey of mainstream news sources immediately makes clear, most people are passionately seized by the Faces of all sorts of creatures.

In Houston a couple of years ago a big alligator from the bayous somehow got lost on a residential street. The officers responding to the panicked calls, officers who were probably terrified themselves, lassoed the alligator, attached the line to the back of a pickup truck, and dragged it on its belly across an asphalt street—all on video. Even in Houston (not exactly a bastion of animal rights activists), and even with an alligator (not the cuddliest of creatures), people were so outraged that city officials had to apologize and promise such a thing would never happen again. Of course, later that day most of those same people without a second thought ate pigs, cows, chicken, fish. The connections were not made, but nonetheless the reality of the Face of that alligator was clearly manifest.

Recently I was doing a lecture series at a church known for its passion and work for social justice, especially for its long-term advocacy for the queer community. I described the young tomato plant I had hoped to purchase and bring to that evening's lecture. I got caught in traffic and could not get the plant, so I asked them to imagine the young plant on the podium, and then I explained that I had planned to propose ripping it out of the dirt and tearing it to pieces right in front of them. There was a collective gasp of horror from that morally sensitive class. They were awakened and seized by love even for the Face of that imagined tomato plant.

With regard to a vast array of Faces, from puppies to elephants to seals to alligators and humans and even plants, the reality of having been seized by love for Faces is stunningly powerful and readily apparent—a reality empirically obvious even as it remains theoretically invisible to predominant streams of modern Western rationality. Consider, for instance, that the reality of the having been seized is so obvious that the existence of those rare individuals whose brains are structured or injured in such a way that they are *not* seized by Faces is a recognized medical condition that describes a psychopathology. At the same time, the reality manifest among the overwhelming multitude of people across history, cultures, and religions who *are* seized by the Faces of others—these are empirical observations—is not theoretically acknowledged and named, and so many conclude that with regard to rational intentional action, insofar as there is such a thing, it all boils down to selfishness or at best enlightened self-interest. I specify "insofar as there is such a thing" as rational intentional action because for many there is no such thing, for, given their theoretical presuppositions, it all must boil down to the prerational, unconscious dynamics of nature and nurture and/or reciprocal, kinship, or group altruism and the like. The failure explicitly to name and acknowledge the reality of the having been seized, that is, the reality of agape, is a significant lacuna in modern Western rationality.

OTHERS AND THE OTHER

My interpretation of Levinas contrasts to an interpretation common among those who read Levinas within mainstream Derridean parameters (I acknowledge that Levinas's phrasing vis-à-vis this interpretive issue is ambiguous). On my reading, I am not seized by *the face of the other*. I am seized *by love for* the Face of the other. That is, it is not recognition of the *immanent* otherness of the other that is key—not the differences in our language, ethnicity, gender, or species—for, after all, these are precisely the immanent distinctions of otherness noticed by those who are racist, sexist, heterosexist, and speciest. The Otherness refers to *the Otherness of the love* by which I am seized for the other's Face—I am not seized by the faces of others, I am seized *by love for* the Faces of others. I am seized by love, and only by virtue of the love that seizes me do I see Faces (which are always mediated by faces, just as the *says* is always mediated by the *said*). That love is itself what is Other, and insofar as this love is not a product of my decisions, intentions, or desires, not a product of my personal preferences, not my love but a love which seizes me for another, which thereby awakens me to Faces, this is precisely the love classically distinguished as agape—not a product of my decision or desire, not a function of reciprocal, kinship, and/or group altruism, but a transcending, Other reality, *a love not from me that seizes me for another (and insofar as it seizes me, a love that seizes me for myself)*.[2]

This, I believe, precisely describes the love that Jews and Christians and those of many other faiths have in mind when they say, "God *is* Love"— and the reality of the divine understood in this specific sense is as apparent, real, and powerful as the reality of our having been seized by love for other Faces. For this reason, I define the essence of faith not in cognitive terms of affirmation or intellectual assent to some assertion or belief, but in existential/spiritual terms of surrender/fidelity to agape: *faith is living surrender to having been seized in and by love for every Face*.[3]

I need to stress one more characteristic of this love. As Levinas realized, the reality of the having been seized is not related to the color of another's eyes or skin, their nationality, or their uniform. So Levinas, who survived five years wearing the yellow star in a Nazi forced labor camp, made clear that this love for others applied even to the Faces of his Nazi captors. In other words, in its transcending purity the love of the having been seized sees Faces without regard to any aspect of the (small "f") otherness of faces. Christians specify this dimension of divine agape by stressing that God's love is *gracious*.

At the same time, Levinas was not a pacifist. He was captured while fighting against the Nazis with the French Tenth Army. On Levinas's understanding, when you are seized in isolation by *one* Face, you are seized by unqualified, gracious love for that Face, and violence is unthinkable (here I will simply note that I disagree with Levinas on this specific point, for I argue we should resist violation of our own Faces).[4] Levinas argues that violence only becomes thinkable when one is simultaneously seized by love for more than one Face (Levinas refers to this in terms of "the third"). When faces are harming one another there is no escape from responsibility to act violently towards some Face, for in such contexts every possible action or

---

2. To be clear, I do not deny the reality of reciprocal, kinship, and group altruism, or of eros, nor do I see them as bad/negative. I insist, however, upon distinguishing and affirming the discrete reality of agape. For an extended defense of the reasonableness of affirming the reality of agape, see my *Reasonable Belief*.

3. See Greenway, *Reasonable Belief*, 105–8.

4. See Greenway, *Reasonable Belief*, 135, for details on my departure from Levinas at this juncture.

inaction will cause or facilitate harm, so one must choose the best option among actions which are all harmful. That is, often we are forced to make ethical judgments where the best action is not a good action but the least bad action insofar as one must act violently towards some Faces in defense of other Faces.

HONEST TO LOVE: FACING UP

It can be easy for those of us who live in relatively peaceful places to imagine we are not involved in the world's violence. But the peaceable spaces we enjoy—our nation states, counties, towns, educational, political, and financial institutions—are *all* in part built upon blood, violence, and injustices that stretch into the mists of prehistory and endure to this day. With specific reference to saying grace before meals at the vast majority of tables, we are all involved in the suffering and slaughter of a multitude of Faces. We are also involved in all that it takes to get that food before us—from the transportation networks, the massive pesticide use, the sociopolitical consequences of capitalist grain markets (where profit is the uber-value), the creation of mega-farms, factory "farms," and a globalized farming system, to the often poverty-level wages and working conditions of farmers, pickers, drivers, and slaughterhouse workers at home and abroad—a network of exploitation, suffering, and despoliation typically lies on our dinner tables.

For such reasons, Levinas concludes, no one is innocent: we are all born already and inextricably complicit. That is why there is no place for simply "giving thanks" before one eats. "Giving thanks" is an expression which ever so subtly facilitates denial of complicity. It is unthinkable one would simply "give thanks" in the context of moral offense, and while in our world there are far better and far worse tables, no table is innocent. So, those who are morally awakened will be incredulous over the very idea of "giving thanks" at any table in this world, for they will be wholly alive to the piercing, awful and awe-full need to *say* grace.

From this perspective, when Christians speak of this world as "fallen" we are not referring to some historical pivot point but, in accord with Levinas, naming honestly and frankly how our real, Darwinian world appears to those awakened to having been seized by love for all Faces, how the world appears to those awakened to the Faces of all the alligators, tomato plants, and workers (Darwin himself, though he failed to understand the connection to Christian doctrine, famously saw the world as fallen in this sense). From this perspective, when Christians speak of "original sin" they are naming how we are born *already* complicit, part and parcel of this unjust, pain-filled world, and of how we are frequently forced to choose the best among options, all bad, in situations where whatever one does a Face will be harmed. While the doctrines of the "fall" and of "original sin" have been unpopular even among theologians in recent years, from this perspective their truth is as clear and compelling as the reality of the inescapable pain and suffering suffusing this vale of tears.

Confronting honestly the character of creation and our existence as creatures in and of it, when Levinas asks, "Is it righteous to be?" he infamously but rightly answers "no." Many people bristle, repulsed by his damning response. Why? First, consider that the manifest reality of widespread awakening to Faces—from horses to puppies to alligators to tomato plants—makes it implausible to suggest the problem is people's insensitivity to the fallen character of reality or even to their inextricable entanglement within it. Wittingly or no, the vast majority of us are awakened and understand the interconnected character of our being in this world. Because of this, while at first it may seem counterintuitive, I suspect a major problem is that at a primordial level people are so sensitive to the realities of the fall and so horrified by their inescapable complicity (what Christians call "original sin"), that they are at a non-self-conscious level desperate to deny their complicity, and so they react against confessing the truth of their complicity, against confessing the truth of the fallenness of our world. They react as if they were about to grab white-hot coals, and in all sorts of individual and collective ways they engage in strident, often angry, denial.[5]

One meets vegetarians and vegans who get fierce at this point. As if somehow their eating is wholly innocent, and as if all other parts of their lives (e.g., economic, cultural, and sociopolitical) are innocent as well. This suggests that one bad reason for being vegan or vegetarian or, at the opposite pole, for drawing thick ethical lines distinguishing humans from other animals (i.e., to assert one's innocence by rejecting the idea that killing non-human animals for food is harmful/violation), or for creating stories about how one's own people is wholly innocent and has a special right to be, is a desire to claim "my place in the sun" (as named and condemned by Pascal), to assert one's right to be, one's innocence.[6] The Jewish and Christian spirituality that *emphasizes grace* while honestly naming the fallen character of our world and our inescapable complicity in and with it (original sin), quite rightly and honestly *says* otherwise.

---

5. I unfold these dynamics at length in Greenway, *Challenge of Evil,* "Part 1: Modern Western Evasions of Evil."

6. Pascal, *Pensées,* 112, as cited in Levinas, *Otherwise Than Being,* vii.

Why this massive denial of complicity or, insofar as it is unwitting, this massive delusion over our innocence? I am suggesting, contrary to first appearances, that it is actually because people are overwhelmingly sensitive to having been seized by the Faces of all creatures. Here I am following an insight of Derrick Jensen in his troubling but valuable book, *A Language Older Than Words*.[7] Jensen is an incest survivor and has experience with denial by both abuser and victim. He understands intimately the way in which denial on the part of the abuser can lead to continuing abuse, which itself actively reinforces denial of the horror of the violation, which would otherwise be too difficult to face. In other words, Jensen suggests that the energy motivating the denial turns in part upon the abuser's horror over the very violation being denied (the horror being so potent that a desire to avoid acknowledging its reality feeds the denial). Moreover, this perverse dynamic encourages further abuse as a means of ongoing assertion and reinforcing of one's denial. Jensen suggests that many cultures are now embroiled in just this sort of perverse dynamic vis-à-vis indigenous peoples, oppressed racial/ethnic groups, women, and animal others. Perpetrators are desperate to deny culpability and so they not only reject all accusation but stridently continue to act abusively in unconscious support of their denial.

If this is correct, then one major reason for resistance to naming all the violence on our tables stems not from hard-heartedness, but from a profound, overwhelming, lurking but latent sense of self-condemnation fueled by unacknowledged *agreement* over the wrong. We resist because we are overcome by a sense that to acknowledge the reality will open us to the pain of the violation. This would explain the ongoing, perfectly obvious, but widely unacknowledged inconsistency of people who care for *some* nonhuman animals, who give them names and take joy in their joy and grieve their suffering, while at the same time they wear and eat other nonhuman animals. This inconsistency is not noticed because obfuscation of the truth protects us from guilt, pain, accusation. The inconsistency also helps to explain why even wonderful people can become reactionary when they inchoately sense that the truth of *their own* unconscious but real self-condemning conviction over their inconsistent behavior is about to be exposed.

SAYING (AND RECEIVING) GRACE

This is why it is so critical to emphasize, for others and for us ourselves, that we are *saying* grace, to lead not with condemnation or judgment, but with openness to having been seized by love. For in the context of the

---

7. Jensen, *Language Older Than Words*.

overall dynamics of agape, honest confession about the fallen character of this world (fall) and about our inescapable complicity (original sin) sounds forth within the context of *gracious love* (i.e., in the context of forgiveness). At this point, emphasizing that we are seized *by gracious love* for every Face is vital, for while the primary focus is upon the other Face, in the dynamic of having been seized *I too* am seized by gracious love. This a love which seizes *me*, seizes me in this sense for myself, delivers to me my own Face as graciously beloved. We are the second Face in the Face to Face, but we too are seized by gracious love.[8]

In addition to the clear self-deception, the resistance and denial derails the possibility of *saying* (and receiving) grace. For to *say* grace, one must first of all open oneself to having been seized by love for every Face. This is the *saying* of agape. Insofar as God *is* love, this is the *saying* of the divine (this is God "speaking"). Our deliberate passivity, our opening/surrender to the *saying* of transcending agape, is at the heart of all prayer. With regard to prayer before eating, an essential part of *saying* grace—there may be other parts—but an essential part is to use words, *said*, to direct our attention to every Face represented on that table, to every slaughtered animal and every plant directly on the table, and to all others of all kinds hurt or killed in the process of getting that food to the table, so that the *said* of our *saying* grace truly *says*. One can dare to do this in a fallen world, where most every table is covered with pain, death and injustice, precisely because opening to the *saying* is opening to gracious love.

To be sure, eating ripe, wild strawberries while walking in a mountain wilderness area is better than sitting inside at a table made of imported, rare wood and eating strawberries purchased in a city market. Vegetarian tables are typically better than meat-covered tables, and vegan tables are typically better still, but no table is innocent. Again, that is why it is critical to stress that the love to which we open ourselves is gracious. As one releases oneself from futile striving for innocence, as one abandons all denial and becomes wholly alive to one's complicity, one is met not with condemnation and judgment, but with love, and in the light of this love one can even be thankful and joyful.

The reality is as incredibly fraught and dynamic and complicated as real life. For while grace is the first and last word, insofar as we must continue to eat literally in order to survive and no table is innocent, grace is never the only word. We live inextricably bound up in and with a fallen world;

---

8. For detailed unfolding of the dynamics of forgiveness I am gesturing to here, see Greenway, *Reasonable Belief*, chapter 8, "Justice, Grace, Forgiveness," and Greenway, *Challenge of Evil*, chapter 6, "Concerning Others and Ourselves: Primordially and Ultimately, 'Yes.'"

and in order to live, to eat, we must continue to harm. I will not pursue this complicated point here, but I think this irreducible, lived tension is what Luther was naming with his famous phrase *simul iustus et peccator*, which means: I rejoice in the lived experience of my redemption but simultaneously I remain convicted over my ongoing and inextricable sinfulness and complicity (I unfold the dynamics of the *simul iustus et peccator* at length in the next chapter).

There is a dangerous temptation here, and that is to try to imagine what a perfectly good table would look like and to focus all one's energy on creating that table. That focus involves a twofold danger. First, there is the danger that the whole point will become personal righteousness and innocence (a form of the denial of our inevitable natural, social, cultural, and economic complicity), not loving action aimed at minimizing as much suffering and maximizing as much joy among creatures as possible. Of course, one wants as innocent a table as possible, but one wants this not for the sake of one's own righteousness, but for the sake of all those Faces who would otherwise be harmed.

The second danger is to narrow one's focus upon eating as if that is the only point of complicity, as if by setting the perfectly innocent table one could avoid all complicity and lay claim to personal righteousness. This is to forget the multifarious character of our inescapable complicity in and with all the suffering and injustice suffusing creation—regarding, *inter alia*, economic, racial, ethnic, gender, cultural, sexual, and/or species oppression and injustice—which is regularly and directly manifest at most tables. I am suggesting that *saying* grace before meals is an especially poignant and pertinent ritual that focuses our attention upon our material complicity not only in regard to our eating, but in regard to our lives generally.

The analogue to *saying* grace within Christian liturgy is the prayer of confession, when congregants confess their personal and corporate sins (*saying* grace is a species of *saying* the confession). Understood and communicated properly, the point of the prayer of confession is not shame or guilt but precisely the opposite, namely, freedom from guilt, forgiveness, and love of and for oneself and one's community—all of which are only truly available when one is honest with oneself. Freedom from guilt cannot truly come where there is denial or avoidance of our complicity and wrongdoing, where there is a rejection of moral reality or of the reality of our ethical ideals. We are dealing at this juncture with the crux not only of Christianity—with its understandings of sin, grace, redemption/salvation; already/not yet; *simul iustus et peccator*—for this nexus of issues, questions, hopes, and affirmations is in various ways at the heart of all the world's major wisdom traditions.

In the light of this recognition of the connection between "*saying* grace" and the crux of all the world's major wisdom traditions, the profound significance of *saying* grace is manifest. For, properly understood—which is, admittedly, perhaps not how it is most commonly understood—but, properly understood, the fraught but ultimately honest, provocative, and salvific act of *saying* grace (and its analogues in other faith traditions) brings humanity's most profound spiritual insights into the regular, public rhythms of our daily lives.

ONLY NATURAL

I want to digress momentarily to reply to an objection sometimes voiced by environmentalists and naturalists, namely, the objection that it is confused to think that there is anything wrong or regrettable about eating nonhuman animals because it is wholly natural, "how the real world really works." In romanticized versions this is expressed in rose-hued affirmations of "the circle of life," and even of utterly unbelievable but straight-faced stories of other animals giving themselves to be eaten (this is one of the points where I depart from Derrick Jensen).

For a hard-hearted version of this "predation is natural" vision, watch the BBC's *Planet Earth*, where—I had this experience with my own increasingly horrified young children—one soon begins to wonder anxiously about every new and wondrous creature that appears on screen, "what's about to eat them?" It's like a slasher film. To anyone who's lived in wilderness or even been on safari, it is obvious that while certainly creation has moments of violence and predation, there is nothing realistic about the unrelenting violence of *Planet Earth* (in fairness, the series was probably edited for an audience ill-attuned to the mostly languid rhythms of real creation). For some, however, the purportedly "scientific" message (in fact scientists are increasingly divided) is clear: those who mourn the strife and suffering suffusing our world of predation need to face up to how the real world really works, to the natural order of things (where "natural," note well, is taken to equal "good"). Notably, this "survival of the fittest," "natural equals good," "might equals right" social Darwinism accords perfectly with a dominating, colonial attitude toward both nonhuman and human others. It should be perfectly obvious to everyone that it is mistaken to equate what is "natural" with what is "good" (it is pretty easy to list human actions that are "natural" and definitely not "good"). We should also protest whenever realism over the realities and possibilities of our world is used to reject or compromise our moral ideals.[9]

Amidst all the indignant, pseudo-scientific rhetoric about "growing up," "getting over it," and "facing up to the way the real world really works" (i.e., about being hard-hearted, though this is rarely stated frankly), it is easy not to notice who is *not* facing up to a manifest reality, who is not facing up to the desperate struggles to escape, to survive, to the grief and suffering manifest among all sorts of creatures to the loss of children, mates, and kin, and to the grief and suffering of humans about the suffering and death of all sorts of creatures . . . even alligators, even tomato saplings. Those of us awakened to the Faces of all creatures know all about the intractable, predatory character of existence and, as should be clear by this point, we have no interest in denying the character of that reality. At the same time, we resist any denial of the character and reality of our moral response to the suffering and injustice. We resist any leveling, simplifying, reductionism, scientism. We affirm the scientific/natural *and* moral realities, *and* we acknowledge/confess the way we are inescapably intertwined with these realities in all their fraught complexity.

RITUAL, SPIRITUALITY, ACTION

As with all good liturgy, the spiritual/ethical effectiveness of *saying* grace before eating does not require complicated reflection. Back in the late 1990s, I taught the first course at Austin Presbyterian Theological Seminary that focused upon love for all creatures. We read the likes of Andrew Linzey, Tom Regan, and Peter Singer, and I threw in my own neo-Levinasian emphases. Several years later, a fairly conservative second-career student from that class, Diane—who had been open but skeptical in the class—was back visiting campus. She told me with a wry smile that her now teenage daughters had pretty much become vegetarian. I asked her how that happened, and she told me that soon after the class had ended her family had begun explicitly to name all the Faces on their table when they prayed before meals, and then they began also to name all the various people who were involved in getting food to their table. Through that practice they were awakened, their desires were reoriented, and they increasingly wanted their table to be as loving as possible, and that was progressively transforming how they shopped and what they ate.

---

9. In this regard, *contra* Kant, "ought" most certainly does not imply "can" (more precisely, "cannot" does not negate "ought").

This proposal of a way of understanding and returning to the practice of "*saying* grace" is consistent with progressive and conservative theology alike, and analogues could be developed for other faith traditions. This practice could sustain and enhance honest awakening, reception of grace, and lives lived in fidelity to having been seized by love for all Faces, including our own. By contrast, to be unwilling to pause and *say* grace, or to pause only in order to "give thanks," manifests and reinforces a hardening of heart. Notably, a culture which in self-ordained sophistication thinks *saying* grace before meals is merely a quaint custom or archaic ritual is in danger of becoming a culture inured to suffering and exploitation generally.

In sum, *saying* names a spiritual opening to having been seized by passion for every Face. Expanding upon Levinas's exclusively anthropocentric focus to include concern for all creatures (flora and fauna), and speaking as a Christian philosophical theologian, in this essay I have explained the ways in which pausing to *say* grace before meals concretely cultivates awakening to the (im)moral realities of our world, and to the salvific reality of *agape*. To this end, I have unfolded: the predatory character of reality in relation to awakening to passion for all others; creation as fallen (a moral, not a temporal/historical category); original sin (as an inescapable, contextual reality, not a condition inherited biologically); the awakened's felt need for confession; impetus to good action; moral standing (of all creatures; manifest through the having been seized); the marked difference between "giving thanks" and "*saying* grace;" and the complicated and existentially/spiritually fraught dynamics—*simul peccator et iustus*—of *saying* grace, and then eating and living morally awake in this fallen world.

If the ritual of *saying* grace were to be understood in this fashion and widely practiced, that is, if the suffering of all creatures (including human laborers) behind our tables were to be regularly and explicitly acknowledged, if we felt and responded to the reality of our tables and our complicity even as we lived in the light of grace, then the practice of *saying* grace before meals would be an honest interruption explicitly naming and publicly witnessing to our inescapable complicity in harmful biological and sociopolitical realities. *Saying* grace would help to derail denial of these realities, and denial of our complicity with them, even as, finally, it also would deliver saving if as of yet not prevailing grace (*simul iustus et peccator*). It would also surely help to create a palpable desire among people across theological and ideological spectrums to act so as ever more fully to minimize the suffering that lies behind our tables, to strive after tables that are as good as possible in this vale of tears.

Significantly, while I am a Christian and have argued within the bounds of neo-Levinasian philosophy and used the language of Christian theology, my reasoning is pertinent to eating rituals in any faith tradition. It is no surprise that parallel eating rituals are already part of the world's major faith traditions, for all who are supremely morally awake—and all the world's major faith traditions have been birthed and sustained by those who are supremely morally awakened—are and ever have been alive to the piercing need to create some ritual way of *saying* grace, of confessing life's unjustifiable, predatory character at a point when, insofar as we are honest and awakened, that character is most regularly, intimately and painfully evident: when we must eat. It is indeed a profound spiritual wisdom that insists upon a pause, a full and considered pause when we are about to eat, so that we might open ourselves to the searing judgment and saving light of agape, that is, so that we might *say* grace.

Chapter 12

Barth and Universal Salvation

A Neo-Calvinist Spiritual Affirmation

My goal in this essay is to bring Christian readers to a sympathetic and affirming understanding of Karl Barth on universal salvation. My argument is spiritual in character. One should anticipate not scholarly essay but scholarly proclamation.[1] This approach results from a conviction that the fundamental obstacle to affirmation of Barth's position on universal salvation is not technical but spiritual. Contemporary reflection on the question of universal salvation needs to be purified of a subtle but devastating denial of sinfulness and our utter dependence upon grace (*sola gratia*). The bulk of the essay is inspired by Calvin and Dostoevsky and is dedicated to "A Spiritual Preparation."[2] I stress living awareness of sinfulness (*peccator*) and

---

1. Those interested in a traditional academic survey of Barth's position and debate over it should consult Greggs's excellent essay, "'Jesus is victor': passing the impasse of Barth on universalism." On my reading, our two essays supplement one another.

2. If one reads Barth's appeals to encounter with "the living person of Jesus Christ" as naming awkwardly the same reality that Calvin names in his appeals to the work of the Spirit, there is scant distance between them. Barth sees christological thinking as legitimate only when "it consists in the perception, comprehension, understanding and estimation of the reality of the living person of Jesus Christ as attested by the Holy Scripture, in attentiveness to the range and significance of His existence, in openness to His self-disclosure, in consistency in following Him as is demanded" (Barth, *Church Dogmatics* IV/3.1, 174). If one reads "as attested by the Holy Scripture" here as the root and core of our knowledge, one runs afoul of Barth's own prescriptions against privileging principles by making a "Scripture principle" ultimate (i.e., confusing the second form of the Word, the words of Scripture, for the first form of the Word, the

of the reality of divine grace (*iustus*) as vital to Christian consideration of universal salvation. When this vital awareness is subjectively realized in full, the spiritual elegance and classic faithfulness of Barth's position on universal salvation is most readily apparent.[3]

A SPIRITUAL PREPARATION

Peccator[4]

An essential element of moral honesty, of spiritual wisdom, of fear, fear of the Lord, lies in unblinking, unmitigated, primordial apprehension of your

---

living person of Jesus Christ). I understand the absolute priority of the living Word to require us to proceed via appeal to no such principle, but according to the "self-disclosure" of "the living person of Jesus Christ." I understand this to be an appeal to the same ungraspable source that Calvin invokes when he appeals to the work of the Spirit. Of course, in *interpreting* the character and meaning of this having been seized, I privilege not myself but the wisdom of the historic and contemporary community, which includes a special place of privilege for the Scriptures. This may not be the most obvious reading of Barth, but I think that it best fulfills Barth's own imperative never to allow any principle to stand in place of the living Word, and thus I find it to be the most generous reading one can make of Barth on this point.

3. When using Christian theological categories, I follow Barth definitively beyond Calvin with his delineation of "the elect" not as some portion of humanity (as in Calvin) but as Jesus Christ, the one elect through whom all are elected. In the wake of Barth's revolutionary shift away from Calvin's classic understanding of "the elect," it became common for commentators to see Calvin's theology as definitively hostile to the idea of universal salvation (which, admittedly, Calvin considered it to be) and to suspect that in principle Barth's theology entailed universal salvation. Nonetheless, I think the overriding spirit of Calvin's theology provides excellent spiritual grounds for Barth's position on universal salvation. I will be suggesting that Barth's shift in understanding concerning the identity of "the elect" is more consistent with Calvin's own most profound spiritual affirmations than was the traditional understanding that Calvin explicitly retained. Indeed, Calvin figures prominently here because I think his spiritual affirmations cultivate the spiritual sensitivities that I am arguing are critical to proper Christian reflection upon universal salvation.

4. Noting that I begin the essay with *peccator*, one prominent Reformed theologian (a former student of Karl Barth) worried that my position was fundamentally Lutheran, not Reformed (as would be appropriate for an essay explicating Barth). As he commented, in terms of the classic debate over the use of the Law, Lutherans "move, epistemologically, from consciousness of sin to gospel, while Reformed move from Gospel/grace to consciousness of sin." Let me clarify, however, that I am here making no claim with regard to this classic debate. As should become apparent, my concern is only with a subtle but critical denial of *peccator* and a correlate denial of our reliance upon God's grace, which haunts the predominant contemporary framing rhetoric and consideration of universal salvation. Both Lutheran and Reformed would affirm the enduring earthly significance of awareness of consciousness of sin and of our reliance upon the grace of God, no matter their stand on the ordering of Law and Gospel or on the use(s) of the Law.

complicity in evil, complicity in causing harm, suffering, anguish. Indeed, the most loving souls suffer rending awareness of their smallest offenses: the rule of their petty grievances; their failures to give aid, to offer comfort or food; their lack of courage to act or even to speak the truth in the face of obvious wrong; their self-absorption; their concern for prestige, fame, and wealth; perhaps the occasions when inattention left their children crushed just when they had needed and dared hope for a word of approval or comfort.

It is utterly understandable, natural, completely common, and also tragic and self-destructive for us to strive to deny that we are complicit in and are ourselves evil. Self-absorption (one form of which is self-righteousness) and inattention are themselves prime aids to our denial, both culprit and shield as we attempt to proclaim our innocence and save ourselves. Today the denial is often aggressive: people dare to become offended or—incredibly—mocking when named sinful; it is in fashion even among some theologians to disdain as juvenile, and even as intrinsically oppressive, any idea of original sin and of the fallenness of creation (personal conviction over which are two critical aspects of *peccator*).

Self-righteous indignation over evil itself, and defense of God in the face of that indignation, constitute two predominant if unwitting modern Western ways of denying *peccator*. The indignation of Fyodor Dostoevsky's Ivan Karamazov in *The Brothers Karamazov* is paradigmatic. Ivan catalogues a horrifying sampling of our inhumanity. Dostoevsky evidently collected Ivan's accounts from contemporary newspapers. Many involve children, and all are so deeply disturbing that I will not rehearse any of them.[5]

At the end of his litany of horrors, Ivan stresses that he does not require an overwhelming collection of horrific happenings in order to take offense. In an age of blunted moral sensitivity, a multitude of dramatic stories may be necessary to stir the conscience. For those with the heightened moral sensitivity Ivan appeals to, however, the despairing tears of a single child abused, alone, and unloved are heartrending, overwhelming, too much. Suppose God *does* exist, says Ivan, suppose God *did* create this world, suppose God *is* all-powerful: well, Ivan concludes, given this vale of tears, God be damned.

Hearing such, Christians have defensively hurried forward with all manner of theodicies, that is, with all sorts of justifications of God. The so-called free will defense, which wisely limits itself only to precluding the necessity of concluding from evil that a good God could not exist, is helpful,

---

5. Section 4, "Rebellion," in Book V, "Pro and Contra," in Dostoevsky, *Brothers Karamazov*.

but neither the free will defense nor any other theodicy is adequate even for Christians on that evening in the morgue when the sheet is pulled back and there lies the bruised, tear-stained face of their precious, missing child.

More than that, any stab at theodicy by well-meaning friends or counselors in such a context is confused and offensive, adding to the evil and suffering. There is nothing in any theodicy that meets those parents where they rightly are, nothing in any theodicy that adequately focuses upon the horror, the emptiness, the imagined pain and despair of their child, or upon their own irreversible loss. To offer up a theodicy is an offense because it is not a response to the parents' grief, not a response to that evil. Theodicy offers an abstract answer to an abstract problem: the problem of evil. So, it is virtually insignificant that no theodicy even begins to compare in existential potency and power with the screaming moral indignation of an Ivan Karamazov. That is, it is virtually insignificant that at critical real-world junctures all theodicies fail. For the real problem is that with the defensive response Christians forget classic Christian confession and faith. To offer up a theodicy is an offense because it masks and thereby denies the evil, redirecting our attention to a logical puzzle about the relationship among God's perfection, God's omnipotence, and the existence of evil.

For similar reasons, Ivan's "God be damned" is also an offense. Ivan's assertion is not the "damn you" the parents may scream heavenward in that morgue. It is not the quivering, angry, anguished, "you have been faithless, O God, where were you? where are you? what are we to make of your vaunted justice and righteousness now?"—this is reminiscent of biblical lament. Biblical spirituality reserves pastoral and existential space for utter lament and even bitter, emotional, broken accusation in the face of overwhelming wrong and loss. Significantly, that is not the character of Ivan's "God be damned."

Ivan recites that litany of evils. Ivan sees the tears of that child. Ivan stands in that morgue. And Ivan is *not* crushed. Ivan is *not* reduced to tears. Ivan is indignant, self-righteous, he is empowered (the strength of the Karamazov), empowered to draw a conclusion—an assertion, not a lament—"this cosmos and God be damned." Ivan's response too redirects our attention away from the evil. In Ivan's case, the evil is not replaced with a logical puzzle. The evil recedes as it is used as a springboard to Ivan's self-righteous, damning-God indignation. That denial too is an offense.

Precisely here we must take caution not to be self-righteously offended by Ivan's offense. See Ivan the living tragedy. Cultivate not indignation but sympathy, pity, even a degree of admiration. Ivan's moral sensitivity to all the evils of the world leaves him in angry, futile protest, and there is no escape. For Ivan, even suicide would be at best an empty gesture and at worst a wrong, a silencing of righteous protest in the face of irredeemable existence. There is a raw power in the defiant screams of accusation, but it is ultimately a helpless and hopeless power, for Ivan asserts himself singularly as judge in opposition to the entire cosmos and its Creator.

Worse yet, Ivan's rebellion only appears powerful. The energy of the defiance itself and also God as an object to push over and against are both necessary for the appearance of power, for they enable a dynamic that conceals the incredible weakness of Ivan's position, which is revealed precisely in Ivan's self-proclaimed strength, for, as we will see momentarily, no one with supreme moral sensitivity and no hope in God could remain as strong as Ivan claims to be without remaining in denial. Dostoevsky makes this point: his delusion of innocence finally broken by realization of complicity in evil, by the end of *The Brothers Karamazov* Ivan lies in a coma.[6]

The true dynamics we are playing with here are clarified if, when confronting someone like Ivan, who is rejecting God based on all the evil in the world, one simply concedes the argument. First, amplify your moral offense to the nth degree. Second (for the sake of argument), drop the idea of God. Now what emerges is the primordial spiritual challenge, the horrifying challenge, the challenge so safely and secretly hidden in angry rejection of God and in all the energy of the debates over the problem of evil. God does not exist. *But you confront precisely all the same evil.* Now the invective so passionately turned against God must be turned against the cosmos itself and—since we are wholly members of that cosmos, since our existence is purchased only at the price of the existence of that cosmos—now the invective so passionately turned against God must be turned upon us ourselves. Now it is not God in the dock needing justification, but the cosmos and us too standing guilty before our own most certain moral convictions.

When Christians respond defensively to Ivan, they confusedly mirror his tragic, death-dealing, unspoken self-righteousness. But Christianity is no less able to name evil than Ivan, no less revolted, no less morally sensitive, no less overwhelmed, no less outraged than Ivan. To the contrary, classic Christian confession—note here the brutal, admirable honesty of classic Christian confession—not only owns and expresses all of Ivan's passion and indignation, it goes further and, where Ivan holds back, pushes the passionate objection beyond the brink. For Christians not only declare the world

---

6. Some may contest my interpretation of Ivan as "self-righteous" by arguing that at this point of the "Rebellion" section Ivan interprets himself via an appeal to the amoral "strength of the Karamazov." But all the energy fueling Ivan's argument in "Rebellion" springs definitively from *moral* offense, thus my description of Ivan as "self-righteous" is more accurate (and more consistent with the arc of his life through the novel) than Ivan's own appeal to the "strength of the Karamazov."

fallen, we confess our inextricable complicity, our coming-to-awareness already fully enmeshed in structures of pain and suffering and oppression, and we confess too our own evil, our own pettiness, selfishness, hatefulness. *Yes*, Christianity proclaims fiercely, our world of pain and predation is fallen. *Yes*, Christianity confesses fiercely, I am also a child of unjust social and political structures (original sin). *Yes*, it continues with equal fierceness, *I* am not only complicit, but I have also intentionally caused pain, suffering, or injustice (intentional sin). Fall plus original sin plus evil intent, all borne home to utter self-awareness: *peccator*.

In stark contrast, Ivan is not crushed by any sense for his complicity or for his own evil. Ivan has implicitly and nonconsciously framed himself off the page as a perfectly righteous judge. His supreme moral sensitivity is ultimately truncated by a delusion, a subtle, nonconscious denial of his own complicity and sinfulness.

A transitional, representative character here, one who takes a decisive step beyond Ivan, might be Judas Iscariot, for Judas not only sees the world as fallen, he becomes wholly convicted of his own sinfulness. Yet it becomes tragically evident that Judas retains Ivan-esque self-righteousness when he makes himself judge and executioner of himself. This is not a comment upon suicide. This is a comment upon the logic of self-annihilation hidden at the heart of all self-righteousness. Judas shows forth a tragedy. His suicide, most especially in the context of the Christian gospel, should not be read as a happy example of justice realized. Judas is an Ivan who has broken through one level of denial but, awfully, still insists upon self-assertion, and as a result the impossibility of one "impossible possibility"—namely, the impossibility of eyes wide open self-affirmation apart from agape in this vale of tears—becomes sadly and literally apparent.

Once one recognizes (as everyone should) the impossibility of this impossible possibility, that is, the impossibility of living through self-assertion, and once one drops Judas's tragic, hopeless, literally self-obliterating defiance, one finds oneself limp, speechless, helpless, hopelessly offended by the world, horrified with oneself, pained, crying, desperate. There is no hope, no energy, no assertion. I am lost, guilty, guilty, *guilty*. Fall plus original sin plus evil intent, all borne home to utter self-awareness: *peccator*.

Notably, *peccator* is the obvious and brutal reality that modern Western rationality—Ivan is Dostoevsky's stand-in for modern Western rationality—*peccator* is the obvious and brutal reality that modern Western rationality furiously, if unconsciously, works to reject.

Let me pause and provide some orientation by specifying theoretically the relevant point *vis-à-vis* universal salvation. First, it is important to specify that, taken in isolation from any experience of *iustus* (i.e., from your sure conviction of your redemption), from this profoundly moral place where we go limp the question of one's own salvation will not naturally arise, for one's attention is wholly hostage to the suffering and need of others. To the degree that the depths of *peccator* are unveiled in a dynamic that involves lived awareness of the grace of God, then there is indeed consciousness of and concern for self. In this instance consciousness of self arises in response to God's grace (i.e., to God's concern for you yourself). So, contrary to what is often thought to be the bounds of possibility, this is a non-self-centered self-concern. Moreover, insofar as God's concern for you is gracious, the intensity of one's comparative sense of *peccator* is not only matched but overwhelmed by a correlatively intense sense of *iustus*. As is so vividly evident in the witness of Luther, amidst the intensity of one's sense of *peccator* one is overcome in wonder by the reality of *iustus*, by truly amazing grace.

All this means that your sense of *iustus* is utterly and wholly accompanied by an enduring sense for *peccator* which remains intense even as you experience *iustus*. Thus, genuine experience of *iustus* is never accompanied by any self-righteousness, is never accompanied by any sense of having received what one deserves or merits. To the utter contrary, experience of *iustus* does not negate experience of *peccator* but intensifies it even as simultaneously (*simul*) it saves.

The non-self-righteous spirituality that knows intensely and simultaneously *peccator* and *iustus* provides the spiritual frame within which the question of universal salvation properly presents itself. That is, very significantly and quite appropriately, the question of the possibility of universal salvation should be framed from this place where I go limp but am delivered in precisely this form: "Salvation? Really? Salvation? Even me, even unto me, how can it possibly have reached—wonder of wonders!—*even unto me?*"[7]

To this point I have argued that indignation over evil, typically coupled in the modern period with bromides hurled at God, along with defensive attempts to justify God, are all actually influential and unwitting ways of

---

7. To be explicit, I have identified a denial of *peccator* and of dependence upon the grace of God that is manifest in a subtle but definitive background presumption that often permeates Christian debates over universal salvation, a presumption that assumes the question of universal salvation has to do first and foremost with those who are distant from us by virtue of comparative works and who are thus at a greater remove from the possibility of being saved.

denying *peccator* (and so, indirectly, *iustus*), and that, as a result, the question of universal salvation has typically *not* been raised in contemporary debate from within an appropriate theological/spiritual frame.

I now address a few other influential ways of denying *peccator* that are equally understandable and tragic and especially significant for us because of how they skew contemporary reflection upon universal salvation. Consider, for instance, dynamics manifest in common readings of Jesus' parable of the sheep and the goats.

> Then he will say to those on his left hand, "You that are accursed, depart from me into the eternal fire prepared for the devil and his angels; for I was hungry and you gave me no food, I was thirsty and you gave me nothing to drink, I was a stranger and you did not welcome me, naked and you did not give me clothing, sick and in prison and you did not visit me."[8]

Who can read these words and not shudder? It is patent that those we number as living saints would be the first to confess how desperately they have fallen short, to acknowledge all the times when they did not visit, welcome, clothe, feed. This is utterly consistent with the parable: it is part of the reason that *the sheep* are surprised. So, how can we who are not saints read this parable without being overcome by horror?

Part of the answer lies in the handy (that is, handy for denial) prominence in the parable of another horror, hell: "You that are accursed, depart from me into the eternal fire prepared for the devil and his angels." Christians often read these lines without experiencing much horror. That, Christians proclaim, is the wonderful thing. We are forgiven. We live by grace. We need not fear hell or Satan's demons. We live with hope for heaven. We live through faith in Jesus Christ. We will approach the judgment seat with confidence, to receive our reward.

There may be some truth in all this. But let me point out several dangers. The first involves a wholly understandable confusion over the nature of "faith in Jesus Christ." Though the confusion is ancient, the ambiguity of this phrase is especially dangerous in our scientific age, for we are especially tempted to understand "faith in Jesus Christ" in the same way that we would understand, "faith that the mean distance to the moon is x miles." In this empirical sense, "faith *in*" means "faith *that:*" faith *that* Jesus was the Son of God, faith *that* Jesus died for my sins, faith *that* I will receive the promise of heaven. That is, in this empirical sense faith names an affirmative relation between you and a truth claim. It is a matter of intellectual assent, not of grace, a human work, not faith.

8. Matthew 25:41–43.

The problem can also be stated in terms of the distinction between *apophatic* and *kataphatic* theology. "*Kataphatic*" means "according to images," this is the *via positiva* and is what most people simply think of as theology. "*Apophatic*" means "apart from all images," this is the *via negativa*, the attempt to open oneself to encounter with the divine by clearing away all concepts and inferences; it names a mystical way that gestures toward sheer openness to the touch of the divine. Barth's *Church Dogmatics* is an exercise in *kataphatic* theology, but Barth realizes that *the apophatic grounds the kataphatic*. This realization is behind Barth's meaning-rich tautology, "God is God," and is also the reason the innermost fold of his threefold form of the Word is precisely where God is most fully hidden. In terms of human reasoning or deduction this means that the *kataphatic* has no other ground than the witness of the Spirit, and that the *kataphatic* is ultimately a poetic gesture unfolding as carefully and humbly as possible—in response to one's having been seized by *simul iustus et peccator* ("at the same time righteous and sinner," "at the same time sinner and righteous") and in conversation with Scripture, tradition, our community, and our time—the beauty and goodness and call of that witness.

In terms of naming the problem with seeing faith in Jesus Christ in empirical terms as a confession of belief, as faith *that*, one might say that it confusedly understands faith to be a matter of assenting to the truth of formulations within the *kataphatic* sphere instead of understanding that the *kataphatic* is ultimately derived from the *apophatic*, that is, instead of understanding the word "faith" itself as a gesture toward the *apophatic* event (i.e., the event of grace, the event of having been seized by agape) that is its origin. Or, perhaps one could say, it confuses faith, an ongoing mode of having been seized in encounter by grace, with beliefs, which are important second-order attempts to articulate the character, implications, and contour of faith.

Or, in a more Barthian vein, perhaps one could say that an empirical interpretation of "faith in Jesus Christ" confusedly mistakes *the words*, the articulations and propositions which testify to the Word, for *the Word*, which is not a proposition, not propositional truth, not a first premise for a science of God, not a thing to be had or assented to at all, but that which stands on the far side as the Subject and originator of revelation, of faith, that which is most fully hidden precisely where it is most fully revealed, the "living person of Jesus Christ" in whom we are embraced by grace.[9]

A more obvious dimension of the confusion of empirical belief with faith is confirmed by the parable itself, for the parable makes it clear that we

---

9. See note 2, above.

cannot talk about saving faith even in terms of one's religion, let alone in terms of any particular doctrinal orthodoxy. According to Jesus' parable of the sheep and the goats, it does not matter if you are Jewish, Christian, Buddhist, Hindu, agnostic, or atheist. The only distinguishing question is this: did you feed, clothe, visit, comfort? After even a moment's reflection upon the beatitudes and other parables and teachings one can realize that this is a constant in Jesus' teachings—whatever saving Christian faith is, the parable makes clear, it is not necessarily related to confessing Christian beliefs or even to knowledge of the name of Jesus Christ.

In sum, modern empiricist rationality, insofar as it leads us to confuse empirical affirmation of beliefs for faith, is a diversion that offers the illusion of a safe harbor wherein we can see ourselves as righteous because of some affirmation, thus illicitly shielding us from *peccator* and preserving as primary our own self-assertion, our affirmation of the truth of one or another belief.[10]

Let me now, second, specify how the horror of hell and the promise of heaven can result in spiritually dangerous motivations. The danger is potent and obvious. The horror is hell, the prize is heaven, and the point is to avoid hell and to get to heaven. This is dangerous because it threatens to make self-interest the motivational heart of Christian belief. This would obstruct love and precisely reverse the gospel of Jesus. For on this understanding the reason to be a sheep, the reason to clothe, to feed, visit, welcome, to confess one's belief in Jesus Christ, is *in order* to be saved. That is, I help others *in order* to save myself. Or, I help others in order to love God *in order* to save myself.

A self-diagnostic question that one may helpfully ask here is, have you proved neighbor? Do you think you're a sheep? To the degree one has any feeling toward "yes," one has, unfortunately, displaced the horror. Not the horror of hell, that is, not the diversion, not the horror that displaces our consciousness of the reality of evil. But the proper horror, the horror that haunts true sheep, the horror which partly explains why the sheep are surprised, the horror of our insensitivity, our failure to love, to act, to care, our failures of courage. "Hence," writes Calvin, "that dread and wonder with which scripture commonly represents *the saints* as stricken and overcome

10. To be explicit with regard to the first danger I identify in conversation with the parable, the problem is a denial of *peccator* and a species of self-assertion that turns "faith" into a work. I respond by developing a distinction between belief and faith that precludes the contention that, for instance, universal salvation is impossible because all have not explicitly confessed belief in Jesus Christ (this may well be the paramount work that illicitly justifies the background presumption identified in note 7). That is, even if it is true that we are saved by virtue of the work of Jesus Christ (as Barth affirms), it is not true that saving faith consists in affirmation of that fact.

whenever they felt the presence of God."[11] Are you neighbor? Are you one of the sheep? "No, no, NO!" cry *the sheep*.[12]

Finally, third, what do we imagine is the sheep's attitude toward the goats? In our anger at evildoers, it is easy to imagine taking pleasure in the long overdue dispensing of justice. Here, in a weak if understandable moment, is Calvin:

> Since we see the pious laden with afflictions by the impious, stricken with unjust acts, overwhelmed with slanders, wounded with abuses and reproaches; while the wicked on the contrary flourish, are prosperous, obtain repose with dignity and that without punishment—we must straightway conclude that there will be another life in which iniquity is to have its punishment; and righteousness is to be given its reward.[13]

First, as Barth would insist, Calvin's "we must straightway conclude" inappropriately utilizes principled human reasoning to dictate the ways of God. Second, at best Calvin here is gracelessly asserting the requirements of justice. At worst, he is indulging a desire for vengeance. In either case: not the attitude of sheep. True sheep love and mourn goats. Third, his distinction between the pious and impious depends upon a denial of *peccator*. How could Calvin, of all people, forget? None are pious.[14]

---

11. Calvin, *Institutes*, 38–39 (emphasis mine). Here we see Calvin not, of course, denying the reality of *peccator*, but characteristically crediting its greatest intensity not to proximity to thoughts about the Law, but to proximity to God (one could affirm this no matter one's position on the possibility of experience of *peccator* absent any experience identifiable as God).

12. To be explicit with regard to the second danger I identify in conversation with the parable, note how this emphasis on proper spiritual motivation for doing justice, loving mercy, and giving witness to the gospel precludes the oft heard objection that if there is universal salvation then there is no reason to do good, love others, or witness to the gospel (for such an objection pivots upon the assumption that ultimately the reason for such actions turns upon self-interest in escaping hell and gaining heavenly reward).

13. Note that in this paragraph Calvin anticipates the conclusions of Immanuel Kant's practical rationality and his religion within the limits of (modern Western) reason alone, which gives us a world which is ultimately just (with an afterlife with reward and punishment) but wholly lacking in any grace.

14. To be explicit with regard to the third danger in conversation with the parable, note how clarity regarding the way those full of godly love mourn those who are lost precludes an often not-so-subtle contempt and even anger towards those who do not confess faith in God and so who are presumed to be outside the sphere of the saved, a not-so-subtle contempt and even anger that is at times clearly discernable in debates over universal salvation (i.e., some people seem not to desire that all might be saved). Regardless of one's convictions with regard to universal salvation, those full of godly, gracious love will profoundly desire and hope that all somehow will be saved.

Despite this unfortunate passage, all of our reflections upon the denial of *peccator*, upon wisdom, upon knowledge of self and of God, are quintessential Calvin. None are pious: that is the enduring wisdom and truth of *peccator*. That is the true, damning horror that afflicts us. Biblical sensitivity to this horror can be stunning. We might ask ourselves, for instance, with what spiritual vision might one look at a man who is so severely paralyzed that the only way he can get about is to be carried by his friends? With what spiritual vision does one see such a man, see such need, and perform a miraculous healing saying only: your sins are forgiven. And then . . . moving on.

What would it be, if we were that person, to be so full of the knowledge of ourselves and of God, so full of wisdom, so full of fear of the Lord, so present to the reality of our own screaming, searing evil, to the true horror, that we would realize the significance of "your sins are forgiven," *iustus*, and be filled with overwhelming joy, begin to live in the present eternally (i.e., saved), without a thought for our enduring paralysis?

What does it say of Jesus, that he evidently expected just such a response from the man? What does it say of the gospel of Jesus, that he could look and be so profoundly concerned about that man's admirable consumption by *peccator* that his paralysis did not even register as a concern to be mentioned?[15]

What I am naming in all this discussion so far is an ongoing and ever more profoundly experienced moment of true moral and spiritual existence. Christianity never denies or minimizes *peccator*. To the contrary, the most profound apprehension of *peccator* may only be psychologically possible for the faithful (that is, within the context of *simul iustus*). For outside of the context of the *simul iustus* the depth and reality of *peccator* may be so overwhelming and damning that it is impossible to bear engaging it—one requires denial (early Ivan), or else one will be driven either to a psychotic break (late Ivan) or suicide (Judas). In any case, the depth of one's realization of *iustus* is directly related to the depth of one's consciousness of *peccator* (a dynamic, spiraling *simul*). The characters of Ivan and Judas can help return

---

15. Matthew 9:1–8, Mark 2:1–12, Luke 5:17–26. Notably, the texts do not note any objection on the part of the paralytic when Jesus proclaims the paralytic's sins forgiven without healing his paralysis. In light of the fact that the texts specify that that paralytic's sins were forgiven because of his faith we should not be surprised to find the text thus indicating that the paralytic understood that the most profound need driving him to Jesus had nothing to do with his paralysis. Note also that even the eventual healing of the paralysis is performed *not* for the paralytic, but in an attempt to break through the hardness of heart of some observers. Finally, note that Jesus' characteristic rejection of the contemporary identification of physical malady with sinfulness is implicit in his separation of the forgiveness of sins from the healing of paralysis.

us to our screaming, desperate need of salvation not from physical death, but from sin. Fall plus original sin plus evil intent, all borne home to utter self-awareness: *peccator*. We are caught as fully and damnably as Ivan and Judas. That is the proper theological and spiritual frame from which one asks about universal salvation, when the one to whom the question most immediately pertains is not some imagined evildoer or "nonbeliever" somewhere *out there*, but when the one to whom the question most immediately pertains is precisely *me*.

Iustus

It is completely understandable but spiritually devastating to deny either the reality of evil or one's complicity in and with it. The power, profundity, completeness, and efficacy of grace are directly related to one's sense of *peccator*. Thus, Christianity does not dodge or minimize the reality of evil. A glancing, superficial, denying confession of sin will correlate with an equally anemic openness to grace. Denial of sin obstructs grace. Markel, the character in *The Brothers Karamazov* with whom Dostoevsky, a Christian, responds to Ivan, testifies to the opposite, to an awareness flowing from purgation which is so wholly open to the other, so wholly loving of the other, that one's own offenses, both intentional and structural, rise up paramount and overwhelming. And though neither Markel nor anyone else (by definition) can explain this divine gift, he can testify that the result of this profound openness and unblinking, unmitigated confession is not a crushing burden, not a hatred of self, not a hatred of the world, but unspeakable riches of grace and love (illumination and union).[16]

Markel is a young man who explicitly and contemptuously dismisses God and his mother's spirituality. He falls ill, however, and it is soon clear that he has only weeks to live. In order to assuage his mother's desperation and grief, he begins to take communion, at first at church, and then very quickly, when he is too ill for church, at home in bed. Consider two excerpts:

> "And I shall tell you, dear mother, that each of us is guilty in everything before everyone, and I most of all . . . you must know that verily each of us is guilty before everyone, for everyone and everything. I do not know how to explain it to you, but I feel it so

---

16. While I cannot develop the point here, I suspect that the transition from purgation to illumination (on the threefold way of the *via negative*) parallels the transition I am identifying in Markel from absolute confession to absolute joy, for while purgation has a moral dimension the move to illumination involves the wondrous loss of concern (without denial) even for the own-ness of one's own culpability.

strongly that it pains me. And how could we have lived before, getting angry, and not knowing anything?" *Thus he awoke every day with more and more tenderness, rejoicing and all atremble with love.*[17]

And:

"Birds of God, joyful birds, you, too, must forgive me, because I have also sinned before you." None of us could understand it then, but he was weeping with joy: "Yes," he said, "there was so much of God's glory around me: birds, trees, meadows, sky, and I alone lived in shame, I alone dishonored everything, and did not notice the beauty and glory of it all." "You take too many sins upon yourself," mother used to weep. "Dear mother, my joy, I am weeping from gladness, not from grief; I want to be guilty before them, only I cannot explain it to you, for I do not even know how to love them. Let me be sinful before everyone, but so that everyone will forgive me, and that is paradise. Am I not in paradise now?"[18]

This is profound testimony to the reality of grace. But the miracle of faith— that which allows Markel to say "guilty . . . I most of all," that which allows Markel to go all the way with and beyond Ivan, all the way with and beyond Judas, to allow *peccator* to be borne home utterly without denial *and not to be crushed, to the contrary* to understand without comprehending that the depth of his continual confession correlates to the depth of his experience of grace, that is, that the depth of his continual apprehension of the depths of his own evil, his own guilt, his own sin, correlates to the depth of his experience of living eternally—the miracle of faith itself stays off the page. From the outside, we can only witness its fruits or hear testimony to its reality.

This is paradigmatic. Our most profound experience of the divine, whether it is of the dramatic, in-breaking variety, or whether one refers to moments in a lifetime of ever-deepening awareness of God's love, are patently such that any description of our experience of having been seized by grace seems a profanation. Even to write of the reality in our journals immediately seems to cheapen it by reducing it to our categories, laying hold

17. Dostoevsky, *Brothers Karamazov*, 289 (emphasis mine). These quotes relate the memories of Markel's younger brother, Zossima, who was nine years old at the time. Later in life, Father Zossima shares these memories with his trusted and trustworthy novice, Aloysha, who gives them voice in the novel.

18. Dostoevsky, *Brothers Karamazov*, 289–90. I substantively expanded upon these reflections on *Brothers Karamazov* and put them into conversation of Iris Murdoch in the context of a discussion of evil in "Part Three: Fyodor Dostoevsky and Joy Eyes Wide Open to Evil" in *Challenge of Evil*.

of it, grasping it, when to the contrary the experience is one of having been seized, of having been lovingly embraced, of being known, judged, and still and finally loved before and beyond comprehension.

There is something so holy, so sacred, so overwhelming, so beyond comprehension about our most profound experiences of the divine, that even to think them in words, let alone to try to describe them to others, seems an immediate profanation. This piercing incongruity generates the desire to distinguish the *kataphatic* from the *apophatic*, and the desire to confess that even so-called *apophatic* theology is still *kataphatic*, distinguished really by its continual reassertion of the desire explicitly and impossibly to gesture beyond itself, to gesture beyond gesture, to say what cannot be said, to overcome itself in an utter opening and testimony to its from-whence.

The story of Wesley's "heart strangely warmed" is so familiar that only upon reflection does one note how charily, simply and quickly Wesley gestures toward a core spiritual experience that revolutionized his life—and in keeping with our emphasis upon "even unto me" we might note that Wesley specifies his experience as one in which he received assurance that Christ, "had taken away *my* sins, even *mine*, and saved *me* from the law of sin and death."[19] After his death, friends accidently discovered stitched into the overcoat of Blaise Pascal a single sheet of paper that memorialized his experience of Monday evening, November 23, 1654. The title, in capital letters: FIRE.[20] Augustine's faith grew slowly over time, but at a climatic point in his *Confessions* he refers obliquely to a spiritual ascent and contact with a Word beyond "speech, in which each word has a beginning and an ending."[21] The ineffable reality bubbles behind the writings of Paul. We hear of his "Damascus road" experience only from others (Acts 9:1–22), and even then, tersely and in minimal and conceptually weak, patently metaphorical terms—weak one suspects out of respect, as if he had felt forced to say something. Paul gives us only a bit more when he speaks with disarming blandness about what would have been an intense experience of transcending intimacy, "hope does not disappoint us, because God's love has been poured into our hearts through the Holy Spirit that has been given us" (Romans 5:5).

---

19. Wesley, *Works*, 250.

20. Pascal, *Great Shorter Works of Pascal*, 117. The one-page-long reflection, commonly referred to as "Pascal's Memorial," says in part: "God of Abraham, God of Isaac, God of Jacob . . . Certitude. Certitude. Feeling. Joy. Peace. God of Jesus Christ . . . Joy, joy, joy, tears of joy . . . I have separated myself from Him: I have fled Him, denied Him, crucified Him . . . Renunciation, total and sweet. Total submission to Jesus Christ and to my director. Eternally in joy for a day's training on earth. *Non obliviscar sermones tuos* [I will not forget your teaching]. *Amen.*"

21. Augustine, *Confessions*, 197.

Calvin, similarly, gestures obliquely to an overwhelming experience of divine grace, making it definitive of faith. Calvin speaks of an inner knowledge, of that knowledge "which alone quickens dead souls, whereby God is known . . . in the person of the Mediator as the Redeemer."[22] In fact, it is in Calvin that one finds one of the most direct testimonies to such an encounter with the Spirit, right at the heart of his *Institutes*, in his definition of faith. Immediately before and after giving his definition of faith, Calvin takes time to caution against confusing faith with empirical affirmation or intellectual assent. Faith, Calvin says, lies beyond the natural capacities of the mind and of the heart. Because of this, writes Calvin, "our mind must be otherwise illumined and our heart strengthened, that the Word of God may obtain full faith among us."[23]

"When we call faith 'knowledge,'" Calvin cautions elsewhere, "we do not mean comprehension of the sort that is commonly concerned with those things which fall under human sense perception. Even where the mind has attained, it does not comprehend what it feels. But while it is persuaded of what it does not grasp, by the very certainty of its persuasion it understands more than if it perceived anything human by its own capacity."[24] The "knowledge of faith," Calvin explains a couple of pages later, "consists in assurance rather than in comprehension."[25]

Notably, Calvin also specifies that faith is not based on the authority of Scripture. To the contrary, one trusts in the testimonies and collective wisdom collected in the Scriptures *because* of one's faith. The Scriptures, then, testify to an experience to which we too must continually open ourselves. The "feeling of full assurance that in the Scriptures is always attributed to

22. Calvin, *Institutes*, 70–71.

23. Calvin, *Institutes*, 551.

24. Calvin, *Institutes*, 559. "Such, then, is a conviction that requires no reasons; such, a knowledge with which the best reason agrees—in which the mind truly reposes more securely and constantly than in any reasons; such, finally, a feeling that can be born only of heavenly revelation. I speak of nothing other than what each believer experiences within himself—though my words fall far beneath a just explanation of the matter . . . Let us, then, know that the only true faith is that which the Spirit of God seals in our hearts" (80–81).

25. Calvin, *Institutes*, 561. In context, Calvin's occasional tirades against doubt are clearly a product of compassion. No one "is a believer," Calvin trumpets, "except [the one] who, leaning upon the assurance of his salvation, confidently triumphs over the devil and death." But, he counters a moment later, "Surely, while we teach that faith ought to be certain and assured, we cannot imagine any certainty that is not tinged with doubt, or any assurance that is not assailed by some anxiety" (562). The stress upon certainty and confidence is not the work of the rigid dogmatist protecting the certainty of his knowledge claims, but the desperate attempt of a loving pastor to open and bolster his flock to a saving experience of God the Redeemer.

faith," Calvin stresses, "cannot happen without our truly feeling its sweetness and experiencing it in ourselves."[26] Scriptures aid us with faithful testimony from those who have been blessed with that "inner knowledge . . . which alone quickens dead souls."[27] In this sense Calvin wants us to, "know that the only true faith is that which the Spirit of God seals in our hearts."[28]

Here, then, is Calvin's definition of faith, a definition that comes in the wake of Calvin's extended exposition upon the depths of our evil:

> Now we shall possess a right definition of faith if we call it a firm and certain knowledge [i.e., assurance] of God's benevolence toward us, founded upon the truth of the freely given promise in Christ, both *revealed to our minds and sealed upon our hearts through the Holy Spirit*.[29]

Clearly, profound experience of the divine lies behind Calvin's confession.[30] Nonetheless, what is the wondrous reality to which this definition gestures? First, note that in accord with the parables and beatitudes, and contrary to the confusion of empirical belief and faith, Calvin's definition of faith does not pivot upon right belief. The Trinitarian references are appropriate but clearly *kataphatic*, they are the terms in which faith is articulated, not the

---

26. Calvin, *Institutes*, 561.

27. Calvin, *Institutes*, 70–71. Or, as Calvin bluntly titles chapter VII of Book I of his *Institutes*, "Scripture Must Be Confirmed by the Witness of the Spirit. Thus May Its Authority be Established as Certain; and it is a Wicked Falsehood that its Credibility Depends on the Judgment of the Church." Elsewhere Calvin writes, "If we desire to provide in the best way for our consciences, that they may not be perpetually beset by the instability of doubt or vacillation, we ought to seek our conviction in a higher place than human reasons . . . that is, in the secret testimony of the Spirit" (78). "For as God alone is a fit witness to himself in his Word," Calvin continues a moment later, "so also the Word will not find acceptance in [our] hearts before it is sealed by the inward testimony of the Spirit" (79). The "certainty [the Scripture] deserves with us," Calvin sums up, "it attains by the testimony of the Spirit. For even if it wins reverence for itself by its own majesty, it seriously affects us only when it is sealed upon our hearts through the Spirit" (80). Calvin reiterates this point in his discussion of faith: "we hold faith to be a knowledge of God's will toward us, perceived from his Word. But the foundation of this is a preconceived conviction of God's truth" (549).

28. Calvin, *Institutes*, 81.

29. Calvin, *Institutes*, 551 (emphasis mine).

30. Thanks to Cynthia Rigby who, after reading this passage in a draft, directed me to "The Author's Preface" of Calvin's commentary on the Psalms, where Calvin explicitly but without specifics describes how he was turned from, "the superstitions of Popery" when, "God by a sudden conversion subdued and brought my mind to a teachable frame . . . Having thus received some taste and knowledge of true godliness, I was immediately inflamed with so intense a desire to make progress therein, that although I did not altogether leave off other studies, yet I pursued them with less ardour" (Calvin, *Commentary on the Book of Psalms*, xl–xli).

Subject of faith. An *apophatic* purification of the *kataphatic* glosses in the definition might be helpful: *faith is overwhelming assurance of the ultimacy of benevolence*. That is, behind Calvin's definition lies the spiritually indubitable having-been-benevolently-seized that is utterly contrary to what, given *peccator*, we might expect. The definition gestures to life in the Spirit without any denial, without any assertion, it gestures to an experience of overwhelming, fully knowing, all-sufficient benevolence.

In the most wondrous moments, to the memory of which we might cling and testify—as have Paul, Augustine, Calvin, Pascal, Wesley, Dostoevsky, and so many others—one is simply silent and thoughtless, living and basking in impossible, utterly undeserved, wondrously real and sufficient benevolence. When the time for words returns, one might confess with wonder and thanksgiving, "In God (i.e., in the reality of having been fully known but embraced) I live and move and have my being." Or a bit more formally, one might define faith as firm and certain assurance of God's benevolence toward us, both revealed to our minds and sealed upon our hearts by the Holy Spirit.

All this, of course, names true freedom in the Pauline sense. Freedom from sin, freedom to life, a living in and through a grace that immediately begets as its fruit love and grace. Have you had someone unexpectedly love and aid you, and in your thankfulness and joy you desire above all to love and help anyone and everyone? Have you ever found yourself unexpectedly helping someone, perhaps at some risk or cost to yourself, and afterwards you find yourself feeling blessed, joyful, meaningful? Have you had an experience of grace, a bubbling joy that overflows and energizes and happily compels your love and effort and even your joyful sacrifice? We do not constantly live in such spaces, of course, but that is the vision, the ideal, the freedom of life experienced in grace that motivates and energizes mission and witness.

And, of course, from that wonderful place you do not just want to help others with their concrete tasks and aims, what you really want to give, what you really want for them, is that they may share in that same divine grace, that saving knowledge, that overwhelming experience of God's benevolence towards them. You are not initiating anything. You are not deciding to give. You are not deciding to love. The love and joy and life bubbles out from behind and below and beneath you. That is what you are really giving when you love. That is what you are inviting others to participate in as clearly as is possible. That is why and how you testify, why and how you witness. You love and you describe love. You do not aim to get people to believe or affirm particular beliefs. You strive to help people past their denial, past their self-assertion, past their self-righteousness, you strive to cultivate within them a humble spirit, to help them open themselves to the divine embrace, to stimulate realization of *peccator* and, *simul*, to stimulate realization of *iustus*.

Simul

The linear progression of my presentation is problematic. The *simul iustus et peccator* describes the living, shifting and complex consciousness of faithful people who remain sinful within a fallen world. We must recognize the enduring dynamism signaled by the *simul*. As we realize *peccator* we are humbled and opened to the grace of God, and as we experience *iustus* we are enabled and enlightened to realize *peccator* with ever more depth and profundity, which then allows us to realize God's grace even more richly and deeply. And then someone cuts us off in traffic and all the depth and intensity and spirituality are compromised in a moment. Of course, over time there can be growth in our spiritual wisdom and depth (and wiser responses in traffic!), but Calvin is comfortingly realistic about the spiritually devastating potential of rude drivers, spiteful, selfish people, and, far more seriously, the awful ways of an unjust world.

KARL BARTH ON UNIVERSAL SALVATION

In all this I have explained why Barth issues a strong "no" to the most significant and pressing dimension of the question of universal salvation. Nothing is more obvious than that there are so many who are indeed lost, who are not living eternally, who are not assured of God's benevolence, who are living desperate lives of denial, guilt, self-persecution, even lives consumed by anger and hatred, lives of impossible denial of *peccator*, lives proportionally closed to *iustus*. This awful reality is heartrending, agonizing. And for those blessed by the experience of the divine benevolence, for those living by grace, bursting with a desire to love and to help others to experience the freedom of forgiveness, to experience the reality of salvation, of eternal life, there is an immediate, irresistible desire to testify and hopefully to save through loving acts and witness.

No matter how much we do, however, in this world of suffering and evil and confusion it seems clear that the vast majority live and die in hell, live and die alienated from God, devastatingly defiant or tragically closed to God's gift of love. On the other hand, the power of our experience of benevolence/love/grace is so awesome and unexpected and overwhelming and beyond any realistic expectation that we find it is impossible to believe that any force could forever stand against it. That is the spiritual energy behind the *creatio ex nihilo*, the spiritual energy that is the rejection of any notion that, ultimately, we are dealing with an admixture of good and evil forces, the confidence in the ultimate triumph of grace, the conviction that pushed Barth forward where Calvin, betrayed (in the same fashion as Augustine) by orthodoxy's mistaken commitment to a logic of sovereignty, was cut short (i.e., cut short theologically, though perhaps not spiritually). That is the conviction that found it unthinkable that God would damn for all eternity any creature, the conviction that Barth expressed in the shift from understanding the elect to be some portion of humans (Calvin) to understanding the elect to be Jesus Christ, the one through whom all are elected.

This is the experience and passion that leads Christians to dare to hope even in life after death, not for our own sakes—though of course we would be thankful for such a gift—but for the sake of so many around us who are living and dying awful, painful, hopeless lives. True sheep mourn the goats. True sheep think, "even unto me? I am guiltier than anyone!" So, true sheep cannot imagine that if even they are included that any ultimately could be excluded.[31]

Still, universal salvation is not a logical conclusion, not a demand, not some requirement we dictate to God. Neither, we should note, is its contrary. One might *speculate*, for instance, that divine creation requires autonomy, that autonomy requires the possibility of a creaturely "no" (Barth's

---

31. Quite wisely and appropriately, there is a present and future aspect to classic Christian expectation and teaching about salvation, about eternal life. The tradition never reduced "eternal life" to "life after death." Salvation names entry into eternal life, which is a transformed way of being in the world *right now*. To be sure, in classic Christian teaching eternal life included life after death, but this dimension of the proclamation is more about the faithfulness of God and less about us, not *vice versa*. An absolutely understandable but spiritually devastating problem unfolds when denial of our own evil extinguishes our desperation for forgiveness of sins. Once that tearing, screaming need has been silenced, the need for and real benefit of eternal life naturally and unfortunately appears to be the prospect of life after death, for a self-centered focus upon my own death as my greatest threat seizes my attention. In this context, the promise of life after death nourishes selfishness. That is, in this context the promise of life after death becomes an obstacle to saving Christian faith. By contrast, the extinguishing of self-interested motivational dynamics, purgation, is the critical first step that opens one to illumination and then union in the Christian mystical tradition.

The question of life after death is one with regard to which many people are understandably fragile, and much sensitivity is needed in probing it. In the case of lost children, for instance, we understandably cling powerfully to hope in life after death. But even here, let alone with regard to some self-interested hope, belief in life after death cannot be a motivation for faith, or even a demand we place upon God. However, hope in life after death (especially for others) accords naturally with our apprehension of God's overwhelming benevolence toward us. It is, in that sense, a hope we all should share (on proper Christian hope regarding life after death see further Greenway, *Reasonable Belief*, 147–49).

impossible possibility), and that the notion of hell as a current and final way of being in the world unto death (and perhaps beyond) is logically required if there are to be truly autonomous creatures. This quite reasonable speculation may even be correct. But that is not to the point. The point is that we do not know. We are in no position to demand or to judge. But we can and should passionately and wholeheartedly hope and pray that somehow all might be saved.

Barth articulates these dynamics with a brilliant set of distinctions. Objectively, Barth says, all are saved through the election of Jesus Christ. But subjectively, that is, at the level of personal conviction, of saving knowledge, only some realize the reality of salvation.[32] Whether ultimately the objective reality somehow works itself out exhaustively, so that ultimately all are subjectively freed to the wondrous, objective truth, that is, whether there is ultimately universal salvation in the subjective sense, we do not know. But, we can say, the hope, not the assertion or demand but *the hope* for universal salvation will be immediate and burning for any who know the "even unto me?" miracle of salvation by grace.

Barth's distinctions allow we who are Christian neatly to summarize a twofold meaning to being saved through the "faith of Christ" (e.g., Romans 3:22, "*dia pisteos Christou*"). First, *objectively*, all are reconciled through the faith of Christ. At the same time, second, *subjectively*, we are reconciled as we experience in and for ourselves the faith of Christ, which the faith of Christ makes available even unto us. This subjective, saving experience of faith, of *simul iustus et peccator*, as this analysis makes clear and as the parable of the sheep and goats illustrates, does not require even knowledge of the name of Jesus, let alone assent to a particular set of beliefs.[33]

---

32. There are subtle differences, so I should note that what I refer to here in familiar language as the "objective" and the "subjective" Barth refers to more precisely and technically as the "ontic" and the "noetic."

33. It is important to stress, against a confusion that Barth's analytic style may inadvertently cultivate, that insofar as *apophatic* apprehension is the root of *kataphatic* confession, that is, insofar as the words merely testify to the Word, which remains most fully hidden precisely where it is most fully revealed, *the subjective is the basis of our objective convictions* (more precisely: the noetic is the basis of our ontic convictions), that is, the subjective experience of God's benevolence toward us is the basis for our claims about the objective work of God. "All are saved through the work of Jesus Christ, the elected one through whom all is elected," then, would be an objective, not a subjective comment. It may well be objectively true, but it is not the basis of nor as certain as the subjective conviction. The subjective is prior to the objective, the *apophatic* is prior to the *kataphatic*, not the other way around. This is critical to stress because without it one may be, even at this late juncture in the analysis, tempted to substitute empirical belief, a human knowledge claim, for faith.

In terms of the question of universal salvation, then, we may say two things with confidence. First, and most importantly, *subjectively*, is there universal salvation? The answer is clearly: *no*, there is not universal salvation—so many around us are living hopeless, raging, guilt-ridden lives. This obvious truth urgently calls forth our ministries of love and witness.

Second, with regard to our desperate, painful, burning question regarding the Ivans and Judases of the world, together with so many relatively innocent who die, some so young and abused (perhaps like that murdered child in the morgue), evidently apart from the love of God, will they ultimately, in some future life, be saved? flourish? enjoy the blessings of God? Well, we do not know. However, the character and overwhelming power of divine grace is such that we hope and pray and, given the amazing, overwhelming power of grace, even passionately expect that somehow the salvation of all in eternity (objectively) may mark the ultimacy of benevolence, the fully realized triumph of grace. We do not know. But, full of grace, we mourn and hope for all, even for the Ivans and Judases.

In short, we are assured that God's grace has reached even unto us, we are aware that not all enjoy this assurance, but we hope that someday this assurance will be a realized blessing for all.[34] As Barth concludes in the final

---

34. Though the issue is tangential to the common scope of the debates over universalism, we must as least note that in our age, when we are become gods on earth, the question of universal salvation should challenge us to consider whether the bounds of our moral and spiritual sensitivity are anthropocentric. Barth has often been charged with theanthropocentrism, with reducing all of theology and divine concern to a relationship between God and humanity. Doubtless Barth is largely guilty of this, and many of his followers clearly are guilty of reducing the scope of their own moral sensitivity and their comprehension of divine concern wholly to humans. However, from the all-inclusive pictures of the peaceable kingdom in the creation and the eschatological accounts, to God's explicit, post-Deluge covenant with all creatures and all creation, to the trees clapping their hands, to Jesus' presumption that all in his audience would agree as a matter of course that one should break the Sabbath out of concern for a sheep, to Paul's "the whole creation groans," to "the Word became flesh"—not male, not Jewish, not human, but *flesh*—the Scriptures reflect a universal love and concern. By effectively obliterating all nonhuman creatures and creation through a rhetoric that puts exclusive focus on the divine/human relation, theanthropocentrism aggressively truncates the universal scope of biblical spirituality and misunderstands the reach of God's saving embrace.

Consider by contrast the spirituality sensitivity of Albert Schweitzer. The scope of Schweitzer's love mirrors that of the Scriptures. Schweitzer urges that one is holy if one, "refrains from afflicting injury upon anything that lives . . . Life as such is holy . . . When working by candlelight on a summer night, one would rather keep the windows closed and breathe stuffy air than see insect after insect fall on the table with wings that are singed. If one walks along the street after rain and notices an earthworm which has lost its way . . . one carries it from the death-dealing stones to the grass . . . One is not afraid of being smiled at as a sentimentalist" (Schweitzer, *Kultur und Ethik*, 331–32, as

sentence of *Church Dogmatics* IV.3.1, where he offers his most mature and complete statement on universal reconciliation:

> If we are certainly forbidden to count on [universal reconciliation] as though we had a claim to it, as though it were not supremely the work of God to which [we] can have no possible claim, we are surely commanded the more definitely to hope and pray for it as we may do already on this side of this final possibility, i.e., to hope and pray cautiously and yet distinctly that, in spite of everything which may seem quite conclusively to proclaim the opposite, [God's] compassion should not fail, and that in accordance with [God's] mercy which is "new every morning" [God] "will not cast off for ever" (La. 322f., 31).[35]

---

translated by Bromiley and Torrance in Karl Barth, *Church Dogmatics* III/4, 349).

Clearly, this stands in contrast to the dominant appropriation of Barth's theology and, admittedly, in contrast to his predominant rhetoric. We must correct for this. But we should remember that Barth cites precisely these words of Albert Schweitzer about minding flies' singed wings and stooping to rescue wayward worms and that Barth immediately comments, "Those who can only smile at this point are themselves subjects for tears" (*Church Dogmatics* III/4, 349). Barth goes on in a few brief pages to reassert Schweitzer's sensitivities, now within the terms of his own theology. In any case, it is clear that we are called to an all-embracing attention and concern, to sensitivity to evil and suffering whenever it afflicts any creature. The question of universal salvation, then, is not a question only about *homo sapiens*.

35. Barth, *Church Dogmatics*, IV/3.1, 478.

Chapter 13

From Cagayan de Oro, Mindanao, Philippines

September 23, 1989

Hi, again! Another hectic month has flown by. In the past three weeks we preached at outreach churches and remembrance services, began four Bible studies (the church midweek, one for the church council, and two at an internal refugee camp—one for adults and one for children), appeared on a Christian television show, led two in a series of six puppet workshops, continued our Visayan lessons, and macheted our way through the brush, dug holes, and planted mahogany seedlings as part of a long-term church project.[1] Before that, at the end of August, we flew to Silliman University in

---

1. Shortly after graduating from Princeton Theological Seminary, in late June of 1989, I traveled to the Philippines with Cynthia Rigby for a year of work as an ecumenical associate with the United Church of Christ in the Philippines. The "ecumenical associate" program was an attempt by the UCCP to model a new paradigm for crosscultural church work (i.e., "missionary" work, which in this case meant largely an exposure program intended to create greater understanding in the sending country—in our case the ultimate aim of the mission was enhanced understanding in the USA). We were officially sent by the Presbyterian Church (USA) but were installed as pastors under the Reverend (now Bishop) Hilario Gomez in the UCCP church in Cagayan de Oro City on Abellanosa Street, and we worked directly and wholly under the authority of the UCCP. This is an early "mission letter" home. My year in the Philippines proved to be one of the most wonderful, enjoyable, meaningful, and influential years in my life. Many people and groups mentioned in passing here would become treasured friends over the coming year. The UCCP provided rooms for us at the church, and we covered all other expenses with monies raised from our home churches and churches we had worked in as students

the Visayas. During our ten-day stay we spoke at the University midweek service and to several small groups. Using the multidimensional example of the four Gospels, we discussed the value of sharing our understanding of the Christian faith from a plurality of cultural and personal perspectives in order to gain a broader and deeper vision of that truth which transcends every individual understanding. We also addressed women's issues in interpretation, discussing select Old and New Testament passages in their historical and cultural context.

The focus of our visit, however, was the four-day National Church Workers Convocation—the United Church of Christ in the Philippines' (UCCP's) National Convention. The Philippines is a country of poverty, corruption at every level of bureaucracy, and raging insurgency. It is a country where twelve UCCP ministers and dozens of church members have been killed in guerrilla attacks. It is a country occupied by three opposing armies. Consequently, while the pastors retain their concern for the spiritual—leading discussions about spirituality, leading prayers, and Bible studies—social, political, and economic issues are priorities. When members of your congregation are caught in a political and literal crossfire, can't afford basic medical care, have only contaminated water, and struggle to eat daily, these sorts of issues become rather immediate priorities.

Scripture too is seen in a different light. The many prophetic and gospel passages proclaiming God's justice and fight for the poor are a rich resource mined triumphantly and hopefully. Passages describing God's gift of life are also investigated. What is it to be fully human? In answer, passages are referenced which treat the nature and conditions of freedom, the significance of land, security of health and nutrition, and the insight that the talents given by God were intended to be developed and nurtured fully.

Perhaps one can best appreciate this distinctive approach after seeing how radically different every aspect of Filipino life is vis-à-vis the US. The most obvious difference is economic. The Philippines has a huge lower class. According to current figures, for a family to live "comfortably" (read "above the poverty level") they need P3500/$175 per month. To be considered *rich* they need to earn $12,500 per year. Tragically, many cannot maintain even the minimum level. Some 49 percent of Filipino families are living below the poverty level. Food accounts for over half the family budget. While

---

($6,000 covered all my expenses for the year). This was the second of a series of monthly letters I sent to our supporting congregations. Almost all the other letters are evidently lost. I was surprised and pleased to find this letter when cleaning out old files a couple of years ago. Note that because the letter is unrevised, some language and some of the ideas are dated. More than thirty years later, my year in the Philippines stands out as one of the most meaningful, impactful, and joyful years in my life.

many products are less expensive here than in the States (e.g., food, local clothes), such commonplace items as hot plates (don't even think about ovens!), electrical and plumbing supplies, soap, sneakers, knives, watches, radios, and heavy industrial goods are sold at United States rates. A small radio or toaster, for instance, is an astronomical P1000/$50! Even items in the United States "Made in the Philippines" are produced in special export zones and might as well be made abroad as far as a Filipino is concerned. This leaves the Philippines in the dubious position of being a major producer of such items as Lee jeans and Timex watches while the Filipino people remain almost wholly unable to buy them.

In this day of the global village, the Filipino is well aware of the living standard of the typical American. The reactions to the discrepancy ranges from what is probably healthy resentment and a feeling of being exploited to unabashed worship of the "promised land"—the United States. One dominant reaction is reflected in the fact that the Filipinos were the largest immigrant group to go to the States last year. The tragedy for the Philippines is that those who emigrate are the brightest and best educated of the Filipinos. While the States benefit from the doctors, nurses, lawyers, and businessmen and women who fought to overcome the odds in a culture of strife and poverty, the Philippines lose their brightest potential for their future and a national inferiority complex is reinforced.

The economic factor is only one dimension in a broader cultural imperialism exerted by the United States simply by virtue of its existence as a large wealthy nation. In the downtown department store a two hundred-seat snack area is perpetually crowded by people watching a large-screen television. MTV, CNN, Major League Baseball, and the NBA are the major offerings. In the evening, most television shows are US network imports (*Magnum PI, Falcon Crest, Star Trek*). Local radio stations play 90 percent American pop and the best stations in Manila have hot shows like *American Top 40*. Elite shops sell American fashion magazines and most store mannequins are Caucasian. As in the States, fashion trends and what is "cool" or "happening" is defined largely by mass media, and in the Philippines the mass media is markedly American.

This infusion of American culture is also evident in education. English is stressed as essential to professional success; children are not allowed to speak their native tongue in elementary school. While there is a body of relatively recent Filipino literature, it is supplemented by extensive reading in American and English literature. Most Filipinos, furthermore, know more about American history than that of their Far Eastern neighbors. Many could name the major US presidents and recite the Gettysburg Address.

Of course, this dynamic between the two nations is not the average American's fault. Nonetheless, it is a definite problem which merits constant consideration in any understanding of our mutual relations. It is, moreover, a dynamic buried deep in the average Filipino's psyche. More than once I have been greeted with the wistful remark, "It's good to be an American, no?" It is said without resentment or envy. There is a sense of awe, respect, and more than anything the unspoken, "Isn't it wonderful to be so lucky? Boy, do I wish I had been lucky enough to be an American." We found that a high compliment is "as pretty as a white woman." And just this morning a pregnant woman said to Cindy, "I hope my baby can look like you when it's born." These poignant statements make you want to scream back, "Yes, I'm glad to be an American, but I'd be just as glad to be a Filipino!" But one quickly learns that such replies, for good reason, are quite simply unintelligible.

Try to imagine growing up in the United States knowing that the best students in your class will probably choose to go to the Philippines so they can get really good jobs. Imagine going home every night and watching Filipino stars on Filipino television shows and listening to CNN talking about weather in the Philippines or what's happening in Manila, Davao, or Cebu. Imagine seeing Filipino wealth and lifestyle you can only dream about. Imagine the front page of every *New York Times* carrying news of Corey's latest decisions. Imagine all the songs on the radio are Filipino songs sung in Tagalog. Imagine really wanting to learn Tagalog so you can get a good job and succeed (although English is fine around the house). Imagine going out and choosing between the best American restaurants and Filipino fast food (both being equally expensive). Imagine wishing that you have been lucky enough to be born a Filipino and not an American. Bring all this to mind at once and remember that you've been viewed with this mentality since birth, and you might begin to understand why many educated Filipinos (for instance Filipino pastors) are openly advocating an unabashed nationalism. You also might begin to realize why this nationalism is by its very nature anti-American.

Because of these dynamics our talks and sermons often stress our equality before God. We emphasize that we are learning from the Filipinos (and indeed we are) insightful new perspectives on Christianity. We explained the Presbyterian and Methodist churches are studying the Philippines in order to learn from them. And we stress that we are all brothers and sisters in one community of faith, that we are created equally in the image of God, that we have worked because God loves us, that we are all equally important no matter who or what we are. We also talk about the joy which can come from a diversity of perspectives in a community, about the value of hearing and learning from and enjoying each other's distinctive differences.

This wide-ranging intercultural context must also form the backdrop for the political question of the continued existence of Subic Bay Naval Base and Clark Air Base. While in the States we may consider the only relevant issues to be those that revolve around the question of the balance of power in the Far East. In the Philippines the powerful United States military presence is the dark center of the cultural, economic, political, and military shadow the United States casts over the Philippines. The bases are a constant, tangible reminder of their recent colonial status, a continuing symbol of their lack of full sovereignty. That is why the New People's Army's reaction is so violent. Ambassador Platt's recent statement that the bases should be retained because they bring $1 billion a year to the Philippines, the loss of which would be economically devastating, served only to exacerbate Filipino anger at being in perception or in essence a pseudo-colony of the United States. While we might consider Platt's statement to be sound economic advice, from a Filipino context it definitely can be understood to mean, "The Philippines have been bought, and if they know what's good for them, they'll stay bought." For a people trying to assert their sovereignty, any perception of mendicancy is anathema.

This problem of domination and fear of pseudo-colonial status is also a live dynamic in the church, as was dramatically illustrated last week by the visit of an American mission board representative. The representative was concerned the church was being "imperialistic" by maintaining a strong Christian institutional presence in a strictly Muslim area. The Filipino church leaders disagreed, stressing its importance. The American representatives reply was, "Well then, we'll cut off support to this area. Then what will you do?" To this hypocritical reply the Filipino church leaders politely responded that if necessary they would certainly find other means of support. This graphically illustrates what is a constant, though usually more subtle, problem with foreign dependence. Reflect perhaps on the subtle but real power that exists in any relationship which involves economic dependence (e.g., parents and the "adult" college student, pastor or missionary and the supporting church). The perspective on each side is easy to understand. From the giver's perspective, one should make sure one's money is being used for uses one thinks justified. This is simply responsible stewardship. But for the receiver, this translates into a form of control and economic dominance which prevents the development of a truly indigenous church under national control and leadership. For the UCCP this is a classic catch-22. A major goal is the development of a truly and purely Filipino church for the Filipino people, a church which is developing a distinctive form of worship, articulation of faith, and fellowship which is most conducive to fostering Christian worship in the Filipino context. But the

UCCP cannot maintain her programs without significant foreign aid, that is, without significant foreign influence.

In any case, I hope I am getting across some of the fundamental dynamics which are structuring the nature of our ministry in the Philippines. One can see how the mission of the church and the message of the gospel must be understood relative to the Filipino context. Where in the States we need to caution against pride, here we need to emphasize the pride we can take in being loved by God, to stress the self-worth entailed in being a child of God. In the States we need to be reminded of the relative insignificance of material wealth, that spirituality, family, and community are the most important part of our lives; here, where family ties in community and faith are incredibly strong because they are all most people have, the church needs to address the social, medical, political, and nutritional needs which threaten the very lives of their members.

One specific example might illustrate how Scripture should be read differently in different contexts. Jesus tells us the two coins of the widow was greater than the much larger gift of the rich man. In the States we quite rightly preach from this that we shouldn't pay attention to the great amount we might give—it is our attitude which is critical. We should not give with the spirit of the rich man but with the spirit of the widow. Don't just give your tithe and feel satisfied, even if it is disproportionately large, but check your attitude and willingness in giving—both materially and in your daily life. But here in the Philippines, that passage carries a very different message of hope and joy. Don't despair that you have nothing to offer God. Don't worry that you can't contribute to the building of the new church or to sponsoring the pastor's salary. God doesn't care how much you give. We learn from the widow that even two coins was a great gift. In the grace of God even the poorest of the poor give just as much as the richest of the rich. Rejoice, for God has made your offering great. God has accepted your gifts as God would accept diamonds and gold. God extends to all of us the wonderful ability to give to Almighty God. When we give from our hearts sincerely unto God the amount simply does not matter. Rejoice and give with great joy, for all our gifts are great in the eyes of God.

As you study various passages experiment with reading them from a "third world" context. It's amazing the new insights which suddenly emerge. This is also an exegetically sound procedure considering that a bulk of Jesus' teachings were directed to the poor, the "third world" of his day (it's also from this group that he chose most of his disciples).

I hope I have been able to communicate the delicate nature of our missionary task here in the Philippines. The obvious danger of having two Americans come in a pastoral teaching capacity is to implicitly reinforce just those images and biases which the church is trying to eradicate. The UCCP ministers are among the best educated people in the country and are highly sensitized to the unfortunate dynamic between American and Filipino culture. For this reason, most are understandably cautious about our involvement here. For our part we are trying to keep our subordination to the national and local leaders very obvious. Our Bible studies are investigative, and while we present new ideas the emphasis is on mutual sharing and dialogue. Our sermons too, as noted above, are carefully crafted to avoid perpetuating unhealthy stereotypes. On the whole, however, these dynamics are much more difficult to deal with than we had anticipated and require constant diligence. They also tend to isolate us from different groups in distinctive ways. Please continue to pray as we continue to learn from and attempt to minister within this context. We grow more informed and effective daily. Pray that we will continue to grow and will be provided with the proper opportunities within which to minister constructively.

SPECIAL BONUS SECTION: "REFLECTIONS ON THE GIVER-RECEIVER RELATION"

One of the most valuable sources of insight for me has been a new context within which to reflect on the existential (that is psychological, spiritual, subjective) dimensions of the dynamic between the beneficent giver and dependent receiver. I am beginning to see that while in my American church context "it is better to give than to receive" may sound like a Christian truism which should be oft repeated in sacred halls; in the land of the impoverished recipient that smacks of a self-righteous, self-affirming elitism and carries the definite connotation that it is also better to be the giver than the receiver. One can imagine the ramifications of the gift coming in the form of a missionary! That is, one can imagine the myriad dangers involved in being perceived as or in any small way becoming a present incarnation of that self-righteous, self-affirming elite.

Another insight which initially startled me was that it is far more difficult to receive than to give. Of course, one could receive as a "taker," considering oneself to be taking from some "sucker" while the taking is good. That would be an easy way to "receive." But to receive grace-full-ly, one must assume an existential stance of need, dependence, vulnerability, and weakness. One must acknowledge to oneself that one is receiving a gift, a gift which cannot be demanded or be perceived as deserved. This is a difficult way to receive. One is reminded of the parallel stance of the dependent infant or child, a stance we self-sufficient adults are loath to adopt. And as the dynamic is delineated one sees that it is precisely that difficult stance we *are* to be assuming as we are accepting entry into God's gift of grace. Perhaps that is part of the reason Jesus chose his first disciples from among the poorest and least educated. Perhaps one of the most profound lessons we can learn from the poor in the Philippines is just this: how to accept a gift in grace.

Reflection on this insight, however, caused me to reconsider and to think that it may be just as difficult to give as to receive after all. Drawing the parallel to God's gift of grace caused me to reflect that I could never give as God gives. God may give in grace through God's own righteous grace, but I never can. God can give what is God's. I can only give what is not mine; I can only give that which is my stewardship. God can give through God's self. I can only give through God's grace. I must realize that my environment and my very being is not my own, but the ongoing gift of the sustaining God. I can only give, then, what is not my own but what is an ongoing gift which I receive. I must remain then, perpetually in the dependent and vulnerable stance of the receiver, the stance of being in grace. Consequently, this is the stance from which I give. The stance of the giver, therefore, is not only as difficult as but identical to the stance of the receiver. In fact, the position of the giver may well be more dangerous than that of the receiver, for the giver is sorely tempted to take, or likely to be deceived into taking, the stance of a God-giver instead of a giver in grace. That is, the danger for the givers is to think they are giving from themselves on the basis of their own righteousness, to dupe themselves into thinking they are giving as only God can give. Instead, they must recognize they give what they receive. They give a gift. They give what is not their own. They should, therefore, assume the same existential stance as the receiver.

These reflections helped me consider anew the problem of the dynamic between giver and receiver (i.e., the common perception of a superior-inferior relationship). Perhaps practical contingencies can be better worked out when the existential dimension is delineated. The giver and receiver can realize that their existential stance of dependence and vulnerability is identical, God being the definitive referent, the existence of both subsisting in grace. Such a consciousness might dissolve the nefarious perception of a superior-inferior relationship. The contingent factor of relative wealth would be recognized as secondary, a consequence primarily of the luck of being born into opportunity. The distinction between giver and receiver may be pragmatically critical but it is existentially irrelevant.

Given this understanding we might perhaps begin to understand "giving" more the way we understand "sharing," especially as we use it in reference to sharing a gift. We can envision the sharing of material gifts throughout the world with universal humility, humility in both the giver and receiver. Our lives in grace and love would naturally entail this worldwide sharing. Appeals to justice, rights, or certain biblical passages would no longer need to be used as coercive means to justifiable (if thereby existentially empty) ends. All could participate in the ability to give and receive as equals in the realm of grace. All could know that within the realm of grace the distinction between giver and receiver is existentially (i.e., spiritually, psychologically, subjectively) irrelevant. We all exist in ultimate relation to God, a God who revises the relationships of all human beings into those of brothers and sisters in one family which transcends all worldly boundaries. "And now I will show you the most excellent way . . ." (See especially the relationship between chapters 12 and 13 in 1 Corinthians.)

Last week Cindy and I visited for the first time an internal refugee camp where we are starting a series of Bible studies. Here families of ten live in shanties the size of a dorm room. The children are poorly nourished, and most families are thankful for two small meals a day. The refugees are squatters, living on unused land they do not own. Two months ago, many lost even their shanties when the owner decided to bulldoze them down. Two leaders from the squatters, our escorts, led us into a clearing in the midst of the shanties. A small square of land had been cordoned off with bamboo poles and palm branches. In the center of the square were a table and two chairs. We were escorted to our seats of honor. About 150 children and adults gathered about the perimeter of the square. Two women brought umbrellas and held them to shield us from the sun. Another began to fan us futilely with a sheet of paper. One of the leaders nodded to someone in the crowd and two large cold bottles of Coke were brought out to us. A moment later a platter of special sweetened rice cakes on banana leaves and an overflowing dish of Chinese noodles, fancy dishes used even by the middle class only for special occasions, were set before us. Our hosts smiled as they placed the food before us and motioned for us to eat. And then they simply stood and waited. No one, not even the two leaders, moved to join us. They all just watched attentively.

I sat quite still. I looked at the children in their ragged clothes as they smiled at me in obvious delight. I knew a Coke would have been a rare treat for them. I looked at the adults, parents who in celebration would not serve their families before me. I looked down again. I wasn't even hungry. I wasn't hungry because an hour before I spent more money than most of them make in a week (around $8) at the Lico-An, a fine Filipino restaurant where I had dined on a splendid lunch of fresh Lapu-Lapu,[2] fried rice, and pineapple

---

2. Lapu-Lapu is the national fish of the Philippines; only after we had been in the

juice. I looked around again. There was no envy or jealousy, just an obvious delight and a trace of anxious expectation. They knew I didn't normally eat their food. They knew I was a rich American. They knew their meager offering wasn't much by American standards. They knew they couldn't impress me. They knew no rich American needed them. They didn't give for any need of mine, or for any self-righteous purpose, nor from any obedience to some external demand, nor as an attempt to impress . . . we were being welcomed as a brother and a sister and they were offering us entrance into their family. They were simply sharing what they had, the best of what they had, because they wanted to give to us, to please us, to invite us into their fellowship. And so they watched us with joy and eager expectation and a trace of anxiety as they offered their best and risked our rejection.

I knew I had no right to eat that food. I knew I didn't deserve it. But I also knew I had to eat and drink thankfully. More than that, I realized that because of the way they were giving to me I could eat and drink thankfully. I also realized that I was being powerfully and violently attacked. That pride which is so much a part of my being was being pummeled. With pride I might have feigned thankfulness and truly eaten in spite. But not with those people. Not even my pride could retain any degree of spite. So, I was pummeled into the most profound humility I have ever experienced as I ate food that I didn't deserve while the squatters watched. I sat in the middle of their shanties and looked at their hungry children and I feasted on those two platters while they watched and forced me to learn how to receive in grace. And because of their teaching I truly feasted thankfully, even happily. And I found my forced humility a welcome thing, for I wasn't humbled before and beneath, I was humbled with them. I was humbled into that community which transcends our worldly boundaries, where all our very real barriers of race, class, and nationality are broken down; where suddenly we are neighbors, where suddenly we are all brothers and sisters. They humbled me to themselves and themselves to me. And as I sat there humbled and feasting, I began to think perhaps one of the most profound lessons we can learn from the poor in the Philippines is this: how to give in grace.

After considering the above reflections I began to think that we might be able to claim and affirm the teaching that "it is more blessed to give than to receive" after all (Acts 20:35). But perhaps what at first sight appears to be a superficial truism is actually one of the most existentially demanding

---

Philippines for some time did Filipino friends share that the fish was named in honor of the chief who killed Ferdinand Magellan, the Portuguese explorer who "discovered" the Philippines while leading a Spanish expedition, which would eventuate in three centuries of Spanish colonial rule.

of passages. Perhaps we wealthy Christians can begin to appreciate what profound humility and thank-full-ness must accompany the realization of being so arbitrarily blessed. Perhaps we can begin to appreciate what it means to give and receive, to share, from a stance rooted in the grace of the only one who is righteous.

>Your humbled brother,
>Bill
>William Greenway
>September 23, 1989
>
>UCCP
>Abellanosa Street
>Cagayan de Oro City
>Mindanao, Philippines 9000

Chapter 14

Dear Gail, About Stan

Dear Gail,

    I have just learned of Stan's death and am so sad to find myself a long way away. I am stunned to hear this news. The phone feels totally inadequate, and there is so much I want to say, and I so wish I were there just to be present and to listen. I will not here in an e-mail try to do any of those things, which I don't think are possible by e-mail. But I wanted to do something and there is one thing that I might offer that might be helpful when the moment is right (which it may not be when you get this, but this is all I could do by e-mail). I thought I could write to share with you an experience which has been of great comfort to me when reflecting on the last moments of my grandmother and of friends like David Miles and, now, Stan. If this is not helpful or is inappropriate, you can of course simply stop reading at any moment.

    I will not detail or dramatize the experience, but there was one occasion in my life—many years ago now—when for about a minute I knew with utter conviction that I was about to die. I cannot adequately articulate the experience, but it was utterly different than anything I had expected. Once that conviction hit utterly, I totally lost all concern for myself; the world turned inside out. I was filled with peace. I was alone, but the people I cared about were wholly and completely present to me. I was wildly happy for them. Not for any specific reasons, but just because they were alive and would experience joy and beauty and love. Everything was beautiful. Not that I actually thought any of this in a considered and explicit way. There was no time consciously to think, consider, reflect. The realization, perspective, ideations—I do not know what to call it—just suddenly washed over and enveloped me.

And then the possibility that I would live unexpectedly came into view, and immediately it was all gone. I was again worried over myself—not selfishness, a good worry for someone who can live but is in trouble.

Of course, I do not know if this is a universal experience, but the dynamics are such that I expect it may be, especially for someone like Stan. At any rate, the experience was so powerful and singular for me that I really believe that Stan may have experienced something like this in his final moments.

Of course, none of this makes Stan's death okay, or takes away the pain. I mean only to comment on this one thing, this one moment. I hope it was not inappropriate or hurtful in any way. I look forward to seeing you very soon.

Bill

Chapter 15

Extinction

I have been asked to reflect upon extinction. First, perhaps because I write during a terrifying global pandemic [April 2020], my thoughts turn to the massive explosions triggered as comet Shoemaker-Levy 9 broke up and slammed into Jupiter in 1994. Jupiter is but a speck in space . . . but so massive 1,300 Earths would fit inside. The spectacular collisions made palpable the extraordinarily slim but shockingly real chance life on Earth might be suddenly, unexpectedly extinguished. By 1998 Hollywood had released *Deep Impact* and *Armageddon* and NASA had initiated a Near Earth Object Search program.

Considering creation's ferocious impulse to life—in acidic hot springs at Yellowstone, in deep ocean vents, in acid baths—and two trillion *galaxies*, I expect life flourishes throughout the cosmos. So, even if life on Earth is obliterated by a massive comet or a nuclear winter, we are probably not talking about the end of all life in the cosmos. Moreover, myriad building blocks of life would likely survive most earthly cataclysms. So, we are probably talking "only" about the extinction of our iteration of life on Earth, not of all life on Earth, nor even the end of Earth teeming with as dazzling an array of creatures as our own iteration, for there is ample time for whole new iterations to evolve.

Yesterday, a news story featuring gorgeous pictures of stars and nebulae urged us to take comfort in the beauty of the universe. Stars and nebulae are stunning, but entities like these do not appreciate beauty. For beauty to exist the sorts of beings that can see things as beautiful must exist. You and I "see" in a profoundly different sense than the Hubble telescope "sees." Ontologically, beauty really is in the eye of some beholder.

It is conceivable, if unlikely, that Mars once teemed with life, but some awful conflagration consumed all life and over the eons every trace of life was erased. If so, then Mars was once seen as beautiful (by creatures on Mars), then Mars was beautiful to none, and then we evolved and beheld, and Mars was beautiful again.

Significantly, all living creatures, even one-celled beings, possess the neurotransmitters and receptors associated with emotions (plants have analogous structures).[1] Thirst, satisfaction, fear, happiness, appreciation of beauty, and so forth are "beheld" in analogous ways by all living creatures. Of course, a tree, for instance, does not conceptualize thirst, but there is commonality in our primordial/precognitive, bodily thirsting.

Aesthetic desire and delight are indexed to personal pleasure/self-interest (*eros*). For mainstream modern Western anglophone philosophy this, combined with description of causal relationships within the world (science), exhausts the parameters of reality—this names all reality for "materialists" or "metaphysical naturalists." Now, *eros* is real and rightly celebrated, and science is invaluable because it allows us to understand and contend with nature's causal flow. But *eros* and science do not exhaust the full scope of reality, for they exclude the reality of freely willing, innovative, self-creating beings like us and—even more devastating insofar as materialism predominates among global elites—*eros* and science exclude moral reality.

Utilitarian theory was nineteenth-century philosophy's best stab at locating moral reality within a naturalistic worldview. Utilitarians defined good in terms of pleasurable/healthy/preferred and defined evil in terms of painful/harmful/unwanted. As frustrated philosophers quickly realized, however, this reduces good and evil to what is good or evil for one or another "me." This reduces ethics to *eros*, for it can name no other reason any "me" may be concerned over what is good or evil for anyone else.

Naturalism's conceptual distortion is poignantly manifest when it subverts Arne Naess's explanation of his exquisite moral sensitivity to a flea—note how modern naturalistic blinders force even Naess, the originator of Deep Ecology, to explain that what is morally basic is the way he *sees himself* in the flea:

> A flea jumped from a lemming strolling along the table and landed in the middle of the acid chemicals. To save it was impossible. It took many minutes for the flea to die. Its movements

---

1. Schoen, *Kindred Spirits*, 44–45.

were dreadfully expressive. What I felt was, naturally, a painful compassion and empathy. But the empathy was *not* basic. What *was* basic was the process of identification, that "I see myself in the flea." If I was alienated from the flea, not seeing intuitively anything resembling myself, the death struggle would have left me indifferent. So there must be identification in order for there to be compassion and, among humans, solidarity.[2]

Most all morally awakened souls have had like experiences with creatures of all kinds, from humans to horses, squirrels to spiders, cats to cardinals. To allow the strictures of naturalism to force us to say that the heart of all such moral dynamics is an identification/concern/encounter *with myself* is a devastating distortion.

In contrast to the naturalism predominant among Western intellectual elites, I affirm a moral reality, the reality of agape, which is manifest when, whether the circumstances are joyful or horrifying, I am seized by the Faces of others. I see smiling newlyweds, the joyful birthday girl, dogs barking and racing around the park and, apart from any decision or desire, I find myself seized by agape, smiling, and joyful. I see the weeping widow, the uncomprehending girl fleeing the flames of the battle, or, like Arne Naess, I see a flea writhing in acid and, apart from any decision or desire, I find myself seized by agape for the widow, the girl, the flea, and I am rent with sorrow and moved to render aid. Insofar as God *is* love, this describes surrender to having been seized by the very Face or Spirit of God.[3]

When I joyfully commune with or mourn a *single* flea, cat, dog, hamster, horse, or human, my having been seized is absolute and unqualified. But we live among a host of Faces in conflicted contexts. If the flea is carrying bubonic plague and the life of that girl or my life is at stake, I may decide to kill the flea, but even then, I would see myself forced in real time to choose the better among bad options, and I would mourn the Face of the flea.[4]

Only individuals, not abstractions such as "species" or "mountains," behold beauty or are seized by or have Faces. Reciprocity is not essential. Even if the flea is only capable of rudimentary *eros* (pleasure or pain), I am still seized infinitely by agape for the flea. With a conceptual sophistication unknown to the flea, I delight in its pleasure, mourn its pain, act responsively. Roughly, the appearance of agape in the world requires response-able beings (i.e., beings which can be seized by agape); in this sense we are God's hands and voice in the world.

---

2. Naess, "Self-Realization," 22, as cited in Greenway, *Challenge of Evil*, 52.
3. I am inspired here by the seminal philosophy of Emmanuel Levinas.
4. Cf. Greenway, *Agape Ethics*.

Any creature that can experience pleasure or pain (*eros*) is a beholder and brings aesthetic value into the world. Any creature that can be seized by the Faces of others (agape), is spiritually response-able, and enables realization of moral/spiritual value in the world. The more plentiful, diverse, and healthy the creatures, the more plentiful, diverse, and robust the aesthetic and moral value in the world. We intuit these distinctions when we sense the contrast between the barrenness of Mars—beautiful to behold but devoid of delighting, creative, response-able creatures—and the fecundity of Earth.

Of course, just a few keystrokes separate us from stories of myriad Earth creatures lost or threatened: passenger pigeons, golden toads, black rhinos, orangutans, gorillas, 30 percent of insects. We live amidst an epochal, anthropogenic extinction event. At its root lies unparalleled scientific advance combined with the leveling of Earth in accord with efficiencies indexed to human desires and, worse, efficiencies predominant global elites (agape be damned) index to maximum near-term economic gain. There is time to change course. Multidimensional change is essential, because for more than a century now we have been increasingly defacing and de-Facing Earth.

We are set apart from all previous generations in human history. We are the proverbial children who have taken control of the starship with planet-destroying weaponry, for over the past three centuries our scientific understanding has grown in wild disproportion to our spiritual understanding. *We are the pivotal generation.* The fecundity and diversity of the plants, animals, river, mountains, streams, and forests which will grace Earth *or not* for the next thousand millennia rests in our hands. "Extinction" names our stupendous challenge. The future of this iteration of life on Earth rests in our hands. Let us strive to ensure future generations will look back and honor our memory with rejoicing.

Chapter 16

The Passion of Torah Is the Passion of Jesus Is the Passion of Lent

Emmanuel Levinas, the celebrated twentieth-century philosopher, grew up as a Russian Jew in Kaunas, Lithuania, just north of Belarus and Ukraine. As a boy, he was forced to flee with his Jewish community when the Russian Revolution swept through Lithuania. As an adult French citizen and Army officer, he spent five years as a captive of the Nazis and his entire immediate family, having returned to Kaunas, was murdered when the Nazis swept through Lithuania on their march into Russia.

Levinas often cited a line from the Christian philosopher, Blaise Pascal: "'That is my place in the sun.' That is how the usurpation of the whole world began."

With that line, Pascal anticipates how ethics grounded in appeals to rights would not only be insufficient for ethics but would be appropriated to justify political and economic imperialism.

The well-known "first fruits" passage of the Torah, Deuteronomy 26:1–12, strives to counter similar imperialistic interpretation of the promised land motif among the Israelites. By the time this text is written, the Israelite conquest of Canaan is done. There is no undoing that, no other place for the Israelites to go. The question is, what will be the character of Israelite rule? The author reminds them of their treatment in Egypt, where it was the Israelites themselves who had been identified as the aliens. Are they going to rule like the Egyptians? The author reminds them that they were poor and isolated immigrants, that their "father was a wandering Aramean." How are they going to treat immigrants?

We know from the history of ancient Israel that the promised land motif was used to justify political and economic imperialism. This is what Jewish prophets called "forgetting God," which in concrete terms meant forgetting the poor, the alien, the widow, and the orphan, forgetting that God promised to bless the children of Abram—a blessing applicable to *all* children of Abram—so that they could be blessing to *all* the families of the earth (Genesis 12).

Our author not only proclaims in this passage what it is to "remember God," but embeds the community's remembering in an annual ritual of "first fruits." In this ritual one takes not the excess, not what remains after we're sure there's enough for us, but "first fruits" of the harvest. Moreover, because this is not just about a once-a-year exception but about marking out a way of living in community, the people are told to take and share not only "first fruits" but a tenth of all that is harvested every third year. They are to "remember God" by sharing all this with the "aliens" in the land—note that in the context of Deuteronomy most of the "aliens" are descendants of peoples who lived in Canaan before the Israelite conquest. One "remembers God" by sharing the first fruits and the tithe so that the "alien, the fatherless, and the widow . . . may eat in your towns and be satisfied." That is what it is to "remember God."

Let's pause to be sure about the reason our author is saying this. It's because they love the aliens, the widows, the orphans, and the immigrants. They cannot make people love each other, but they can remind the people of times when they themselves were needy, when they were seen as strangers in the land, and of what they thought of those who welcomed and aided them, and they can say, "remember God," "go and do likewise."

But is this first-fruits philosophy realistic? Indeed, don't we know that it is patently unrealistic? *Why not* assert my rights? *Why not* establish means and security for me and mine first? I mean, let's be real, haven't modern philosophy and science established that that is how the world really works, that the "state of nature" is primordially a "war of all against all"?

Moral idealists like our biblical author are naïve and dangerous, because in the real world it's a struggle for survival, and those who do not know how to play the game get eaten alive. So, go with the flow, form strategic alliances, do long-term assessments, and work to align others' interests with your own, especially if they are powerful.

Ideals are great if you can afford to have them, but a "first fruits" philosophy is insane, because in the real world people who refuse to compromise, refuse to accept reality and play the game, people who get stuck on their moral ideals, who do not play by the rules of *realpolitik*, in the real world—and this is actually true, I'm not setting this up to undo it later, this is true—*in the real world people like this get crucified*...

It is this hard truth that binds the Torah's "first fruits" passage to the crucifixion of Jesus and Lent. This connection is obscured by an understandable but massive confusion over how to understand Jesus' crucifixion and Lent, a confusion most obvious in penal substitutionary understandings of atonement.

I say this confusion is understandable because not just among Christians but in religions around the world one finds a primordial conviction that the only hope of making up for evil is if, in a tit-for-tat exchange, some equally great evil is done in return. Accordingly, one finds sacrificial rituals in religious traditions across the world where one does harm to oneself or to some other creature to make up for some other evil. Tragically, this increases harm in the world and compounds the offense. This point deserves more careful and compassionate discussion than I can commit to it here, but let me stress that even people who articulate such theories of atonement have, insofar as they have indeed found forgiveness, have found forgiveness in divine grace (which substitutionary atonement theories misunderstand).

Womanist theologians like Delores Williams and JoAnne Marie Terrell[1] have been particularly important in awakening us to the problematic ways in which substitutionary understandings of atonement sanctify and even glorify suffering itself, suffering for the sake of suffering, and confusedly think that somehow perpetuating new evil—torture and killing—will undo past evil. Such understandings of atonement lead Christians to see God as somehow pleased or satisfied with Jesus' suffering and death on the cross, pleased with the suffering and death itself. This is manifest when people are asked, "What does the 'passion' of 'Passion Week' and the 'passion' of 'the passion of Jesus' refer to?" and answer, "The cross, the suffering and death of Jesus on the cross."

There are two confusions here that it is especially vital for us to name and correct. First, there is nothing inherently good about suffering, pain, and unjust death, nothing good about the suffering, pain, and unjust death

---

1. See especially Williams, "Black Women's Surrogacy Experience," and Terrell, "Our Mother's Gardens." See also, Greenway, "Greenway on Delores Williams" and "Greenway on Terrell."

of Jesus. Second, the God who is love did not delight in the suffering, pain, and unjust death of Jesus and does not delight in the suffering, pain, and unjust death of anyone else.

But then what precisely is the passion of Passion Week? The passion of Passion Week is the passion of Jesus, agape, not suffering, agape incarnate, agape so perfectly incarnated in Jesus that Jesus remained true to this passion, to agape for every Face to the death, even death on a cross. It is vital to realize that the cross was a horrifying form of execution used by imperial Rome to terrorize subjugated populations into submission. As the theologian Marit Trelstad notes, in 4 BCE the Romans "simultaneously crucified two thousand Jews suspected of rebellion. Mass crucifixions of Jews continued through and beyond Jesus' time, numbering into the tens of thousands."[2] The civil and ecclesial authorities did not execute Jesus so that humanity's sins might be forgiven, to appease God, or as some sort of bloody payment in a tit-for-tat economy. Jesus was executed because he lived surrender to having been seized by love for all the Faces that surrounded him, and so he spoke clearly and forthrightly about that which was loving and good and against what was unloving and evil. Jesus thereby threatened powerful figures and systems of exploitation and oppression, and precisely as one would expect in a fallen, selfish, and violent world, those figures and systems responded to the threat by crucifying him.

Jesus did not falter. The triumph manifest in the cross is the triumph of surrender to the passion of having been seized in and by love even in the face of massive imperial power and the threat of imminent torture and death, it is the triumph of faith, of fidelity to agape, to the God who *is* love, over desire for personal well-being and survival. In Jesus' fidelity to having been seized by love for every Face that surrounded him, even unto death on a cross, we see, in the words of Emmanuel Levinas, a man who in the passion of agape was led "to fear injustice more than death, to prefer to suffer than to commit injustice, and to prefer that which justifies being over that which assures it."[3]

God did not delight in the suffering and murder of Jesus. God delighted in Jesus' fidelity to love for all Faces, fidelity to the passion of agape, fidelity to the love of neighbor which *is* the love of God, even unto a cross.

---

2. Trelstad, "Lavish Love," 116, citing Elliott, "Anti-Imperial Message of the Cross," 168.

3. Levinas, *Entre-nous*, 132. This paragraph and the one previous are lightly edited quotations from my *Reasonable Belief*, 162.

The idea that Lent or Passion Week are about the suffering and death of Jesus in and of themselves tames Lent, domesticates it by neutralizing its social critique. Christians can think of this in very practical terms: if you give something up for the Lent that is not directly tied to justice for some neighbor, if giving up something simply creates suffering, if it is not about living surrender to having been seized by agape for some other Face, then you have missed out on the joy and truth of participating in the passion of Jesus Christ.

There is a debate in New Testament studies over how to translate *"pisteos"*/"faith" in relation to Jesus Christ (e.g., Romans 3:22, 25; Galatians 3:26). Are Christians called to have faith *in* Jesus Christ or to have the faith *of* Jesus Christ? But these are false alternatives. For to have faith in Jesus Christ *is* to have the faith of Jesus Christ, is to share in the passion of Jesus Christ.

That is the passion Christians like me should remember and recommit ourselves to when we break the bread and drink the cup. That is the passion of Lent, the passion of Passion Week, the passion of Jesus, the passion for justice, the passion for neighbor, the passion of sheep, the passion of good Samaritans, the passion of *kenosis*, of incarnation, of Christmas, the passion of Isaiah and Amos and Micah, the passion of Bodhisattvas, of Siddhartha, of Gandhi, of Levinas, the passion behind the Five Pillars of Islam, the passion which experiences this vale of tears as *dukkha*, a burning, and it is the passion of the "first fruits" philosophy of the Torah.

It is also a passion systemically elided from the categories of modern rationality and absent from "the rooms where it happens" across the globe, to devastating effect. Just for starters, everyone with this passion would have joined with South African Anglican Archbishop Thabo Makgoba in accusing the US and EU of COVID-19 "vaccine apartheid" for their long-standing denial of patent waivers and threats to punish any countries who infringed upon patents for COVID vaccines.[4] A "first fruits" philosophy would have insisted upon patent waivers and would have us ask not just about first fruits, but about third and fourth fruits, whether or not it was moral for us in the United States to get second and third doses of COVID vaccine if US foreign policy was by design denying vaccines to millions of poor people across the globe. And this is "just for starters." All of this is connected to what has happened in Hong Kong, in Ukraine, in the Northern Triangle, to the plight of refugees at the US/Mexico border, to the withering of the Arab Spring, to the "school-to-prison pipeline,"[5] and on and on. For

---

4. Lerner, "South African Archbishop Denounces Coronavirus Vaccine Apartheid."
5. See especially Alexander's devastating *New Jim Crow*.

a brilliant assessment of the problematic geopolitical dynamics and realistic suggestions for redress, see Pope Francis's encyclical *Laudato Si'* (2015).[6]

Let me close with some thoughts about how Christians might celebrate Ash Wednesday and Lent, thoughts that connect Lent to the Torah's "first fruits" philosophy.

First, consistent with Deuteronomy 26's emphasis upon the alien and the impoverished, it seems Lenten celebrations should attempt to include or at least explicitly to name and remember those who are alien to their communities, people from other faith traditions, other ethnicities, races, or socioeconomic classes, especially those who are poor. Lent should not be a most exclusive season, a season just for Christians, but a most inclusive season, a season for those from any tradition who surrender to the passion of Lent.

Second, consistent with the Torah's "first fruits" philosophy, especially as it is realized in the passion of Jesus, who spoke love to power even unto the cross, both individually and communally "giving up something for Lent" should involve naming and committing time, social and political capital, and money to redressing some injustice, some violation of the poor or those considered alien. If you are yourselves poor and powerless, this might mean embodying the passion of Jesus by offering a word of encouragement or a gesture of love. What distinguishes simple self-deprivation from true Lenten sacrifice, from participation in the faith of Jesus Christ, participation in the passion of Jesus Christ, is that true Lenten sacrifice is self-deprivation or risk which is directly related in word or deed to the love of God which *is* love of neighbor, to the passion of Lent—for the most privileged of us, this should probably involve speaking love to power.

Two closing thoughts. First, all this means that the Lenten season is continuous with the Advent and Christmas seasons. Those who give something up for the sake of giving something up during Lent miss out on the joy of giving something up out of love for others, on giving rooted in surrender to the gracious love of God, miss out on a way of participating in the love of God. When one's giving is rooted in surrender to agape, it feels like a blessed opportunity, not like "giving something up." So Lent is simultaneously a joyous season like Advent and Christmas and, with its termination in the cross, ultrarealistic about the character of this world. But this world does not triumph. Surrender to having been seized by agape for every Face, surrender to the passion of Lent, to the passion of Jesus, brings profound joy

6. See also Greenway, "Care for our Common Home."

in this world despite its crosses and yields resilience. We are not ignorant of the reality and power of real-world social, economic, and political dynamics, but we neither see them as true to the ultimate character of reality nor do we surrender to them.

Second, full surrender in true Lenten celebration yields palpable communion with agape that enfolds us and holds us and lifts us up. Communion in the passion of Lent, communion in our shared surrender to agape is so powerful and glorious that it instills in us reasonable hope that somehow it is not this world but agape that has the ultimate word.

In other words, it is from true participation in the passion of Lent that Easter hope is born. We Christians are mistaken if we endure Lent so we can get Easter. It is true celebration of Lent—full surrender to the passion of Lent, to the passion of Jesus, the passion of the prophets, the passion of the Bodhisattvas and Siddhartha and the Prophet Muhammad, peace be upon him—it is full surrender to that passion that gives birth to Easter hope, to hope in Nirvana or the Pure Land, to the hope that in some unimaginable way agape is the ultimate Word for each one of us. Get this backwards, ground everything in the promise of some heavenly reward, and one will miss the joy of communion with the God who *is* gracious love.

Chapter 17

The Flowering of Faith in the Light of Agape

WHY FAITH MATTERS

Our troubling context and the scapegoating of faith

I want to start by telling you what troubles me. I'm going to abbreviate this, otherwise we could be here for weeks! It's a familiar list, and I'm sure you could easily add to it. I'm troubled by global species loss projected at 50–70 percent over the course of this century, and by the loss already of 70 percent of insects in parts (and maybe all) of Europe and North America. All by itself, this epochal level extinction event, especially since it involves massive loss at the foundations of the food chain, threatens human civilization.

I'm troubled by the loss of potable water all around the world, and with repeated attempts by corporations to buy global fresh water sources like the Great Lakes or the ice fields of North America in order to turn water into a cornered commodity that could make oil seem cheap. We do not need oil to live, but water is necessary for life, which is why water, if supplies were cornered, could be more valuable than oil—"blue gold" many call it.

I'm troubled by corporate efforts to genetically modify seeds so they can be patented and owned to capture global markets in corn, rice, soy, wheat, and other grains that feed the world. If these seeds have contracts stipulating that no seeds from the crop can be used for replanting (so new seed must be purchased annually), these GMOs put national food supplies directly into the pockets of transnational corporations.[1] Unfortunately,

---

1. "Can Farmers Save and Replant GMO Seeds?"

mainstream Western media portray resistance to GMOs by the leaders of poorer nations as backward, not as savvy responses from leaders wise to the insidious maneuvers of colonizers and profiteers.

I'm troubled by an unprecedented concentration of global wealth and power and a growing gap between the wealthiest and poorest across the earth. I'm trouble by the forced migrations of multitudes across the globe. Migration is not a crime, but those forced to migrate by global systemic poverty and violence are innocent victims of injustices rooted in systemic inequities. Here in the States, I'm troubled by multigenerational poverty and systemic injustices indexed to race and class.[2]

While my writings make it clear that I am on the left end of the political spectrum, I am troubled by a rise in sectarian and hateful speech and violence on all sides of all sorts of divides, and I am mindful that the totalitarian horrors of the twentieth century were rooted in extremist ideologies and personalities from both the right and the left.

I'm troubled by climate change as a great magnifier of all other global challenges.

And in the face of these and other major challenges to the flourishing of earthly communities, I'm troubled by the caricaturing and scapegoating of the world's historic wisdom traditions. To be sure, all these great systems of understanding have been misappropriated to justify exploitation and oppression. From the elites of India justifying the caste system to the elites of Europe and the Americas justifying colonialism and slavery, the Scriptures of all the world's wisdom traditions have been appropriated to justify the greed and selfishness that was always people's real motivation. Horrific examples of misappropriation of all the world's historic wisdom traditions and of modern equivalents (like Marxism or Maoism) are easily multiplied.

There are and always have been corrupt and immoral religious leaders—the world's Scriptures themselves explicitly and repeatedly warn against false prophets and "wolves in sheep's clothing." But, contrary to common caricature and scapegoating, people typically do not exploit others to fulfill Scripture. The British East India Company and the Dutch West India Company were not missionary organizations. The Spanish conquistadors may have said, "God, gold, and glory," but few are naïve enough to think the Spanish monarchy, Cristóbal Colón, Hernán Cortés, and Ponce de León conquered or enslaved indigenous peoples of the Americas more (if at all) for God than (above all) for gold and glory.

---

2. See Alexander's penetrating analysis in *New Jim Crow*. Alexander notes that many of the systemic injustices related to mass incarceration are indexed not only to race, but also to class.

And while English and then Anglo-American slavers and plantation owners were quick to misappropriate Scripture to justify their racist savagery, and even to attempt to brainwash their victims, few are naïve enough to think anyone has enslaved people primarily out of fidelity to their faith. The core motives have always been selfishness, greed, and a lust for power.

Notably, because the Christian Scriptures emphasize liberation, slavers' attempts to use these Scriptures as instruments of oppression were a spectacular failure. As Black slaves in the United States were quick to notice, at the heart of the Jewish and Christian Scriptures is the story of God's liberation of the Israelites from slavery and Jesus' declaration, quoting Isaiah, that he came to "proclaim release to the captives . . ." (Luke 4:18, NRSV).

Recently, people generally hostile to religion talk as if the world's faiths and Scriptures predominantly affirm and encourage exploitation when, by contrast, all the world's faith traditions were birthed as great movements of resistance against greed and exploitation. The central writings, saints, and prophets of every major religious and wisdom tradition overwhelmingly speak against injustice, greed, and exploitation, and on behalf of love, justice, generosity, and forgiveness.

This scapegoating of the world's faiths, common among global elites, is far from innocent or harmless, for it conveniently isolates religious traditions and lifts them up for condemnation while leaving unnamed and shielded from view the enduring greed and selfishness that still motivates exploitation and causes so much suffering in our world. In particular, the scapegoating of faith leaves unnamed and shielded from view the corporate entities that for centuries now have been the actual, on-the-ground forces that organize, enforce, and profit intentionally and mightily from exploitation.

For instance, it is not uncommon to hear how missionaries went to colonized people and gave them Jesus while taking their gold. This tends to place the blame upon missionaries and fuels bitterness and suspicion towards Christianity and other faiths. While missionaries certainly had their shortcomings, and a very few got rich, most lived in country and remained poor. More important, if one goes to the Philippines, South Korea, or majority Christian countries in Africa or Central or South America, one will overwhelmingly find people who want to keep their now thoroughly indigenized varieties of Christianity (many of these countries are now sending missionaries to the West), but they want their gold back and they want an end to *ongoing* economic exploitation and control by global secular elites.

In relation to the scapegoating and marginalization of the world's wisdom traditions, I'm very concerned about a global hallowing out of democracies and rise of oligarchies. I am concerned over the rise of capitalist oligarchies in China and their sphere of influence that betrays the ideals of Mao for a good and just society. I am concerned about the rise of capitalist oligarchies in Russia and its sphere of influence that betray the ideals of Marx for a good and just society. In both cases, these developments are also a betrayal of faith traditions predominant in those regions of the world (Hinduism, Buddhism, Taoism, Confucianism, and Christianity, among others). I am equally troubled to see in the West a rise of capitalist oligarchic dynamics that betray the democratic ideals even of Adam Smith, let alone the ideals of the American and French revolutions and of the great faiths predominant in the Western world (Christianity, Islam, and Judaism, among others).

Across the globe, I am troubled by the rise of cartels and corrupt civil orders and by staggering economic inequities that are forcing mass migrations of desperation—this is not good migration, not people happy and eager to explore the world, but people forced to leave their native lands, to take desperate risks, and to suffer exploitation for the sake of their families and themselves.

I'm concerned about the fact that we humans are now, regarding the future of life, veritable gods on earth. The future of this iteration of life on earth—I say "this iteration" because if we blow it there will be future iterations of life (earth has lots of time)—but the future of *this* iteration of life on earth, determination of which plants, animals, rivers, forests, and mountains will exist on earth in two hundred years and which will be lost to us forever, determination of this future now lies in our hands.

Over the course of the past three hundred years, we have gained unprecedented power over the earth. This warp speed advance in technological power is unparalleled in human history. At the same time, our social, ethical, and political forms are just where they ever were—and may be in decline. We are the real-life version of science fiction stories in which children are left in charge of the star cruiser with weaponry that can destroy planets, and we desperately hope they will somehow find the wisdom to see their way through without blowing up a planet or themselves. We must strive to grow up morally and politically before we cause tremendous, perhaps even apocalyptic suffering and death.

I recently had a second-career student, smart and very successful in his first, C-suite career, say to me about climate change, "Nothing will happen until capital decides to make something happen." He may be right. But the logic of capitalism traffics at best in relation to individual self-interest and at worst in relation to whatever maximizes some corporate entity's near-term profit. To think capitalist logic will react adequately, let alone ethically, to global challenges like climate change is hopelessly magical thinking. If he is right, if in the "real world" we must rely on "capital," then we—especially our children and grandchildren—are in real trouble.

Reasons for hope

Now I want to say some of what encourages me. I am encouraged a lot, and a lot of that encouragement is local. I am a professor of philosophy, ethics, and Christian theology, and I'm encouraged by my students and colleagues, by all the energy at the graduate school in theology in Austin where I teach, by the passion and analytic power of our faculty and students. While secular elites' scapegoating of the world's wisdom traditions obscures this reality, across the globe there are seminaries and divinity schools of all faiths full of people likewise focused upon thinking through and working for what is good.

Our faculty come from scholarly and ministerial walks of life, but our students, especially our many second-career students, come from all walks of life. They are engineers, computer programmers, teachers, doctors, soldiers, lawyers, bankers, nurses, politicians, and journalists. They bring from and take back to their professional and home communities a passion for what is loving and just. Indeed, precisely that passion led them to engage in serious study of theology, ethics, history, pastoral care, and philosophy in the first place. I find that inspiring. I feel similar encouragement when I speak at churches across the United States and find them full of passionate folk who are committed and intelligent and working for what is loving and just.

I am encouraged by the trustees of my school. Many of them are themselves elites, rich and powerful people with resources and wealth enough to be doing whatever they want with their lives, but they are invested in my graduate school, and in their churches, and in other institutions that are focused upon what is loving and just.

I am inspired and encouraged by protestors I read about from across the globe who are taking courageous action, making sacrifices, and taking risks in fidelity to justice and love. I am encouraged by them—not by those whose rhetoric is vengeful or self-serving—but by the multitude of protestors whose passion for justice is rooted in love, and whose concern extends not only to people like them, but to all people and all creatures. I am inspired when I see protestors acting in the spirit of Isaiah, of Micah, Amos, and Siddhartha, in the spirit of Mahatma Gandhi, Václav Havel, Nelson Mandela, Vandana Shiva, and Berta Cáceres, in the spirit of prophets, saints, and martyrs from all the world's faith traditions who over the centuries have led struggles for justice. There is a wonderful, passionate, loving vibrancy out there, and in that I find great hope.

All of this explains why faith matters, for what we desperately need today is spiritual awakening, a spiritual revolution on a par with the scientific revolution of the seventeenth and eighteenth centuries. Powerful secular forces are aligned against spiritual awakening. They are bent upon scapegoating faiths while they deny the reality of agape and ethical realism, thereby hobbling global struggles for justice. But global spiritual awakening is not beyond the bounds of possibility. I have in mind the sort of moral transformation that in similar circumstances gave birth to Hinduism and Buddhism, and which in other ages gave birth to Judaism, Christianity, and Islam. This sort of spiritual awakening inspired the progenitors of all the great faith traditions of the world, and there is reason to be optimistic we might ignite a global interfaith awakening in the twenty-first century.

MORAL REALISM AND SPIRITUAL AWAKENING

The reality of agape

One brilliant modern source for moral awakening is the philosophy of the celebrated Jewish philosopher Emmanuel Levinas (1906–1995), a soldier in the French Army who was spiritually awakened during five years of captivity in a Nazi hard labor camp. What Levinas realized and confessed from the heart of the Shoah was that nothing is more sure or significant than the ethical reality of being taken hostage by the faces of those who are being tortured and murdered and screaming out, "do not hurt me," "do not kill me." In that moment, Levinas proclaims, when we are taken hostage by those faces, we are taken hostage by a reality more surely real than any of those modern systems of understanding that would have us dismiss that reality as something epiphenomenal, as some sort of social or evolved construction, meme, or ideation—we are taken hostage by a moral dimension of reality.

In profound debt to Levinas, but modifying his thought slightly, I speak of awakening to having been seized *by love for* every Face. I capitalize "Face" to distinguish the Face manifest in the event of having been seized by love from the face manifest to our five senses.

In a word, I find myself seized by a passionate concern *not from me*—that is, not a product of biological or social conditioning, nor of any desire or intentionality on my part—a passionate concern *not from me* that *seizes me for every Face*. This is an exact description of the sort of love called agape. There are other types of love. For instance, eros, which is my own immediate desiring from and for myself. There is nothing wrong with eros, nor is there anything wrong with reciprocal or kinship altruism and all the other forms of love, but they are not agape.

The reality of agape is familiar in our daily living. We see children squealing with delight in the surf at the beach. We see the shocked faces of survivors of the tsunami, broken bodies strewn about in the background. We are not at first objective, detached, neutral, and only then deciding what we think. No, insofar as we are not by nature or through repeated hardening of heart psychopathic, whether they are scenes of joy or scenes of horror, we are *instantly*, before decision or reflection, joyful or horrified. The singular passion by which we are seized in both contexts, the singular passion enflaming our joy or, in other circumstances, our horror, the palpable spiritual force over and against which we must exert ourselves if we decide to harden our hearts and react differently, that spiritual force is agape.

Most people, including most modern Western intellectual elites, whose philosophies leave no conceptual space for realist affirmation of agape, are nonetheless profoundly awakened to the reality of agape in their daily lives. They are awakened to and are immediately seized by agape when they see children squealing with delight at the beach or the anguished faces of survivors of the tsunami.

Imagine this morning I brought in a bunch of sticks gathered from the parking lot. I hand them around and ask you to break them into pieces. You would break them without a second thought. However, and *do not* imagine this, for it is brutal—I use it because for whatever reason most of us are awakened more easily in the face of brutality—say I did the same thing with a cat. The cat is bound, and I ask you to break the cat. My hope and expectation is that you are repulsed at the very thought of breaking the cat, that you are offended I would even suggest such a horror. Your response is the manifestation of the reality of you having been seized by agape for the Face of the cat. To be clear, if any one of you would break the cat without a second thought, that would not be a counterargument but cause for grave concern.

For most of you, indeed, I expect for all taking time to consider this argument, even if I talked about an oak or tomato sapling, had it right here and wanted someone to take it and to rip it out by the roots and kill it for no reason at all, most of you would again be immediately repulsed. That response is you having been seized by agape for the Face of that sapling.

Again, I use brutal examples because we are typically awakened more easily when confronted with evil, but the reality of having been seized by love for Faces is also manifest in contexts of peace and joyfulness. You're at a birthday party and as you watch the children playing joyfully, you find yourself smiling and joyful. You're at a park and you see dogs bounding around off leash, happily chasing each other in an open field, and again you find yourself joyful and smiling. You have been seized by agape for the Faces of those children and those dogs.

It is important to be precise at this point, for even many scholars (including Levinas!) speak of being seized by the Faces of the children, the cat, or the sapling. It is critical to realize that you are not seized by the Face of the cat. You are seized *by agape for* the Face of the cat. You are seized *by agape for* the Face of the sapling. You are seized not by the Face but *by agape*, you are seized *by agape for* all Faces. Indeed, it is precisely through having been seized by the moral reality of agape that Faces are manifest.

Insofar as we are awakened to agape, we are surrounded by a glorious sea of Faces of all creatures of every kind. In this vale of tears, however, wherein vast multitudes of creatures are suffering and abused, spiritual awakening is infinitely painful. This does not count against the power and reality of agape. When Faces seize you in horrible circumstances evil is not an obstacle to having been seized, not a reason to deny the reality of agape. *To the contrary, it is precisely in the face of evil that our conviction over the reality of agape gains unparalleled power.*

To be sure, in moments of horror we do not want the pain of having been seized by agape for the one in agony. We may desperately want to look away from horrific suffering. But looking away requires exertion, for the primordial reality is the reality of having been seized by agape for those who are suffering or persecuted.

Contrary to the confusion of secular rationality, which sees evil as an obstacle to faith, far from evil standing as an obstacle to faith it is precisely in the context of the greatest evil that we are seized by agape, by the divine, by the God who *is* agape with the most conviction.

Not only is agape as powerfully manifest in contexts of horror as in contexts of joy, it is the burning reality firing our horror or joy. In surrender to agape, we are filled with urgent motivation to act in fidelity to agape. This answers what for modern rationality is the vexing question of motivation in ethics. For if I am seized in contexts of horror, I am horrified and immediately move to resist the horror. If I am seized in contexts of joy, I am joyful and immediately move to enhance the joy.

To be sure, agape is not irresistible: you can harden your heart. Hardness of heart can grow. Over time you can so harden your heart that you barely even notice any Faces. But while we can harden our hearts, this is nonetheless a hardening over and against a reality that manifestly *is there*. What I am unfolding here as primordially *existing* is a force as powerful and as plainly real and universal as gravity.

"God" or "the divine"

All this means that, understood strictly and literally in the precise sense of "God *is* agape" and "agape *is* God," "God" or "the divine" signifies a reality precisely as real as our joy over the flourishing of Faces and our horror over their violation. For monotheistic traditions like Judaism, Christianity, or Islam, insofar as God *is* love and love *is* God, having been seized by agape for every Face *is* having been seized by God for every Face. For monistic streams of traditions like Buddhism, Hinduism, or Jainism, insofar as love *is* the divine and the divine *is* love, having been seized by agape for every Face *is* having been seized by the divine for every Face.[3] Again, "God" or "the divine" signifies a reality precisely as real as our joy over the flourishing of Faces and our horror over the violation of Faces.

The essence of faith

At this point I can define the essence of wholly reasonable faith. This definition of the essence of faith is so primordial that it applies both to monotheistic traditions (e.g., Christianity, Islam, or Judaism) and to monistic traditions (e.g., Buddhism, Hinduism, or Jainism). Here it is: *faith is living surrender to having been seized by agape for every Face, including one's own.* This means that insofar as I do not harden my heart to agape, which is to say, insofar as I actively—with all my heart, soul, mind, and strength[4]—surrender to having been seized by agape for every Face, including my own, I am faithful, faithful to agape.

Note the short but vital proviso, "*including one's own.*" The "including one's own" makes clear that in the event of having been seized by agape for others, we ourselves are seized and held by agape.[5] This love for self is not the self's own love for itself. That is, this is not eros—again, there is nothing wrong with eros, but eros is not agape. Agape is gracious love one

---

3. Obviously, while this is a profound and significant affirmation of the divine and, note well, an entirely reasonable and plainly true affirmation of the reality of the divine—hardly insignificant in a "secular age"—it is a minimalist identification of what we signify with "God." I want to be clear that I am not denying that God may be truly described with other terms and categories. God may be not only the force we designate with "agape" but a person, perhaps even triune. Whatever the more specific categories, they should still be consistent with, "God is love/agape" (which is at the heart of the confessions of all the world's faith traditions).

4. This is a reference to Scriptures which are celebrated in Judaism (Deuteronomy 6:4–7) and Christianity (Mark 12:30–31).

5. Notably, Levinas does not specify the "including my own" proviso.

receives for oneself insofar as one does not harden one's heart but surrenders to having been seized by agape.[6]

So, it bears repeating, *faith is living surrender to having been seized by agape for every Face, including one's own.* Insofar as I surrender to having been seized by agape for every Face, including my own, I am faithful, faithful to agape.

THE UNIVERSAL REALITY OF AGAPE AND THE FLOWERING OF FAITH

Universal and global dimensions of agape

Since what we signify with "agape," like what we signify with "gravity," is an aspect of reality, it is not just a human or earthly reality, but an independent, universal reality. If, as theists believe, God is not only agape but also in a traditional sense Creator, it is most reasonable to expect that there is life all over the cosmos, for it is absurd to think that God created 100 billion galaxies but created life on only one planet of one star. Or, if there is no "Creator" in the traditional theistic sense, but just a primordial impulse to life in the cosmos—as appears increasingly likely as we find life flourishing in Yellowstone's boiling, acidic geysers or in hypersaline anoxic basins in the depths of the Mediterranean Sea—then in that case too it is most reasonable to expect that there is life all over the cosmos. We are far more likely the rule than the exception.

In other words, if there is a Creator or if there is not, it is most reasonable to expect that there is life all over the cosmos. In any case, the point is that since what we signify with "agape," like what we signify with "gravity," is an aspect of reality, not just a human or earthly reality, but an independent, universal reality, it is also reasonable to expect that sufficiently intelligent beings elsewhere in the cosmos will undergo and theorize the reality we signify with "agape" just as they will undergo and theorize the reality we signify with "gravity" or "curvature in spacetime."

When I consider that agape is a universal reality, I think not only about intelligent beings in other parts of the cosmos, but about people who once

---

6. I unfold this in far more detail in *Reasonable Belief*. While my publishers had good reason for using this title, in the book it becomes clear that reasonable *faith* is distinct from and prior to reasonable *belief*. Note that while I argue it is vital to distinguish agape from eros (and philia, and kinship altruism, and so forth), I am not saying agape is good and eros is bad, though agape may delimit the range of good eros (for instance, affirmation of agape as divine excludes erotic pursuits that violate agape by exploiting or abusing others).

lived where I now live, which we now call "Austin, Texas," in the days of Isaiah and Micah, or in the days of Jesus, Augustine, or Aquinas. I also think about those who lived along the Amazon, the Huang He ("Yellow River"), or the Ganges in those days. I remember that what we signify with "agape" is as real and manifest as what we signify with "gravity." And I realize that people from all ages and places would have developed their own ways to name, discuss, and respond faithfully to agape.

If, as I am suggesting, all faith traditions developed in response to the reality of agape, that would explain why our profound but bare description of the lived undergoing of "having been seized by agape for every Face" is in accord with the spiritual heart of Buddhist, Christian, Hindu, Islamic, Jain, Jewish, and Wiccan spiritualities and, to my knowledge, with the spirituality of every historic faith tradition on earth—including, presumably, the faith traditions developed among long since vanished ancient peoples in what we now call the Americas.

Obviously, all these traditions signify with different words, but at their heart is awakening to the same reality, to agape. I would argue, for instance that when Christians say, in the light of the witness of the Holy Spirit, that is, in the light of the force of agape, that this world is "fallen," they are at one with Buddhists who say, in the light of spiritual enlightenment (awakening to agape), that this reality is *dukkha*, a burning. Note that "fallen" is not an historical category but an ethical category. That is, to say the world is "fallen" is not to say that once upon a time the world was perfect; it is to say that seen in the light of agape this world is a vale of tears. In this sense, again, Christians who say the world is "fallen" are at one with Buddhists who say, in the light of spiritual enlightenment (awakening to agape), that this reality is *dukkha*, that is, who say that in the light of agape this world is a burning.

Likewise, because the light of the transcending power of agape is not extinguished but burns even more intensely in the face of the horrors of this world, a flame of hope in the transcending power of agape reasonably endures across faith traditions, hope that in some way beyond imagining agape is the ultimate word for every creature, hope in Nirvana, hope in the Pure Land, hope in Heaven.

Agape, faith, and belief

Significantly, the event of having been seized by agape for every Face originates in a reality before and beyond words, concepts, and beliefs. This is faith without conceptual/analytic content. Of course, we humans live as linguistic, thinking beings in the world. So, we immediately *think* our lived undergoing of having been seized by agape. Thereby the lived undergoing is signified and enters the realm of concepts, understanding, beliefs. When the lived undergoing is thought, conceptualized, understood, articulated in terms of beliefs and calls to action, *that* is the "faith seeking understanding" celebrated teachers and prophets of all the world's faith traditions have been engaged in for millennia.

This means faith is not the product of understanding. Faith is not a concept or a belief in something, no matter how warranted. Faith is not a conclusion, no matter how reasonable. Faith is not the product of an intentional decision to believe something, no matter how good or understandable one's reasons. Faith is certainly not an irrational leap to affirmation of some belief. Faith is surrender to the force of agape. Note that "surrender" here signifies not an action but *not taking* an action, namely, not hardening one's heart to agape. So, more precisely, faith is not hardening one's heart but actively living surrender to having been seized by agape for every Face, including one's own.

All this clarifies how faith is distinct from and prior to belief, for beliefs exist in the realm of understanding, whereas faith names spiritual surrender to having been seized by a nonconceptual reality we use words to name. Consider a third-century Hindu woman in what we presently call India, a ninth-century Islamic man in what we presently call Saudi Arabia, an eighteenth-century Qom woman in what we presently call Argentina, a twentieth-century Jewish woman in what we presently call France: *like all of us, each of these people will immediately think their lived undergoing of what we signify with "agape" from within the words and traditions into which they have been born and raised.* That is simply and honestly to name the conceptual finitude intrinsic to our creaturely condition. It no more entails relativity in ethics, where we develop theories in relation to the lived undergoing we signify with "agape," than it does in physics, where we develop theories in relation to the lived undergoing we signify with "gravity."

We all must accept our finitude and particularity, and within the bounds of that acceptance I have been urging both a nonexclusive celebration of our particularities and of diverse ethno-cultural-religious forms of life *and* a nonrelativistic celebration of the singular reality of "agape," a reality celebrated across faith traditions.

Faith, then, is primordial existential surrender to agape, and is prior to belief. This isolates the prelinguistic event of faith—not hardening one's heart to having been seized by agape for every Face, including one's own—that lies at the heart of the great systems of understanding that are Baha'i, Buddhism, Christianity, Hinduism, Humanism, Islam, Judaism, Wiccan, and all the rest. To reiterate, all these traditions have carried harmful systemic distortions and have been misappropriated to evil ends, but those misappropriations are not consistent with the predominant teachings of the prophets and saints remembered and revered by those traditions, for affirmation of agape is at the heart of the witness of the most venerated writings, saints, and prophets of all the world's great faith traditions.

Against metaphysical dogmatism

Let me digress momentarily to caution that many intellectual elites, especially those in the humanities, including many scholars of religion, will resist my argument fiercely because they are bewitched by metaphysical naturalism, which has no conceptual (metaphysical/ontological) space for moral realism, let alone agape. This is why modern academic elites are famously afflicted by a crisis of foundations in ethics, by a legitimization crisis and interminable debates over sovereignty in political theory, and why they have recently been making facile stabs at "materialism 2.0," or at "expansive" or "liberal" naturalism—"facile" because the revisions are far too weak to anchor real-world ethical protest.[7]

Let me stress, in anticipation of the howls of metaphysical naturalists, that the relationship I am describing between our nonlinguistic, lived undergoing of agape and our thinking of it is not some stupefying appeal to mystery, for it parallels exactly our nonlinguistic, lived undergoing of downwardness or weight and our thinking of it in terms of "gravity" or "curvature in spacetime." Lived undergoing of downwardness or weight is a primordial, nonconceptual encounter with a reality which we then conceptualize, just as lived undergoing of having been seized by passionate concern for others and ourselves is a primordial, nonconceptual encounter with a reality which we then conceptualize. Just as we signify lived undergoing of the force of downwardness with "gravity," so we signify lived undergoing of the force of having been seized by passionate concern with "agape." The dogma of metaphysical naturalism is so strong, and current prejudice against faith traditions is so deep that I will explicitly note once again that all of this is wholly reasonable.

On the unity and plurality of earth's faith traditions

All of this means that the idea of an inevitable sectarianism among the world's religions, let alone secular elites' frequent depiction of religions

---

7. See, for instance, De Caro and Macarthur, eds., *Naturalism and Normativity.*

primarily as irrational sources of worldly terror, is neither innocent nor true. For the idea that the world's faiths are mainly at odds with one another masks their shared fidelity to agape, and it cuts us off from the reality of a massive, global, interfaith consensus calling all to condemn greed and selfishness, to feed the poor, heal the sick, clothe the naked, visit and defend the persecuted, and to work to ensure maximal flourishing and happiness for all creatures (remember the cats and saplings!). The consensus over such matters among the world's faiths is so overwhelming that it justifies and should motivate immediate political action to address the world's most pressing needs and inequities.

Unfortunately, the idea that the world's faiths are at odds with one another is so widespread that as soon as I name diverse faiths the threat of sectarianism looms—as if Abraham, Black Elk, Isaiah, Jesus, the Prophet Muhammad, Siddhartha, and all the other founders and saints of the world's great religious traditions, as if, if they were all to get together, they would want to fight one another. What do we imagine these folks, if they were transported together into today's world, would say to us about our world, about what is needy, what is important, about the vast inequities of wealth and power, about the devastation of creation and the exploitation of creatures, about what our goals and actions should be as we move forward?

To dissipate sectarian tendencies, it is helpful to think of faith traditions in an aesthetic modality. For instance, think of diverse faiths the way you think of diverse but renowned works of art. Consider symphonies. Some symphonies are works of genius. Some are mundane, even deadening. There are no criteria out there which we can use to adjudicate objectively among symphonies, but we can still distinguish among the great and the mundane with a high degree of surety. Moreover, we are thankful there are many different great symphonies, and we hope for and celebrate the creation of daring, new symphonies. In similar fashion, we can appreciate the diverse ways of organizing communities and affirming life and naming and living in fidelity to agape that we find among the world's great and emergent faith traditions.

Diversity among the world's faiths should be celebrated because they multiply ways of living in loving and just communities that are beautiful, creative, and enlivening. The same is true for diversity within religious traditions. Christianity, for instance, is richer because it is unfolded in an array of Baptist, Catholic, Episcopal, Mennonite, Methodist, Orthodox, Presbyterian, Quaker, Wesleyan, and other traditions.

But this aesthetic affirmation of pluralism is not unqualified. For insofar as the source of all faith is agape, the aesthetic modality is curtailed the moment agape is violated. There is no place for celebration of diversity but only for resistance where any tradition violates agape. The world's great faith traditions can be seen as historically deep, highly refined, multiauthored poems, all of which are responses to the same reality of agape and all of which are striving and largely succeeding, if imperfectly and incompletely, to testify to and responsibly to incarnate that same transcending reality. But there is no place here for affirmation of moral or spiritual relativism for, it is worth repeating, there is no place for celebration of diversity but only resistance where any tradition violates agape.[8]

Obviously, there are significant issues over which there is enduring ethical disagreement among reasonable and good people both within and among faith traditions. Debates over quandary issues will always be with us. But disagreement over quandary issues should not result in wholesale condemnation of any tradition or in worries over ethical relativism when there is also massive, overlapping ethical consensus among faiths across the globe over what is clearly loving and just.[9] Just as we can distinguish core areas of surety in physics from more peripheral areas where there is still uncertainty and debate, so we can distinguish core areas of surety in ethics and faith traditions from more peripheral beliefs where there is still uncertainty and debate.

On the one hand, then, there are glorious differences in the ways various faiths interpret agape and order loving lives. On the other, there is profound consensus among diverse traditions about agape and about the essence of faith as surrender to having been seized by agape for every Face. Again, this latter point is not merely academic, for among all the faiths of the world there is massive, overlapping ethical consensus that, if acknowledged, would have profound implications for social programs, political policies, and transnational treaties of vital significance for billions of humans and tens of billions of other creatures.

The flower of faith blooming in the light of agape

I drew a picture to represent my vision of the relation among agape and the world's diverse faith traditions. I call this "The Flower of Faith Blooming in the Light of Agape." At the center of the flower is the fundamental event of having been seized by the reality of agape. No conceptual content. No beliefs. Just the raw reality of our lived undergoing of agape.

Flowering out from this center are the petals of the flower, each a different color. Each petal represents a different faith tradition. Here I include

---

8. Parts of the previous paragraph are lifted verbatim from Greenway, *Reasonable Belief*, 154.

9. I take "overlapping consensus" from Rawls, *Political Liberalism*.

even relatively young traditions like Secular Humanism. (Have you heard the joke about the Jew, the Hindu, and the Muslim arriving at the pearly gates? They're greeted by St. Peter and begin their tour of heaven. As they walk by a walled-off area, St. Peter asks them to please be very quiet. "Why?" they ask, and St. Peter says, "Oh, that's where the Humanists are . . . they think they're the only ones here!" We need to include everyone, everyone who has "surrender to having been seized by agape" at the heart of their faith).

Again, each petal represents a faith tradition, each is a different color, and then within each petal there are different hues (e.g., cobalt, sky, and navy hues of blue) and then tints of color which represent different streams of understanding within each faith tradition. For instance, within the multihued petal of Christianity, and overlapping at many points, especially near the center, there would be Catholic, Orthodox, and Protestant hues, and within the Protestant hue there would be Presbyterian, Baptist, Methodist, and Wesleyan tints . . . all within the petal of Christianity.

The Flower of Faith, Blooming in the Light of Agape

The hues increasingly overlap with one another nearer the center of the flower, which signifies the primordial, lived undergoing of having been seized by agape. All the petals with all their hues and tints, that is, all the world's historic faiths in all their diversity are rooted in the same event of having been seized by agape. The tints become more discrete the further one moves towards the periphery of each petal, which signifies differences over precise doctrines (for example, in the petal of Christianity, differences over doctrines of incarnation, Trinity, atonement, salvation, Eucharist, and the like). Likewise with the other petals of diverse faiths, that is, likewise with Buddhism, Humanism, Judaism, Islam, Jainism, and Wiccan, in all their variety. All flower from and are the flowering of agape.

In sum, the force we signify with "agape" is the shining force which, if we do not harden our hearts, seizes us with passionate, gracious love for all Faces of every kind, including our own. The force we undergo and signify with "agape" is as real as the force we undergo and signify with "gravity." None of us live at the level of sheer undergoing of gravity or agape. We immediately *think* our lived undergoing. Moreover, because we each emerge at specific points in history with specific cultural-linguistic ways of understanding, we inevitably think the event in terms of the words and traditions we have been born into. But all true faith traditions, monistic and monotheistic, are rooted in lived undergoing of agape. This means (let me reiterate) that in stark contrast to the distortions of secular understanding, that insofar as "the divine" or "God" *is* agape and agape *is* "God" or "the divine," "God" or "the divine" is as directly manifest and as surely real as our horror over the violation of Faces and our joy over their flourishing.

CHRISTIANITY AND THE FLOWER OF FAITH

The view from my petal, Christianity

Amidst the flowering of agape on earth I live in the petal of Christianity, as everyone invariably lives in one petal or another. So, I understand fidelity to agape in Christian terms. As a Christian, I follow a person who in his life and brilliant teachings was faithful to having been seized by agape for every Face. In Jesus' life and teachings agape is brilliantly manifest. Moreover, Jesus remained true to having been seized by agape for every Face in a militarily and politically fraught context of oppression and empire. He remained true to agape even when it took him to death on a cross. Though this vital knowledge is largely forgotten in recent centuries, in the first century everyone knew the cross as a symbol and weapon of imperial power deliberately designed to terrorize subjugated peoples into submission.

In the face of injustice, terror, and even death, Jesus did not waver in his fidelity to agape but spoke love to power. That is where Jesus is very much like those protestors who give me hope, and where he is like prophets and saints from faith traditions across the globe. Christian Scripture invokes Jesus and his fidelity all the way to death on a cross as inspired and inspiring in precisely this sense. This is how the cross of Jesus and his unwavering fidelity to agape spoke to the early community of Jesus followers when, it bears repeating, all knew the cross as a fearsome weapon of oppression, a torturous form of execution reserved especially for insurrectionists who threatened imperial powers.

We who are Christian can take due pride in being followers of Jesus. But this is not an exclusivist pride. It is not a pride that refuses to admit the historical and contemporary shortcomings of Christianity. It is not a pride which needs to put others down. It is the sort of humble, honest pride that it wants others also—Buddhists, Latter-day Saints, Muslims, Navaho, Qom, Sioux, Wiccans—to have in their own faith traditions.

Speaking as a Christian, agapeic understanding of the relation among faith (lived surrender to agape) and belief (culturally contingent ways of understanding what we signify with "agape") is wholly consistent with the witness of Jesus. So, if we ask, "Is Christian belief an essential aspect of Christian faith?" we rightly answer "no" because the essence of Christian faith does not require affirmation of Christian beliefs, or even knowledge of the name "Jesus," for faith is not Christian belief but what Christian belief is *about*. Faith is living surrender to having been seized in and by gracious love.

This distinction between the essence of Christian faith, on the one hand, and Christian belief, on the other, can sound radical, but it is precisely this understanding of faith that Jesus unfolds in his parable of the sheep and the goats (Matthew 25:31–46). In the parable only one set of questions separates sheep from goats: Did you feed the hungry, clothe the naked, welcome the stranger, visit the sick and imprisoned (e.g., those in debtors' prison)? According to the parable, it does not matter if you are Jew, Gentile, Samaritan, Christian, Muslim, Buddhist, Sikh, Roman, Greek, Confucian, Apache, or Alpha Centurion. The question is, did you feed, clothe, welcome, visit? In a word, have you lived surrender to having been seized in and by love for the Faces of others? Have you lived faith?[10]

---

10. Portions of this paragraph and the one previous quote from Greenway, *Reasonable Belief*, 150–51.

This affirmation about the essence of Christian faith is also at the heart of Jesus' parables of the prodigal son, the unforgiving steward, and the good Samaritan.[11] My understanding of the relation among agape, faith, and belief, then, is in complete accord with the most celebrated parables of Jesus.

It is vital for Christians to distinguish *faith in* Jesus Christ from *beliefs about* Jesus Christ. In Greek, the phrase commonly translated "faith in Jesus Christ" in the Gospels and epistles is just as correctly translated "faith *of* Jesus Christ." Scholars have long debated which translation is correct, but what is most consistent with the actual teachings of the Christian Gospels and epistles is not an either/or but a both/and: to have faith *in* Jesus Christ is to share in the faith *of* Jesus Christ. Or, one might say, to have faith in Jesus Christ is to share in the passion of Jesus Christ. But what precisely is the passion of Jesus Christ?

It is common for Christians to speak of the final week of Jesus' life as Passion Week. What precisely is the passion of Passion Week? The passion of Passion Week is the passion of Jesus, agape incarnate, agape so perfectly incarnated in Jesus that Jesus remains true to this passion for every Face to the death, even death on a cross. Jesus lived surrender to having been seized in and by love for all the Faces that surrounded him, and so he spoke clearly and forthrightly about that which was loving and good and against what was unloving and evil. Jesus thereby threatened powerful figures and systems of exploitation and oppression, and precisely as one would expect in a fallen, selfish, and violent world, those figures and systems responded to the threat by crucifying him.

To be a Christian, a follower of Jesus, is to accept the passion of Jesus Christ as one's own. When we who are Christian affirm the cross of Jesus as an icon of our faith, and confess ourselves to be followers of Jesus, we celebrate a surrender to having been seized in and by love for all Faces so utter and complete that it remained faithful unto death, even death on a cross.[12]

But what about classic Christian claims that Jesus is God incarnate, one person of a divine Trinity that is one and three without separation or admixture, the one through whom a personal God achieves reconciliation with all who believe? And must not some one or another among mutually incompatible Christian doctrines of atonement or Eucharist be correct? Yes, obviously, some set of more specific beliefs, some understandings of divinity, some understandings of the role of Jesus Christ and the cross, or of the Prophet Muhammad, or of Siddhartha, may be more correct than others.

---

11. See Greenway, *Reasonable Belief*, 129–32, 137–39, 155–61.

12. Portions of this paragraph and the one previous quote from Greenway, *Reasonable Belief*, 162–63.

But all human understanding may fall gloriously short of the transcending reality, and at this juncture none of us has access to special knowledge which allows us to make definitive judgments about such specific, rarified beliefs.

Again, within faith traditions just as within the natural and social sciences we can distinguish core areas of surety from areas of increasing uncertainty at the periphery of our understanding. For example, Christians can enjoy the highest surety about "God is love" but should admit to decreasing degrees of surety as they move towards specific doctrines of incarnation, atonement, or Eucharist. Above all, every doctrine is to be evaluated for its fidelity to agape. If it's not loving, it's wrong.

Within the wide bounds of what is faithful to agape, happily, the diverse petals of the flower of faith, in all their wondrous diversity, bloom brilliantly and on the whole faithfully in the light of agape.

"But," I still hear, "do not different faiths make irreconcilable claims about God and salvation? For instance, Christians believe God is in some sense a person, that Jesus Christ is God incarnate, and that it is through the life and work of Jesus that all are saved. Not only do Buddhists not agree with any of these claims, but major streams of Buddhism believe the divine is a transcending but impersonal reality and see salvation in wholesale release from the distortion of individualism. How, then, can Buddhists, Christians, Jews, or Muslims be faithful to their respective traditions without affirming their own faith and rejecting others'?"

In the modern West there have been two predominant responses to the reality of the incompatibility of different belief systems. Both were visible in an annual, interfaith retreat I took students to for many years. My students and those from various other Christian and Jewish traditions included both conservatives and progressives—and let me stress right up front that the overwhelming majority of all the conservative and progressive students were wonderful people. Still, we would usually end up with a stark divide in the community. Students who were conservative and those who were progressive from different traditions would end up hanging around with one another at coffee breaks and meals, conservatives with conservatives, progressives with progressives.

The conservatives all stridently rejected one another's beliefs, but they strongly agreed about the need stridently to reject each other's beliefs and that, ironically enough, was such a powerful source of agreement that it united them over and against the progressives from their respective traditions, whom they viewed as pretenders. On the other hand, the progressives from diverse traditions would also hang out together, convinced that the specific beliefs of their tradition should never be put ahead of their fellowship, and united in their contempt for the intolerance of the conservatives.

Each year students were asked to organize services of worship. The conservatives would design services using language particular to their traditions and exclusive of all other traditions. The progressives would design services using only language common to all traditions, excluding all language exclusive to any one tradition.

This all reflects the predominant conservative/progressive either/or of modern interfaith relations, and on this either/or both sides have weaknesses. Conservative understandings tend to be sectarian and intolerant. Progressive understandings tend to be disconnected from the specific beliefs of any faith and anemic.

I am attempting to step beyond this either/or with a distinction between faith and belief and a correlate distinction between the ethical and the aesthetic. In a word, I have argued that in an *aesthetic* modality we can wholly affirm the disparate and irreconcilable *beliefs* of diverse faith traditions while, simultaneously, in an *ethical* modality we can affirm an *essence of faith* common to all faith traditions and, standing on that common ground, we can reject beliefs that violate agape. That is, we celebrate diverse and incommensurable forms of fidelity to agape, different faith traditions, while rejecting any beliefs that violate agape.

Our awakening to agape does not allow us to resolve quandary cases, where good and reasonable people disagree over what is loving. Given the limitations of human understanding, in real life we can always expect to confront quandary cases. In contrast to secular rationality, however, awakened rationality can map regions of ethical ambiguity on a plane that is grounded by an affirmation of moral realism, and that includes vast areas of ethical surety.

I believe this affirmation of the flowering of faith in the light of agape can be affirmed in all faith traditions, but I can only speak with authority in terms of my own Christian tradition. I need theologians, priests, and philosophers from Bahai, Buddhist, Humanist, Latter-day Saint, Muslim, Navajo, Wiccan, and other faiths to justify this distinction using the conceptual categories of their respective traditions.

CONTRA INDIVIDUALISM: COMMUNITY AND COMMUNITIES

Ancient Jewish wisdom

One final point. It is not enough to be faithful and to be Buddhist, Jain, or Latter-day Saint on one's own. It is essential to be part of an ashram, church, mosque, shrine, sweat lodge, synagogue, or temple, some local community that meets regularly, wherein we encourage one another, reawaken one another, love one another, reflect together, concretely minister to one another, name and resist what is selfish, unjust, and hateful, concretely minister to others, and publicly speak love to power. This is what it is for us to live concretely in the world as Christians, Hindus, Humanists, Jains, Jews, Muslims, Navajos, or Wiccans. This is how we together strive to make the reality of agape manifest and effective in the world. This is what it is to be peoples of faith, peoples living surrender to having been seized by agape for every Face.

We all might join Jews in remembering the momentous formulation of the call of Abram near the beginning of the Torah:

> Now the Lord said to Abram, "Go from your country and your kindred and your father's house to the land that I will show you. I will make of you a great nation, and I will bless you, and make your name great, *so that you will be a blessing*. I will bless those who bless you, and the one who curses you I will curse; and *in you all the families of the earth shall be blessed*." (Genesis 12:1–3, NRSV)

The Israelites, like peoples of all faiths, struggle to live up to the call to agape. Nonetheless, the call of Abram articulates a solution to the hard riddle which confronts us when I encourage us with pride to affirm and understand ourselves not just as generic people of faith, but as Apache, Hindu, Jain, Jew, Muslim, or Wiccan, and as members of some particular ashram, church, mosque, sweat lodge, temple, tribe, or nation. For the blessing of Abram, in complete accord with a vision of the flower of faith blooming in the light of agape, speaks directly to the dangerous challenge of sectarianism.

First, God calls upon Abram to leave his country, his kin, his family, in a word, to become a migrant, a stranger on the face of the earth. This does not mean we all need to leave our native land and family, but it does mean that these should not have our prime allegiance, none should be the prime source of our identity, security, and concern. This constitutes a strong stand against tribalism and nationalism. At the same time, it is clearly not a stand against tribes or nations, for in the very next sentence God promises to make of Abram's descendants "a great nation."

This greatness, however, is the gift of God, that is, the gift of agape, which means that "great" here does not signify self-made, conquering, wealthy, or flourishing over and against others. Significantly, this "over and against" sort of "great" is precisely the sort of "great" rejected in the immediately preceding Tower of Babel narrative, which sees divine blessing in diversity (i.e., the scattering into diverse tongues/peoples).[13] Also significant, this "over and against" sort of "great" that is rejected in the call of Abram is the problematic "great" of the social Darwinism that is in fact predominant in secular society and world affairs. "Great" in the light of agape means something very different from what it means for modern rationality, for it means being "great" in relation to what is loving and just. In the light of agape, a great nation is a loving and just nation, a blessing to all nations.

We have and will likely forever organize ourselves into diverse peoples and nations. This can set the stage for xenophobia and strife. But utilizing our aesthetic sensibilities, and insofar as love is not compromised, we can celebrate and delight in this wondrous diversity and work towards truly just, inclusive, and democratic governance for all peoples.

I stress "democratic" because there is an increasingly actualized danger in our secular world of political domination by corporations and oligarchs. Corporations, by definition, understand "great" in terms of shareholder value—see, for example, the ethically devastating laws of incorporation of the State of Delaware in the United States (where more than a million business entities are incorporated). Delaware's laws stipulate that no concern over workers, other creatures, or creation can trump fidelity to profit. Oligarchs, historically, always end up abusing their power and exploiting, even murdering thousands of people. Contrary to the false contentions of today's corporate media and oligarchs, peoples organized into democratic nation-states need not be enemies or progenitors of strife, and contrary to the not-so-subtle suggestion of many contemporary elites, wars did not emerge with nation-states.

Recently, elites have been talking about growing beyond the stage of nation-states. They substitute "nation-states" for "democracies" because they do not want people to understand they are talking about "growing beyond" democracy. But it is democracies which emerged as nation-states in response to the tyranny of elites (usually royal elites) in the eighteenth to twentieth centuries. Some elites today are dedicated to democracy, and to what is loving and just, but the globally ascendent elites who are looking to "grow beyond nation-states" do not specify what political forms are in the process of replacing nation-states, for currently the best bet would be on a combination of oligarchies and exploitative transnational legal regimes crafted by trade and corporate representatives. Because of these dynamics I

---

13. In a brilliant address delivered upon his induction into the *Academia Peruana de la Lengua Española*, Gustavo Gutiérrez relates the predominance of any single language to empire and domination and, accordingly, interprets the scattering of the people into diverse languages at Babel as divine intervention which liberated oppressed laborers from domination (Gutiérrez, *Essential Writings*, 65–73).

stress working towards truly just, inclusive, and *democratic* governance for all peoples.[14]

Insofar as agape is not compromised, we can celebrate and delight in wondrous diversity among peoples and traditions. At the same time, we can be for our own nation and people, as long as being for our nation is consistent with fidelity to agape for all nations and all peoples. So, we can be for the United States of America if being for the USA (for all Americans) is a way of being for Mexico (for all Mexicans), and for Canada (for all Canadians), and for China (for all Chinese), and we can affirm and delight in the traditions of the United States as long as that goes hand in hand with celebrating the distinctive traditions of other cultures (insofar as our or others' traditions remain faithful to agape).

Moreover, instead of aiming to negotiate international treaties that ensure that we, or a certain class of citizens (e.g., economic elites), benefit at the expense of other nations or other classes of citizens, we can idealize as our goal the formation of international treaties meant as far as is possible to maximize the flourishing of all creatures in all nations. This will require—no naïve idealism—countering the selfish nature of humans' and corporations' amoral, laser focus upon profit. The groundbreaking work of celebrated economist Elinor Ostrom (the first woman to win the Nobel Prize in Economics) suggests this is possible, and Pope Francis's encyclical *Laudato Si'* makes concrete, savvy suggestions for giving these ideals real-world traction.

Regarding faith, you can be for your local ashram, church, or temple insofar as that means also being for the Hindus, Muslims, and Wiccans down the street. For we do not exist either as generic, global people, nor as isolated monads. We invariably exist as people in some community or another and we can do that faithfully—in fidelity to agape—insofar as being for our community is also about being for what is loving and just in other, diverse communities.

---

14. This paragraph was written years before Vladimir Putin's Russia invaded Ukraine, which confirms my concerns and the importance of affirming and working to support democratic nation-states (which many Western nations, included the United States, have in fact long failed to do). Democratic ideals appear to be endangered in Western democracies, including the United States, in complex ways not limited to right-wing factions—including, for instance, laws passed in the 1990s that resulted in the devastation of the fourth estate, that undercut our society's safety net, or that encouraged irresponsibility in the financial sector. Or consider the Citizens United decision or the government's failure to rein in the brutal excesses of a predatory health care industry in a fashion untold numbers of nurses and doctors would champion.

After metaphysical dogmatism: a new Enlightenment?

Twenty-first-century understanding in the areas of faith and ethics is like that of medieval science before epistemological and methodological developments sparked the scientific revolution. Scientific Enlightenment, however, has been accompanied by conceptual collapse in the areas of faith and ethics. Ideally, my neo-Levinasian theorization of the reality signified by "agape," and my distinctions among faith, belief, ethics, and aesthetics can contribute to epistemological and methodological developments that could spark another conceptual revolution, yielding a moral and spiritual Enlightenment that would free us from both religious and metaphysical dogmatism and enable unprecedented progress in our understanding of ethics and faith in fidelity to agape.[15]

Reason for hope: salt of the earth

In the light of all of this, what are the solutions to the scary challenges I named at the beginning of this meditation? I have no exact and complete idea, and neither does anyone else. The issues are too big, too complex, and evolving too fast. Significantly, however, our faiths are full of people who are in the world: teachers, CEOs, street workers, politicians, doctors, nurses, auto mechanics, salespeople, bankers, writers, lawyers, entrepreneurs, and members of chambers of commerce. And this is where there is reason for hope. This is where Jesus' "be salt of the earth" metaphor is just perfect. What we need is for people in all faith communities from all different walks of life to live faith, that is, to live surrender to having been seized by agape for every Face, to be focused not upon increasing material power, security, and wealth—though one must attend to these—but to be first and last about creating a world that is as loving, just, and vibrant as possible.

To be sure, we act faithfully in all these ways knowing we will never create a perfectly just world. The Hebrew prophets together with the prophets of every major religious tradition sagely make their visions of a perfectly just and peaceful reality eschatological (i.e., beyond the bounds of human possibility) even as they call people to struggle for what is loving and just

---

15. Elsewhere, I develop this neo-Levinasian understanding into an empirically testable philosophical theory: Moral Realism Theory. Moral Realism Theory affirms and celebrates modern science, it affirms and celebrates poetic self-creation and authentic being in the world, and it also affirms, celebrates, and strives to be faithful to the lived undergoing signified by "agape." More precisely, it celebrates the flowering of faith in the light of agape, and in fidelity to agape it bids us all unite in the quest to make our world maximally loving and just.

in the present. That is, we are called to the struggle even though we will never make all things perfect—there is "ought" without "can." We can have the hope, I think the reasonable hope, that the gracious "Yes" of agape will somehow be the final word for every creature and all creation, but that is not an end we can accomplish. We do not act because we are part of a cause or assured of success, nor to qualify as good Buddhists, Christians, Humanists, Jews, Muslims, Sioux, or Wiccans. We act in fidelity to the reality of agape, in fidelity to having been seized by agape for every Face.

Ideally, we will come together from all walks of life in our local communities of faith—our ashrams, churches, sweat lodges, synagogues, and temples—and we will love and support and inform and rejuvenate one another. We will use our communities to minister to the world. We will go into diverse walks of life where we have expertise and influence, and we will act as salt of the earth. Day by day we will work together in big and small ways—offering an encouraging or chastening word here, making a minor or major decision there—to make life for our neighbors (including all creatures!) and ourselves better rather than worse.

Let us all together open our hearts and live surrender to having been seized by agape for every Face of every kind. Let us glory in blessing others and in being blessed. Let us be nourished and flourish in the light of agape. Let us work to make the world more loving, more just, more wondrous, more beautiful. Let us strive after the global flowering of faith in the light of agape.

Bibliography

Agamben, Giorgio. *The Time That Remains: A Commentary on the Letter to the Romans*. Translated by Patricia Dailey. Stanford, CA: Stanford University Press, 2005.
Alexander, Michelle. *The New Jim Crow: Mass Incarceration in an Age of Colorblindness*. Tenth Anniversary ed. New York: New, 2020.
Augustine. *Augustine: Earlier Writings*. Translated and edited by J. H. S. Burleigh. Philadelphia: Westminster, 1953.
———. *Confessions*. Translated by R. S. Pine-Coffin. New York: Penguin, 1984.
———. *On Christian Doctrine*. Translated by J. F. Shaw. Mineola, NY: Dover, 2009.
Badiou, Alain. *Saint Paul: The Foundation of Universalism*. Translated by Ray Brassier. Stanford, CA: Stanford University Press, 2003.
Barker, Margaret. *Creation: A Biblical Vision for the Environment*. London: T. & T. Clark International, 2010.
Barth, Karl. *Church Dogmatics III/4: The Doctrine of Creation*. Translated by G. W. Bromiley and T. F. Torrance. Edinburgh: T. & T. Clark, 1961.
———. *Church Dogmatics IV/3.1: The Doctrine of Reconciliation*. Translated by G. W. Bromiley and T. F. Torrance. Edinburgh: T. & T. Clark, 1961.
———. *Die Kirchliche Dogmatik, Dritter Band, Die Lehre Von Der Schopfung, Vierter Teil*. Zurich: Evangelischer Verlag A. G. Zollikon, 1957.
Beauchamp, Tom, and James Childress. *Principles of Biomedical Ethics*. 6th ed. Oxford: Oxford University Press, 2009.
Buber, Martin. *I and Thou*. 2nd ed. Translated by Ronald Gregor Smith. New York: Charles Scribner's Sons, 1958.
Calvin, John. *Commentary on the Book of Psalms*. Translated by James Anderson. Grand Rapids: Baker, 2003.
———. *Institutes of the Christian Religion*. Edited by John T. McNeill. Translated by Ford Lewis Battles. Philadelphia: Westminster, 1977.
"Can Farmers Save and Replant GMO Seeds?" American Farm Bureau Foundation for Agriculture. Washington, DC, 2024. https://www.agfoundation.org/questions/can-farmers-save-and-replant-gmo-seeds#~:text=However%20C%20when%20farmers%20the%20following%20year.
Clausen, Rebecca, and Stefano Longo. "The Tragedy of the Commodity and the Farce of AquaAdvantage Salmonâ." *Development and Change* 43:1 (2012) 229–51.

De Caro, Mario, and David Macarthur, eds. *Naturalism and Normativity*. New York: Columbia University Press, 2010.

De Lazari-Radek, Katarzyna, and Peter Singer. "The Objectivity of Ethics and the Unity of Practical Reason." *Ethics* 123 (October 2012) 9–31.

———. *The Point of View of the Universe: Sidgwick and Contemporary Ethics*. Oxford: Oxford University Press, 2014.

Debaere, P., et al. "Water Markets as a Response to Scarcity." *Water Policy* 16 (2014) 625–49.

Dostoevsky, Fyodor. *The Brothers Karamazov: A Novel in Four Parts with Epilogue*. Translated by Richard Pevear and Larissa Volokhonsky. New York: Vintage Classics, 1991.

Elliott, Neil. "The Anti-Imperial Message of the Cross." In *Paul and Empire: Religion and Power in Roman Imperial Society*, edited by Richard A. Horsley, 167–83. Harrisburg, PA: Trinity International, 1997.

Ellis, Fiona. *God, Value, and Nature*. Oxford: Oxford University Press, 2014.

Francis, Pope. *Laudato Sí: On Care for our Common Home*. Vatican City: Libreria Editrice Vaticana, 2015.

Garcia, Ismael. *Dignidad: Ethics Through Hispanic Eyes*. Nashville: Abingdon, 1997.

Goodstein, L. "Percentage of Protestant Americans Is in Steep Decline, Study Finds." *New York Times*, October 9, 2012.

Greenway, William. *Agape Ethics: Moral Realism and Love for All Life*. Eugene, OR: Cascade, 2016.

———. "Animals." In *The Dictionary of Scripture and Ethics*, edited by Joel Green, 69–71. Grand Rapids: Baker Academic, 2011.

———. "Animals and the Love of God." *The Christian Century*, June 21, 2000, 680–81.

———. "Before and Above All, *Agape*: On the Essence of Faith." SARX, December 2015. https://sarx.org.uk/articles/christianity-and-animals/before-and-above/.

———. "Care for our Common Home: William Greenway on *Laudato Si'*." *Eerdword*, July 13, 2015. https://eerdword.com/care-for-our-common-home-william-greenway-on-laudato-si/.

———. *The Challenge of Evil: Grace and the Problem of Suffering*. Louisville: Westminster John Knox, 2016.

———. "Eternally Incarnate: Advent in Genesis." *Journal for Preachers* 39:1 (Advent 2015) 30–36.

———. "Extinction." *Unbound: An Interactive Journal on Christian Social Justice*, April 23, 2020. https://justiceunbound.org/extinction/.

———. *For the Love of All Creatures: The Story of Grace in Genesis*. Grand Rapids: Eerdmans, 2015.

———. "Greenway on Delores Williams on Surrogacy, Cross, and Redemption." https://www.youtube.com/watch?v=TWq4xNSpHtU.

———. "Greenway on Terrell on Sacramental Sacrifice." https://www.youtube.com/watch?v=9ypMmlnu4Ds.

———. "Jesus as Moral Philosopher: The Parable of the Good Samaritan." *Insights* 128 (Fall 2012) 15–22.

———. "Karl Barth, Albert Schweitzer, Emmanuel Levinas and 'Love for All Creatures' as a Quintessential Aspect of Christian Spirituality." In *Issues in Ethics and Animal Rights*, edited by Manish A. Vyas, 168–77. Delhi, India: Regency, 2011.

———. "Life Sacred: Recovering the Seven Days of Creation Narrative." In *God's Earth is Sacred: Essays on Eco-Justice*, edited by Jenny Phillips and Cassandra Carmichael, Kindle locations 3441–3750. Washington, DC: National Council of Churches, 2012.

———. "Peter Singer, Emmanuel Levinas, Christian *Agape*, and the Spiritual Heart of Animal Liberation." *Journal of Animal Ethics* 5:2 (Fall 2015) 45–58.

———. *A Reasonable Belief: Why God and Faith Make Sense*. Louisville: Westminster John Knox, 2015.

———. "Seized by Love: Teaching, Ministry, and Augustine's 'Teacher.'" *Windows* 131:1 (Winter 2016) 21.

———. "To Love as God Loves: The Spirit of Dominion." *Review and Expositor* 108 (Winter 2011) 23–36.

Greggs, Tom. "'Jesus is victor': passing the impasse of Barth on universalism." *Scottish Journal of Theology* 60:2 (2007) 196–212.

Gutiérrez, Gustavo. *Gustavo Gutiérrez: Essential Writings*. Edited by James B. Nickoloff. Minneapolis: Fortress, 1996.

Hardin, Garrett. "Discriminating Altruisms." *Zygon* 17:2 (June 1982) 163–86.

———. "Lifeboat Ethics: The Case Against Helping the Poor." *Psychology Today* 8 (1974) 38–43.

———. "Tragedy of the Commons." *Science* 162:3859 (December 1968) 1243–48.

Heidegger, Martin. *Being and Time*. Translated by Joan Stambough and revised by Dennis Schmidt. Albany: State University of New York Press, 2010.

Hill, Peter. "Are All Commons Tragedies? The Case of Bison in the Nineteenth Century." *The Independent Review* 18:4 (Spring 2014) 485–502.

Hobbes, Thomas. *The Leviathan*. Amherst, NY: Prometheus, 1988.

Huemer, Michael. "Singer's unstable meta-ethics." In *Peter Singer under fire: The moral iconoclast faces his critics*, edited by Jefferey Schaler, 359–79. Chicago: Open Court, 2009.

Jensen, Derrick. *A Language Older Than Words*. White River Junction, VT: Chelsea Green, 2004.

Jill-Levine, Amy. "The Many Faces of the Good Samaritan—Most Wrong." In *Christian Ethics Today* 20:1 (Winter 2012) 20–21.

Kinzig, A., P. Erlich, L. Alston, L. Arrow, S. Barrett, T. Buchman, G. Daily, B. Levin, S. Levin, M. Oppenheimer, E. Ostrom, and D. Saari. "Social Norms and Global Environmental Challenges: The Complex Interaction of Behaviors, Values, and Policy." *BioScience* 63 (2013) 164–75.

Kraak, Sarah. "Exploring the 'Public Goods Game' Model to Overcome the Tragedy of the Commons in Fisheries Management." *Fish and Fisheries* 12 (2011) 18–33.

Krier, James. "The Tragedy of the Commons, Part Two." *Harvard Journal of Law and Public Policy* 15:2 (Spring 1992) 325–49.

Leopold, Aldo. *A Sand County Almanac*. New York: Oxford University Press, 1987.

Lerner, Sharon. "South African Archbishop Denounces Coronavirus Vaccine Apartheid." *The Intercept*, February 12, 2021. https://theintercept.com/2021/02/12/covid-vaccine-south-africa-apartheid/.

Levinas, Emmanuel. *Difficult Freedom: Essays on Judaism*. Translated by Seán Hand. Baltimore: The Johns Hopkins University Press, 1997.

———. *Entre-nous: Thinking-of-the-Other*. Translated by Michael Smith and Barbara Harshav. New York: Columbia University Press, 1998.

———. "Ethics as First Philosophy." In *The Levinas Reader*, edited by Sean Hand, 75–87. Oxford: Basil Blackwell, 1989.

———. *Of God Who Comes to Mind*. Translated by Bettina Bergo. Stanford, CA: Stanford University Press, 1986.

———. *Otherwise Than Being or Beyond Essence*. Translated by Alphonso Lingis. Pittsburgh: Duquesne University Press, 1998.

Linzey, Andrew. *Animal Rights: A Christian Assessment of Man's Treatment of Animals*. London: SCM, 1976.

Malka, Solomon. *Emmanuel Levinas: His Life and Legacy*. Translated by Michael Kigel and Sonja Embree. Pittsburgh: Duquesne University Press, 2006.

Marion, Jean-Luc. "A Phenomenological Sketch of the Concept of Gift." In *Postmodern Theology and Christian Thought*, edited by Merold Westphal, 122–43. Bloomington: Indiana University Press, 1999.

McChesney, John. "The Changing Face of America." Aired on National Public Radio, *All Things Considered*, September 27, 2000. Transcript produced by Burrelle's Information Services, Box 7, Livingston, NJ 07039.

Metzger, Bruce, and Roland Murphy, eds. *The New Oxford Annotated Bible*. New York: Oxford University Press, 1994.

Miles, Charles A. "In the Garden." Hymn, 1913.

Naess, Arne. "Self-Realization: An Ecological Approach to Being in the World." In *Thinking Like a Mountain: Towards a Council of All Beings*, edited by John Seed, Joanna Macy, Pat Fleming, and Arne Naess, 19–31. Gabriola Island, BC: New Society, 1988.

Nygren, Anders. *Agape and Eros*. Translated by Philip Watson. London: SPCK, 1957.

Ostrom, Elinor. "Coping with Tragedies of the Commons." *Annual Review of Political Science* 2 (1999) 493–535.

Outka, Gene. *Agape: An Ethical Analysis*. New Haven: Yale University Press, 1977.

Pascal, Blaise. *Great Shorter Works of Pascal*. Translated by E. Cailliet and J. C. Blankenagel. Westport, CT: Greenwood, 1974.

———. *Pensées*. Translated by A. J. Krailsheimer. New York: Penguin, 1966.

Penn, Dustin. "The Evolutionary Roots of Our Environmental Problems: Toward a Darwinian Ecology." *The Quarterly Review of Biology* 78:3 (2003) 275–301.

Phillips, Jenny, and Cassandra Carmichael. *God's Earth is Sacred: Essays on Eco-Justice*. Washington, DC: National Council of Churches, 2012.

Proudfoot, Wayne. "Religious Belief and Naturalism." In *Radical Interpretation in Religion*, edited by Nancy Frankenberry, 78–92. Cambridge: Cambridge University Press, 2002.

Rawls, John. *Political Liberalism*. New York: Columbia University Press, 1993.

Rorty, Richard. *Contingency, Irony, and Solidarity*. Cambridge: Cambridge University Press, 1989.

Ryan, Richard M., and Edward L. Deci. *Self-Determination Theory: Basic Psychological Needs in Motivation, Development, and Wellness*. New York: Guilford, 2017.

Santmire, Paul. *The Travail of Nature: The Ambiguous Ecological Promise of Christian Theology*. Minneapolis: Fortress, 1985.

Schoen, Allen. *Kindred Spirits: How the Remarkable Bond Between Humans and Animals Can Change the Way We Live*. New York: Broadway, 2002.

Schweitzer, Albert. *Kultur und Ethik*. München: C. H. Beck, 1960.

———. *Out of My Life and Thought*. New York: Henry Holt, 1933.

———. *Out of My Life and Thought: An Autobiography*. Translated by Everett Skillings. New York: Mentor, 1953.

———. *The Philosophy of Civilization II: Civilization and Ethics*. 3rd ed. Translated by Charles Thomas Campion and revised by Lilian M. Rigby Russell. London: Adam & Black, 1946.

Sidgwick, Henry. *The Methods of Ethics*. 7th ed. London: Macmillan, 1907.

Simmons, Frederick V., and Brian C. Sorrells, eds. *Love and Christian Ethics: Tradition, Theory, and Society*. Washington, DC: Georgetown University Press, 2016.

Singer, Peter. *Animal Liberation: The definitive classic of the animal movement*. New York: Ecco, 2009 (original 1975).

———. "Ethics and Intuitions." *The Journal of Ethics* 9 (2005) 331–52.

———. "Famine, affluence and morality." *Philosophy and Public Affairs* 1:3 (1972) 229–43.

———. *How Are We to Live?* Amherst, NY: Prometheus, 1993.

———. *Practical Ethics*. 3rd ed. Cambridge: Cambridge University Press, 2011.

———. "Reply to Michael Huemer." In *Peter Singer under fire: The moral iconoclast faces his critics*, edited by Jeffrey Schaler, 380–94. Chicago: Open Court, 2009.

———. *Rethinking Life and Death: The collapse of our traditional ethics*. New York: St. Martin's Griffin, 1994.

Smith, Adam. *The Wealth of Nations*. New York: Modern Library, 1937.

Sober, Elliot, and David Sloan Wilson. *Unto Others: The Evolution and Psychology of Unselfish Behavior*. Cambridge: Harvard University Press, 1998.

Taubes, Jacob. *The Political Theology of Paul*. Translated by Dana Hollander. Stanford, CA: Stanford University Press, 2003.

Terrell, JoAnne Marie. "Our Mother's Gardens: Rethinking Sacrifice." In *Cross Examinations: Readings on the Meaning of the Cross Today*, edited by Marit Trelstad, 33–49. Minneapolis: Augsburg Fortress, 2006.

Trelstad, Marit. "Lavish Love: A Covenantal Ontology." In *Cross Examinations: Readings on the Meaning of the Cross Today*, edited by Marit Trelstad, 109–24. Minneapolis: Augsburg Fortress, 2006.

Van Vugt, Mark. "Averting the Tragedy of the Commons: Using Social Psychology to Protect the Environment." *Current Directions in Psychological Science* 18:3 (June 2009) 169–73.

Waldau, Paul and Kimberley Patton, eds. *A Communion of Subjects: Animals in Religion, Science, and Ethics*. New York: Columbia University Press, 2006.

Wesley, John. *The Works of John Wesley: Journals and Diaries I (1735–38)*. Edited by W. Reginald Ward and Richard P. Heitzenrater. Nashville: Abingdon, 1988.

White, Lynn, Jr. "The Historical Roots of Our Ecologic Crisis." *Science* 155:3767 (March 10, 1967) 1203–7.

Williams, Bernard. *Truth and Truthfulness: An Essay in Genealogy*. Princeton: Princeton University Press, 2002.

Williams, Delores. "Black Women's Surrogacy Experience and the Christian Notion of Redemption." In *Cross Examinations: Readings on the Meaning of the Cross Today*, edited by Marit Trelstad, 19–32. Minneapolis: Augsburg Fortress, 2006.

Žižek, Slavoj. *The Puppet and the Dwarf: The Perverse Core of Christianity*. Cambridge: The MIT Press, 2003.

Index of Names

Abram. *See* Abraham
Abraham, 162, 170–71
Agamben, Giorgio, 27n4
Alexander, Michelle, 150n2
Amos, 146, 153
Aquinas. *See* Thomas Aquinas, Saint
Aristotle, xviiin6, xix
Augustine, Saint, vii, xviiin6, 20n6, 26, 116, 119, 121, 159

Badiou, Alain, 27n4
Barth, Karl, vii, x, 44, 46–57, 102–24
Beauchamp, Tom, 5n19
Black Elk, 162
Buber, Martin, 68n9, 89n1
Burge, George, 66–67, 70, 72

Calvin, John, vii, x, 102, 102n2, 103n3, 111–13, 117–21
Cáceres, Berta, 153
Childress, James, 5n19
Clapp, Jesselyn, ix
Clapp, Rodney, ix
Clausen, Rebecca, 79
Colón, Cristobal, 150
Cortés, Hernán, 150

Darwin, Charles, 75, 93, 98, 171
Darwinian, Darwinism. *See* Darwin
De Caro, Mario, xivn1, 161n7

De Lazari-Radek, Katarzyna, 9–11, 13, 9n34
Debaere, Paul, 79
Deci, Edward, xivn1
Derrida, Jacques, xviiin6
Derridean. *See* Derrida
Descartes, René, 41, 51
Dostoevsky, Fyodor, 102, 104–7, 114–15, 119

Fiona, Ellis, xivn1
Francis of Assisi, Saint, 43, 75, 77, 81
Francis (Pope), 147, 172

Garcia, Ismael, x, 17
Ghandi, Mahatma, 146, 153
Goodstein, L, 80n31
Gomez, Hilario, 125n1
Gregg, Tom, 102n1
Gutiérrez, Gustavo, 171n13

Habermas, Jürgen, 3
Hall, Stan, vii, x, 136–37
Hardin, Garrett, 76–79, 81n32
Hare, R. M., 3
Havel, Václav, 153
Heidegger, Martin, xviiin6, xix, 11–12
Hill, Peter, 79
Hobbes, Thomas, 5n20
Huemer, Michael, 5n18
Huff, George, 67

Hume, David, 5n20

Isaiah, 42, 146, 151, 153, 159, 162
Iscariot, Judas, 107, 113, 123

James, William, 18
Jensen, Derrick, 95, 98
Jesus of Nazareth, vii, viii, x–xi, xviii, 3, 17–25, 27–30, 51, 77, 84, 109–11, 113, 132, 142, 144–48, 151, 159, 162, 165–68
Jill-Levine, Amy, 20n6

Karamazov, Alyosha, 115n17
Karamazov, Ivan, 104–7, 114, 123
Kant, Immanuel, xix, 99n9
Krier, James, 77n19

Lapu-Lapu, 133n2
Leopold, Aldo, 86
Levinas, Aminadav, xvn3 (brother of EL)
Levinas, Boris, xvn3 (brother of EL)
Levinas, Dvora, xvn3 (mother of EL)
Levinas, Emmanuel, vii, x, xiv–xv, xviii, xviiin6, xix, 1, 2, 11–16, 20, 27, 32, 38–39, 46, 48, 50–54, 88–94, 100, 140n3, 142, 145–46, 154, 156, 157n5
Levinas, Gurvitch, xvn3 (father of EL)
Levinas, Raïssa, xvn3 (wife of EL)
Levinas, Simone, xvn3 (daughter of EL)
Linzey, Andrew, 1, 38, 47, 86, 99
Longo, Stefano, 79
Luther, Martin, 33, 97, 108

Macarthur, David, xivn1, 161n7
Magellan, Ferdinand, 133n2
Makgoba, Thabo, 146
Malka, Solomon, xvn2 and n3
Mandela, Nelson, 153
Mao Zedong, 152
Marion, Jean-Luc, xviiin6, 22
Markel, 114–15 (brother of Father Zossima)
Marx, Karl, 152
Mauss, Marcel, xviiin6
McChesney, John, 67, 70
Miles, David, 136

Micah, 146, 153, 159
Moses, 3
Muhammad (the Prophet, PBUH), 148, 162, 167
Murdoch, Iris, 115n18

Naess, Arne, 86, 139–40
Noah, 35, 42, 84
Nygren, Anders, xviiin6

Ostrom, Elino, 80, 172
Outka, Gene, xviiin6

Pascal, Blaise, 94, 116, 119, 142
Patton, Kimberley, 38
Paul, Saint, 26–28, 116, 119, 123n34
Penn, Dustin, 75n9
Plato, xix, 2, 77n19
Platt, Nicholas, 129
Plotinus, xviiin6
Ponce, de León, 150
Proudfoot, Wayne, 17–18, 23

Rawls, John, 3, 79n23, 163n9
Regan, Tom, 99
Rigby, Cynthia, 118n30, 125n1, 128, 133
Rommel, Erwin, xiv
Rorty, Richard, xvn5, xviiin6, 19
Ryan, Richard, xivn1

Santmire, Paul, 47
Sartre, John-Paul, 3
Saul, of Tarsus, 28
Schweitzer, Albert, vii, x, 43–57, 70, 123n34
Sidgwick, Henry, 5n20
Siddhartha, Gautama, 146, 148, 153, 162, 167
Simmons, Frederick, xviiin6
Singer, Peter, vii, x, 1–16, 38, 47, 72n13, 77n20, 86, 99
Shiva, Vandana, 153
Smith, Adam, 3, 76, 79, 152
Snodgrass, Gail, vii, x, 136–37
Sober, Elliot, 77n20
Sorrels, Brian, xviiin6

Taubes, Jacob, 27n4

Terrell, JoAnne Marie, 144
Thomas Aquinas, Saint, 159
Trelstad, Marit, 145

Waldau, Paul, 38
Wesley, John, 116, 119
White, Lynn, Jr., 46–47, 74–77, 80–81

Williams, Bernard, xivn1
Williams, Delores, 144
Wilson, David Sloan, 77n20
Wimer, Matthew, ix

Žižek, Slavoj, 27n4
Zossima (Father), 115n17

www.ingramcontent.com/pod-product-compliance
Lightning Source LLC
Chambersburg PA
CBHW031428150426
43191CB00006B/449